Lion of God

Lion of God
Copyright ©1994 by Multnomah Bible College

Library of Congress Cataloging-in-Publication Data
Bohrer, Dick
    Lion of God / Dick Bohrer
        p.   cm.
    ISBN 0-9640330-0-3

94-075841
CIP

Published by Multnomah Bible College

Editor: David Sanford
Cover Design: Multnomah Graphics/Printing

Printed in the United States of America

94 95 96 97 98 99 / 10 9 8 7 6 5 4 3 2 1

Lion of God

A biography of
John G. Mitchell, D.D.

by
Dick Bohrer

Dedication

To the Eby/Mitchell
family—
in more ways than one,
the lion's pride

Forward

I have a feeling this book would not have been written if John G. Mitchell had his way. However, in the measure it exalts the Lord Jesus Christ, it would have his approval.

John G., like John the Baptist, felt deeply, "He must increase, but I must decrease."

But his dear wife, Mary, who knew him better than anyone else, felt that the memories of his life would leave readers more in love with the Lord Jesus than occupied with her husband.

And I agree, having served with him and under his spiritual leadership for 58 years. We were together at Central Bible Church and Multnomah School of the Bible, both in Portland, Oregon. I lived with the Mitchells in their home and fished with them the waters of the San Juan Islands and Vancouver Island. Under his leadership as chairman of Multnomah's trustee board, I served as president.

I came to know his heart and to love the stories of his childhood and of his pioneer evangelism on the Canadian prairies. His Bible classes and Bible conference ministries, his radio broadcasts, and his shepherd care of his flock at Central Bible Church made Dr. Mitchell a blessing to countless thousands.

And Dick Bohrer agrees. He agrees that the memories of Dr. Mitchell as recalled by the heart-warming stories he told, as recorded in Mary's journals, and as recounted in the testimonies of his many friends and colleagues would form a beautiful reflection of the Saviour Dr. Mitchell loved and served.

And, *not* incidentally, Dick has done a good job in letting John and Mary and their friends tell the story. He has preserved the idiom and the feelings of all who have joined to give us the portrait and the *patent* of John G. Mitchell. Dick, as one of our grad students, was devoted to Dr. Mitchell as his teacher. When Dick joined our faculty as teacher of journalism from 1963-79, he served for three years as Dr. Mitchell's song leader and choir director at Central Bible Church. He left Multnomah to become editor of *Moody Monthly* magazine and then professor of journalism at Liberty University.

And you will agree, too. Jack's life *did* reflect the Saviour he loved.

So throw another log on the fire, settle down in your favorite chair, and let your heart be warmed by reading about John and Mary Mitchell—that childless couple who had thousands of spiritual sons and daughters.

Be sure to have a box of tissues at hand.

—Willard M. Aldrich

Author's Preface

I treasure a letter Mrs. Mary Mitchell sent me when she received a copy of my *Right With God*, her husband's commentary on the Book of Romans. A short time later she was with the Lord. She wrote:

Dear Dick:

John Van Diest has brought me a copy of the book of Romans, right from the press. I understand it is not in the store yet. I am so grateful to him.

I do not know, Dick, how I can ever find words to tell you how very much I appreciate the work you have done. It is excellent. You have preserved John's words and illustrations so well I can almost hear him speaking as I read.

I do not remember what I wrote when you sent me a copy of the tribute you had written, but I want you to know that I think it is beautiful. It brought tears as I read it again.

Both John and Willard have talked with me about planning to write memoirs of John. They said that you would be working with them on this. I surely hope you will. You knew and loved him well. I have been giving them notes of his early life and our work together during our 61 years of marriage. I hope it will be helpful.

I am sorry that I have not written you more often, but I am limited in strength these days.

Sincerely, in our Saviour's love,
Mary

* * *

In another letter, she wrote, "You spoke, Dick, of writing the story of John's life. There is no one I would rather have do it."

When one is so commissioned, he cannot but respond.

* * *

During the memorial service for Dr. John G. Mitchell, Mrs. Eleanor Yost made the following remarks before she sang:

When Dr. Mitchell's niece, Mrs. Marty Eby Katcho, visited him in the hospital during his last illness, she asked him, "Uncle John, give us a verse."

He waited a while.

And then he quoted the third verse of this song that I'm going to sing:

"Oh, I am my Beloved's and my Beloved's mine.
He brings a poor, vile sinner into His house of wine.
I stand upon His merit. I know no other stand—
Not e'en where glory dwelleth—in Emmanuel's land."

And she told me that it wasn't just once, but three times he repeated this verse. So you know this song, "The Sands of Time Are Sinking," must have been very special to him.

I'd like to sing the other three verses for you now:

"The sands of time are sinking. The dawn of heaven breaks.
The summer morn I've sighed for. The fair sweet morn awakes.
Dark! Dark! hath been the midnight but dayspring is at hand.
And glory, glory dwelleth in Emmanuel's land.

"Oh, Christ, He is the Fountain, the deep sweet Well of Love.
The streams on earth I've tasted. More deep I'll drink above.
There to an ocean fullness His mercy doth expand.
And glory, glory dwelleth in Emmanuel's land.

The bride eyes not her garment but her dear bridegroom's face.
I will not gaze at glory but on my King of Grace.
Not at the crown He giveth but on His piercéd hand.
The Lamb is all the glory of Emmanuel's land."

* * *

In my editor's note prefacing Dr. Mitchell's volume on the Book of Romans, I mentioned that finally our pastor, teacher, friend would receive the praise he so fully merited—the "Well Done" from his Saviour's lips. On deeper reflection and from my many years editing this man's expositions and now writing this book on his life, I would not be surprised if he shrugged off even that praise. To him, indeed, and to me, the Lamb he loved and served so long must receive *all* the glory.

Acknowledgements

I would like to thank Mrs. Verna Eby and her family as well as my friends and former co-workers at Multnomah School of the Bible for their great help and cooperation in bringing together the information necessary to compile this remembrance. Mrs. Irene Scruggs and our friends in the Stewardship Department of the school were particularly solicitous and hospitable during the months of April 1991 and June 1992 when my wife Betty and I returned to Portland to work on this book. Their prayer support has helped us through the difficult times . . . . Many people gave me interviews and others would have if we had had the time. My great thanks to those who are included in this book. My apologies to those friends who are not . . . . Four papers have given me very real help for which I am grateful: "Recollections" by Mary Mitchell, "The Early Years" by Harley K. Hallgren, "History of Central Bible Church 1921-42" by Wilfred L. Jensen, Jr., and "The Sutcliffe Years" by Vincent P. Turturice. The latter three detailed the history of Multnomah School of the Bible and Central Bible Church . . . . For her encouragement and editing skills, I give deep thanks to my Betty . . . . Mrs. Celia Wiebe assembled the pictures and, along with Mrs. Bonnie Weiss and Dr. Willard M. Aldrich, read the developing manuscript and gave great encouragement. Mr. Verne Davis of Multnomah stayed with this project to its conclusion. Without him, the manuscript might well have remained in a drawer.

I have tried to search out Dr. Mitchell's definition of what makes a man of God. It seems to boil down to with what he fills his mind and his minutes—both on and off his knees and to "a consuming passion for Christ and great longing to know the Book." . . . May his life encourage us all to be men and women of God.

—Dick Bohrer
MSB Grad, 1951

Contents

Chapter One

The Measure of a Man

When he could illustrate a point, Jack Mitchell did not hesitate to tell stories on himself:

I think of an experience I had way back in the Dark Ages—1919—when the flu epidemic was on, raging down through and especially on the prairies of Canada—and I had started to hold some meetings. I had just started out to preach; and I was away up there in Saskatchewan, about 20 miles from nowhere, having meetings in a schoolhouse.

And, because of the flu, we had to stop the meetings. And the man I was staying with—his son, daughter and six children lived in the big house and I lived with the old man in a little old shack over there. And they had over 640 acres of ground.

All of them had the flu, and I spent a whole week nursing this family through the flu.

And then came the question. The old man said, "I'm getting disturbed because I need my summer fallow done."

"Well," I said, "don't worry. I'll do it."

And he said, "You ever plow?"

"Never worked on a farm in my life."

I was raised on the sea. If you want a boat, I can run a boat for you. I could drive a tractor, but no plows. He had a 16-gang plow, and he had an old Rumley oil engine. (You folks wouldn't know. This was the Dark Ages I'm talking about.) It had four great big cylinders, and it ran on coal oil. You started it up with gas. Each cylinder had its own carburetor. So I started it up with gas.

And he said, "Now, you get in there, and I want that piece plowed." He pointed out which one.

And I looked across the fence. It was about half a mile through. It was a great big field. I don't know how many— a hundred, hundred and fifty, two hundred—acres in the field. So I got up on top of this old Rumley oil plow, and he said, "When you get there, you pull that rope and all the gang plows will go down."

So I started off and pulled the rope. And he ran after me and jumped on the platform by the gangs and made me stop the engine.

I said, "What's the matter?"

He said, "Where you going?"

I said, "I'm going over there."

He said, "Look back there."

I looked back. And I said, "Oh, I catch on."

So what I did was to hike to the other end of the field. I took my shirt off and put it up on a stick and put it up in the air. And then I just kept my eye on my old shirt.

I just wanted to get to my shirt, you know. That kept me on a straight course. Once you get your first furrow, it's easy to get the next one. You just follow right along.

But the first one is like that. When I started off, you see, I was just running that old engine. I didn't care about the plows. But when I got my shirt there, I held a straight course. I plowed a straight furrow. That's the thought you have in this verse— II Timothy 2:15.

"Study to show yourself approved."

Unto your teacher?

No. No-no-no. "Unto God. A workman that needeth not to be ashamed. Holding a straight course through the Word of Truth."

Have I made myself clear on that?

John Greenwood Mitchell did make himself clear on that. He plowed a straight furrow, his eyes on his Goal, for 97 years.

How does one even begin to assess the significance of such a man?

You can trace his ancestry and his own beginnings. You can document the major changes in his life and watch as he develops the character that colored his adult years. You witness his leaving home, his conversion to Christ, his choice of vocation and wife, his changes in ministry. And you talk to his friends.

A man's friends gather when he has left this life and gone to meet his Saviour, and so there is no better way to begin a biography of the man than to listen as his friends record his significance. Sometimes, their remarks can become a table of contents of his life.

Dr. Joseph C. Aldrich, president of Multnomah School of the Bible, did this when he spoke at a memorial service for Dr. Mitchell at Central Bible Church soon after the old man died. He said:

Dr. Mitchell was one of those kinds of people that everybody wants to own. I remember I thought we (Aldriches) were the only ones that called him "Uncle John." And I was always as a youngster a little bit chagrined when I'd hear newcomers using that term of endearment—"Uncle John."

Some of us haven't grown up enough to forget that he's our "Uncle John."

Dad and I have often compared Dr. Mitchell to a fire-station horse—highly trained. Those animals could be harnessed and out of the fire station door in 11 to 12 seconds when the alarm rang. When the alarm rang, they were all business.

I want to tell you if you've never been at Multnomah and sat under Dr. Mitchell's teaching that, when the classroom bell rang—no matter how weary Dr. Mitchell was—he came alive. Strength from above coursed through his being and like a fire-station horse he moved more than his share of weight.

I think we'd agree that few men exalted Christ as he. I think we'd agree that few men loved Christ as he. And I think we'd agree that few men longed to see Christ as he.

I guess a whole myriad of thoughts and reflections come to mind when you think about a unique, choice servant of God like Uncle John.

I reminded Auntie Mary that my earliest childhood memories include being enchanted with slugs crawling across the sidewalk in their back yard and receiving a box of grapefruit delivered annually at Christmastime.

I remember Auntie Mary and Uncle John showed up one time unexpectedly, and my mother absolutely was chagrined because the house was not in order. But how could it be with nine kids?

When I reflect on Dr. Mitchell, I see a young man walking the Canadian prairies and praying all night for the lost. In my mind's eye, I see a young man alone preaching his heart out to the boulders and stumps. I see him paying a telephone operator in a remote community to place a general call and invite people to come to a revival service. I can almost hear the wagon teams, the buggies, the horses moving toward the church or grange hall as they came to hear this young evangelist preach. Sometimes there was no light, and he preached to an audience he couldn't see.

It still amazes me that, as an itinerant evangelist during the Canadian depression, it was not unusual for him to drive across the prairies with virtually no gas in his car.

I can almost hear him and old man Erickson fighting off a pack of wild dogs to save the life of a seriously wounded pig. I see him kneeling with the owner to ask God to spare the pig's life, and God answered the prayer. Early the next morning, the barn resounded with a litter of 12 healthy pigs, two of whom became God's tool to lead another rancher named Murphy to Christ.

I see Dr. Mitchell preaching an evangelistic series in Radville as people are throwing rocks at the building. One evening, as they were having a prayer service, these people came and nailed the door shut with ten-penny nails; and the congregation had to go out the back way. It was at Radville that they threatened to put the fire hose on him if he ever showed up at the roundhouse. So Uncle John went down to the roundhouse and he talked to the boilermakers and the machinists—his kind of people.

I can see rifles pointed at him by suspicious moonshiners who thought he might be a federal agent. He invaded their turf with the gospel, and many found Christ.

I can see him going to preach and no bridge is around, and so he crossed the Cleveland Rapids every day in a canoe paddled by an Indian to go and share the gospel out in the remote areas of the state of Oregon.

I can see him at Dallas Seminary, studying into the wee hours of the morning with his roommate, my Uncle Roy.

Tucked away in bits and pieces in my mind are at least a thousand sermons that I heard him deliver as many of you have.

From the balcony of the old Behnke-Walker building many of us could hear his Scotch-Irish—his Geordie accent—urging us to love the Saviour and suggesting we ought to read our Bibles.

From earlier correspondence with my father, I read of his heart for the Northwest and his great desire to see it reached for Christ.

I see the names of many families reached and touched by his ministries. I started to list some of those and I thought no, I can't do that. Some people would be left out, but you know what I'm talking about.

From my childhood days I see him spellbinding many with his famous candle story.

How many birthdays have we celebrated? How many candles have we seen blown out? How many weddings and funerals have we been to when Dr. Mitchell presided?

*Who can forget Romans or his "Spiritual Life" classes? Or singing "The Lion of Juder" and "There Is a Fountain Filled With Blood?" Who can forget the **Know Your Bible Hour** program? I can still see the twinkle in his eye when he was asked to tell another fish story or talk about the days of his youth or his beloved wife Mary who reputedly caught the most fish.*

Who can forget the yellow bus fleet and the thousands of

kids reached by released-time classes? And Trout Creek camp?

His love for students will always stand out. His love for Christ has marked all of us.

I can see him coming through the door of my office, usually apologizing for interrupting me and staying anyway.

And then he flopped down and we'd talk. And then without exception, with no warning he'd just start to pray. . . .

Now, let us pray:

Father, blessed in Your eyes, precious in Your eyes is the Homegoing of Your children.

Father, we suspect that Heaven is full of joy as this one that you waited so long to bring Home finally came Home.

His love for You was so great we wonder sometimes how You were able to leave him here as long as You did, but we thank You that You did.

And, Father, as we who are alive and remain reflect on the life that he lived and the dedication that he demonstrated and the commitments that drove him, we as Elisha would pray that somehow by Your grace those qualities could touch each one of our lives.

And, Father, we pray that we could have a growing desire to know You as he knew You. . . .

And, now, as we celebrate that one of Your choicest servants in now in Your presence, we also commend ourselves to You in Christ's Name. Amen.

Chapter Two

Always Ready

The Mitchell family was enjoying a late supper when a distant booming of the harbor guns signaled that a ship was in distress. In the late 1890s, townsmen still fired cannons in storms to signal when ships had crashed on the rocks.

At the first sound of the guns, three young boys flew out of their chairs and down the steps of their upstairs flat before a detaining hand could hold them back.

South Shields in Northern England, a century ago, prided itself on being a town that was always ready to face any kind of emergency. Its harbor, on the northeast corner of England where the Tyne River flows into the stormy North Sea, had a reputation for danger. Sailing ships trying to make port often foundered in the high seas that swept across the rocky shore.

Back in 1867, the town had organized a pilots association to help captains bring their ships in. Already the first English town to maintain boats for rescue operations, South Shields bolstered its reputation when builder William Wouldhave constructed the first unsinkable lifeboat.

On the night the Mitchell boys ran breathlessly the long mile from their home to the beach, the sea was running high and great waves were crashing against the shore. The whole town turned out, its young men ready to rescue sailors clinging to the ship impaled out on the rocks.

But the head pilot decided it would be impossible to launch the boat in the heavy seas, and so he refused to open the boathouse door.

"Open it, Father, open it," his sons called to him.

"No! It's too much! The sea's too high."

"Open it, Father. They'll die oot there."

"You'll die gettin' them. I canna let you do it, boys."

"If you will not go, we will!"

The sons of the pilot broke open the door and pulled the boat to the water. Many men helped, plunging deep into the surf; but each time the boat was thrown back on the sands. Finally, a huge wave swept it out to sea.

For almost two hours, the people watched. They shouted when a wave lifted the boat high and moaned when it disappeared. They watched their men reach the ship and pluck off the sailors. They were delirious when the boat returned to the beach.

Shouting and crying, the people lifted their lads to their shoulders and carried them through the town.

The next day, bold headlines in the papers read, "Shields is always ready."

I have heard John tell this story many times, and always he would add, "The motto of our town was 'Always Ready.' "

I feel that this could be the motto of his life. He was always ready to commit himself fully to the work God had given him to do. He was "ready always to give an answer to every man. . .a reason of the hope that was in him" (I Peter 3:15).

—Mary Mitchell

South Shields sits on the cod banks of the North Sea, up where Mother England rears her back and hunches west to guard herself against Nordic blasts—and Scots she's never learned particularly to like. Despite hundreds of years of trying, she never could keep Scotsmen from leaking over the border and mingling with the Brits and the Irish who had settled along the coast.

She coined the nickname, "Geordies," speculation has it, as a sneer word to ridicule the Northumbrians—the hybrids who dwelt beside the River Tyne. Some think the word helped the purer bloods on both sides of the English-Scottish border to describe the descendents of those who, like the Israelites of old, chose to ignore their own Promised Land and to intermarry with alien tribes who lived across their "Jordan."

More likely, "Geordies" derived out of "Georgies," the popular name of a coin that bore the superscription of St. George; and, thus, as a derogation, it may have been meant to mock the industry and thrift of the "penny-pinchers" who lived along the River Tyne.

But citizens of South Shields in County Tyne And Wear had more to do in the early 1890s than care a twit about what critics thought.

Daily, fishermen left the harbor and coursed out the mouth of the Tyne, past wrecks of schooners sagging on the rocks, to harvest herring, cod and mackerel from the sea. Farmers trundled produce and herded livestock to the docks. Shipbuilding, import and export, and all the trades that thrive in a coastal farming town served by a broad flowing river filled the air with rattles and clanging and callings and noise as every house and tenement, every shop and factory bustled with industry and vigorous living.

Even children, dragged from their beds, fed and shoved out the door by energetic mothers, had to attend school from age three and stay there eight hours a day. They gorged on heavy doses of arithmetic, grammar, French, Latin and advanced geometry, administered by lively teachers in a day when people thought a mind was made for stretching. By age 11, with their own energy charged and their noggins full, most youngsters left school, ready for life, having had the equivalent of a modern high school education.

One South Shields girl, Isobel Huntley, traveled to America with her first husband, James Pierson, back in the

1850s when a trip on a sailing vessel took three months and passengers had to take food to last the entire journey.

She and her husband settled in Kentucky to raise their children. During the Civil War, a Southern neighbor in a rage shot and killed James for siding with the North. The man threatened Isobel with death if she reported him. Frightened, she returned to England with her two sons and later married Joshua Greenwood, a talented musician, teacher of music and organizer of bands popular in those days. He was a widower with a son and daughter.

She then bore three more children—Joshua, who became a bandmaster and an assistant to a Dan Godfrey, an internationally known band leader; David, who became a professional musician in London; and Lavinia, who married James Mitchell, a marine engineer. They, in turn, named their children Joshua, John, David and Isobel.

When John Greenwood Mitchell (called "Jack" his life long by those who knew him best) was born on December 5, 1892, the family lived in a five-room upstairs apartment in one of several tenements owned by their grandfather Greenwood. It stood on Hyde Street in an area of town known as "The Lawe," an eminence that overlooked the entrance to the river from the sea.

The apartment was heated by a large open fireplace in the kitchen. The children would hurry from their beds in the morning to dress on a big hand-woven rug in front of the fire—the favorite spot on cold winter mornings. It was here, too, that all the cooking was done.

We cooked over the open fire, Jack would tell folk later. *There was a little fender. We would sit on the fender when we were kids and get the fire. If you needed toast, you put bread on a long fork and put it right in front of the coals. And you cooked on top in a little oven alongside. You pushed the coals in there. My job was to bring in the coal every morning, you know. I always kept the bucket full of coal.*

Breakfast porridge, made fresh each morning, boiled in a

double boiler on the grate.

"It was wonderful porridge," he would say years later. "It was so thick you could walk across it if you wanted. It would really stick to your ribs."

What wasn't finished for breakfast appeared fried for lunch. What wasn't eaten for lunch they got for dinner. It never went over to the second day. The boys learned early to gulp it down in the morning so it wouldn't keep coming back to haunt them all day long.

During those early years as a family, the father spent most of his time away from home as a sea-going engineer. But with the birth of her youngest boy David, Lavinia put her foot down.

"James, these three boys need their father. I want you to stay home."

He said, "But I've signed up to sail on the S.S. Garthorn. We're goin' to South America."

She answered, "Well, if you go, you need not come back."

He didn't go. And, later, they learned that the S.S. Garthorn had gone down at sea with no survivors.

His mother, a "wee woman," had a strong personality and high moral standards. Though loving, she ruled with an iron fist. Jack would boast, "My mother could take her slipper off and give us a crack with it and get it back on her foot before the first yell got out."

And she knew how to lay down the law.

When I was growing up, sometimes my mother would put things in the living room (we called it the "front room") and shut the door. Then she would say, "Now, you children, don't go into the front room today."

We weren't even thinking about going into the front room. We were in the kitchen most of the time. But when Mother said, "Don't go in there today," what do you think we did?

Sometimes she would put butterscotch candies on a high shelf and warn us to keep away. And suddenly there was nothing we wanted more than those butterscotch candies.

She caught the boys trying cigarettes and whaled the tar out of them. They could smoke when they got to be 21, but no sooner if she had anything to say about it.

Although they did not attend church nor make any profession of Christianity, Jack's parents did permit other influences to make a mark on him. When he was eight years old, they let him join a boys' choir that sang every day at Evensong in St. Hilda's Church. He always spoke highly of the chorus master who, he felt, made an impact for godliness on his life. Dressed in his black cassock with white surplice, Jack sang until he was 12 and his voice began to change.

His parents also let him attend mission Sunday School classes where the children won prizes for learning Bible verses. He always wanted to be the one to learn the most.

They let Grandfather Greenwood take charge of the boys' musical education. He taught them the piccolo, cornet, flute, Flugelhorn and even the French horn. He kept them busy practicing and copying music, so busy that Jack told how the boys would take turns sliding down a pipe outside their window so they could play for a while with neighbor boys. They desperately loved to play.

But Grandfather Greenwood desperately loved his brew. He would sew drinking money in his coat linings to hide it from his wife. His delirium tremens amazed and frightened the Mitchell boys and gave them a life-long abhorrence of alcohol.

Eleven months of the year, they attended school. But, oh! how they looked forward to August, their only vacation month. They loved the warm days of summer when they could fish and swim in the sea. If the tide was low, they would swim out to the wrecks and dive deep in the still waters inside the rusting hulls.

Jack stuttered from childhood, a malady that lasted into young manhood; but it didn't seem to interfere with his childhood education. He finished school at age 11 and began to work at the Reidhead shipyard, catching red hot rivets for the riveters. In no time, he learned a new language.

"Those old riveters would curse at me, and I'd curse them right back. I picked it up in less than 24 hours, I tell you."

But he didn't dare do it at home.

"One day, I came home. I was mad about something and I just cursed like a trooper. Boy!

"My mother said, 'Come here, son. Come here.' She took a bar of soap and got hold of me. She wanted to stick it in my mouth.

" 'B-r-r-r-r-r! I won't d-d-do it ag-g-g-gain!' I yelled.

"After that, I talked one language down at the shipyards and over here at home I talked another one."

Though she wouldn't tolerate nonsense, Jack's mother did recognize fun when she saw it. She was frying eggs one day when he, at age 11, got to teasing her. As she turned around to give him "a crack," he put his elbow up to ward off the blow. She hurt her hand. She got so mad, she turned around and picked up the frying pan and whaled at him with it. Up went his elbow again—right through the frying pan. Eggs and grease and soot went everywhere.

I thought sure I was gonna get it now. You see, there was so much soot on the pan. I don't know how many years old the old frying pan was, but you wouldn't know it because it had so much soot on it.

But she just stood there and laughed to beat the band. Just laughed. That's the kind of mother to have, I'll tell you.

She was—she was a wonder!

Other women in the family also made their mark on the children. Grandmother Mitchell lived with them for several years. She loved to sit in her rocking chair beside the fire. Her husband died when Jack was a young child so he didn't remember him.

The boys loved to visit their father's sister, Sarah, who lived in Hexam several miles' walk away; and they loved to go to their maternal grandmother's apartment to hear tales of

America—how she had to take enough food to last the three months, how people in America walked across rivers on ice in the winter, and especially how her husband was killed arguing in Kentucky.

There was a reason for their interest. Geordies loved to argue, and these young Geordies loved to fight.

"When I worked in the shipyards, we would fight every day," Jack said.

The men and women who worked on and around the ships would tease the boys and get them to fight one another. And then they'd bet on which boy would win.

Oh, the thrill when you hit a fella and got him in the nose and out came the blood. It just made you feel—"Ooo, I'd just like to go some more."

And when we were done, we would go down to the river—our shipyard was right by the river—and wash ourselves off. You know, the blood and all. And then we'd go home together arm in arm. You know, no envy, no bitterness about it. Just a good old fight.

See? You have to live among the Irish to get this idea, you know. They just love to fight. Yes, just love to fight.

And in his nineties, Dr. Mitchell would challenge the young men in his Bible classes to meet him in the hall for a fight.

"Sometimes, I want to call you fellows out. Sometimes. I'll take my glasses off, just for the fun of it. Boy, that'd be wonderful. I'm too slow on my feet, that's the trouble."

But it wasn't fighting that almost took his life.

Young Jack at age 11 was standing on a plank with a riveting team, high up on scaffolding that hugged the hull of a ship. Beside him on the plank stood a little box of cinders. One man would heat a rivet white hot and throw it in that box. Jack would pick it up with tongs and put it in a hole in the hull plates. One man behind the rivet and two on the other side would pound it into place.

Normally, he would have stood between the riveters and the box. For some reason this day, he was standing on the end of the plank.

"When the man behind the rivet stepped onto the other plank, the plank I was on went up and I went down."

If the bottom of the ship had been built up, he would have been killed, falling nearly four stories. But he went right between the ribs to the ground.

"I got myself up and walked up the ladder again. People were amazed I wasn't killed. But you have to remember that the Lord takes care of His own—even before they know Him," he said later.

It's doubtful he ever told his mother. He had had enough of a scare.

Lavinia still kept her eye on him when he turned 13. She let him go to work two years in a hardware and bicycle shop. Then he apprenticed in Ray's Marine Engineering shop. But when he wanted to attend evening school to study marine engineering, she warned him, "You be home by 10 or have a good excuse if you come home late, I tell you."

He would work in the shop from 6 o'clock in the morning until 5:30 at night. And then, three nights a week, he would go down to the marine school where he was taught mathematics and machine designing.

One night, he came home after 10.

When I came in, my mother took her slipper off and I dove under the dining room table.

Now, my brother—you know, in those days, you only had two bedrooms in the house. I slept on the top of the stairs on a little cot, and my brother was on a little couch right near the dining room table.

When I dove under the table, I rolled under his bed and pulled his pillow with me.

So mother got down on her knees. By this time, she'd got a stick. She was mad because I dove under that table. So she pounded at me with that stick. And every time she reared back and hit the pillow, I yelled.

Years later, she and Jack were reminiscing about the old days when the boys were kids.

And I said, "Mom, do you remember the night that I dove under Josh's bed when you went after me?"

"Yes," she said, "and that was one time that I r-r-r-really gave you a good licking."

And I said, "You know, Ma, you never hit me once."

"I never hit you once?"

"No," I said, "I grabbed Josh's piller and every time you hit the piller, I yelled."

My mother could stand under my arm. And she got up. I was in my late twenties at the time.

She said, "I've got a good mind to lick you noo."

And I laughed and said, "Well, Ma, you go right ahead and lick me noo."

She said, "I would, but I'd hurt myself more than you, you big lug."

Jack, at 13, made the mistake one whipping of telling her, "Ya! You d-d-didn't hurt me at all!" She laid hold of him and made up for it.

"But I tell you one thing," he said later, "I never ran to the neighbors when I was hurt. Who do you think I ran to? My Ma."

She did her best to keep her boys from the evils around them.

She would say, "Remember, John, you're a Mitchell."

After he gave up the sea, James Mitchell, the father, worked as an engineer at the local docks; but he was restless. He made one trip to America but returned because he couldn't find any work. No one was hiring because a depression had cut out many jobs. He returned to the States in 1908 with his eldest son Joshua. This time, they were able to find good jobs and soon sent for the family to join them.

Jack loved his England. He was deeply sad to leave. He never forgot the sights and sounds of his boyhood home, and he never lost the Geordie brogue that stamped its accent on his tongue.

On their arrival in America, the Mitchells lived for a time in Missouri, then moved to Chicago and Pittsburg. Jack, at 16, was able to get jobs as a full-fledged machinist.

But the cold winters in Illinois and Pennsylvania aggravated his sister Isobel's health, so much so that a doctor advised the Mitchells to take their daughter to a warmer climate. So in 1911, they moved with her to Dunsmuir, California. The rest of the family chose to scatter with Joshua returning to England, David going to New Mexico and Jack to Winnipeg, Manitoba, where he worked in a machine shop for a year.

It was betting on the horses that got him into Canada to begin with. He was working in a machine shop in Pittsburg and went to Winnipeg with an Irish friend whose uncle had race horses of his own. They bet on his horses and lost their money. So they both got a job in a machine shop on the night crew. When his friend had earned enough money to buy his ticket, he went back to Pittsburg. But Jack stayed on, perhaps feeling more at home at this time in a British nation than he had in the States.

The thought of being a machinist the rest of his life nagged him. In that shop, he asked a man who had lopped off a couple of fingers on a band saw to tell him how the accident had happened. Demonstrating just how he did it, the man cut off another one.

Jack watched a second man who seemed quite content having worked on the same machine for more than 20 years.

Not that the men weren't bright—but, deep down, Jack wanted to become a doctor. He tried to enroll at Brandon College in Manitoba. He would get his college credits there before applying to McGill University medical school.

But Brandon put him off because he didn't have enough credits in language.

In the process of working on the machine shop night crew, he met a Scot who had the same academic language deficiency Jack did. Brandon officials had told them both that if they could pass an examination covering 120 pages of Haggarty's Latin text, they could save a year or so.

Jack studied days and propped his text up in front of

him during his night shift at work. By fall, he had mastered his Haggarty's Latin; and he stayed at Brandon College from 1912 to 1915. He earned part of his expenses waiting tables.

I had three tables with ten to a table. When I brought the tray around, they all ducked their heads. I had only 30 people to wait on, but the work was hard. I barely kept on my feet long enough to get through.

While making out his first schedule, he signed up for Greek at the encouragement of his roommate, James Smith, the only other one who had signed up for the course. Later, when Jack entered seminary, he was grateful for the three years of Greek study.

He and James received the highest honors in the school that year. His roommate had the highest scholastic record, and Jack was awarded the Governor General's medal as the best all-around student.

The student newspaper, "The Brandon College Quill," November 1915 issue, reported his contribution to the musical life of the college at a literary society meeting:

"A programme given in the chapel was most enjoyable, especially a scene 'Tenting' and the quartette rendered by Messrs. Chapman, Mitchell, Carlson and Stone."

Mention of his contribution to the athletic life of the college appeared in the November 1914 issue:

"Old Warhorse Rutherford was right there with the mile walk. Andy put out his chest at the tape and won what looked a dead heat from Happy Mitchell."

The students, appreciating his sunny disposition, called Jack "Happy."

The November 1915 issue also stated:

"In the boys' event, Hurley, who won (the 100 yard dash) two years ago, was forced to take second place, Mitchell being first, with Masterton third. . . . The handsome Moffat won the shot-put by heaving the shot 25 feet 7 inches. 'Happy Mitchell' was a good second, with his old room-mate, Smith, third."

The December 1914 issue lists him as treasurer of the

literary society and as a debater:

The first inter-class debate for the year '14-'15 was held Friday, Nov. 20th, when Theology and Hash clashed! The appropriate and interesting resolution read as follows: 'Resolved that the Monroe doctrine provides adequate protection for Canada against invasion.' The Theological 'word mongers' represented by T. H. Harris, B.A., and E. Davis defended the proposition, while James Smith and John Mitchell attacked. The affirmative was given the decision."

The play on words, "Theology and Hash," probably referred to Jack's service in the dining room and the fact that he and his roommate were debating religion majors.

When Canada began making preparations to enter World War I, Jack tried to enlist in the Armed Forces. At that time, it was an all-volunteer service. His application was repeatedly rejected because he had flat feet. He went back to college and trained that winter in the University Battalion and applied again without success. He decided that, since all his friends had enlisted, he could help the war effort best by leaving school and going back to a machine shop to make war materiel.

He found a job as night foreman in one place for a year. When that shop burned down, he moved to Medicine Hat in Alberta for six weeks and then to Calgary, tooling up big shops that handled high explosives.

"And, while I was there, I went out on the street one time with a little Irishman who used to be in Brandon College. And he asked me where I was going to church, and I said. . ."

A little Irishman asked a little question on a street in a town way up in Western Canada. That one question and the events that followed changed Jack Mitchell's life and, subsequently, lit a fire that burned in his heart across the Canadian prairies.

Chapter Three

Something Happened

Jack loved to relive the events that led up to his conversion.

When I went to Calgary, Alberta, to take over a tool and die job in that city, I met a fellow I went to school with in Manitoba, in college, who sang in the same quartet I did. He was a little Irishman by the name of McNulty. He was pastor of a little Baptist church on the east side of the city. He asked me where I was going to church, and I said I wasn't going to any church.

He asked me where I was staying, and I told him I was staying in the YMCA with three other fellows. If we weren't playing basketball, we were in some sort of mischief or playing poker or whatever we did to while away our time.

After I had been there about a month or so, he came to me and he said, "I'm leaving my little room in the home where I am, and I am going to be married."

"Oh?" I said. "Congratulations."

And he said, "I would like you to take this room because this little widow I'm renting from needs someone to room in her home. She needs the money."

That was fine with me. So I just took my things and went down to this home. But when I got there, I found he wasn't leaving until the next week; and I confess to you that I didn't appreci-

ate spending two or three nights sleeping in the same room as a
preacher, an Irish one at that.

The question was incidental: "Where are you going to church?" It was followed by an even shorter question, just as direct: "Where are you staying?"

It was probably no more than that. They were just two college friends who met on the street, chatted briefly and parted. Jack learned only then that McNulty was pastor of a little Baptist church across town.

The mustard seed of that conversation germinated in his consciousness for a month or so before McNulty looked him up again. In the interim, another mustard seed began to grow.

Jack had gone for a haircut with no way of knowing that his barber was a practicing Christian determined to obey an impression he had received in his morning devotions that he witness that day.

In came Jack Mitchell. On went the sheet and out came the scissors.

Introductory patter over, here came the first thrust.

"You know, the Bible says there is none righteous, no, not one."

"Don't give me that," came the answer. "I'm just as good as any of 'em."

"Oh? That so?" Out came the Testament. "Looka here. 'For there is no respect of persons with God.' "

Jack Mitchell didn't like that. He wanted to get that haircut over and be on his way.

The barber put his Testament aside. "Just remember that, while all have sinned and come short of the glory of God, we are justified freely by His grace through the redemption that is in Christ Jesus."

No response.

While he was shaving around the edges, he said, "Jack, it

is free to us—but it cost God His Son!"

No response.

On came the hot towel. Out came the lotion. Off came the sheet with a shake. Jack reached for his pocket.

Smith, the barber, put a friendly hand on his shoulder and said, "I'm not so interested in the price of a haircut, Jack, as I am in the cost of your soul. Christ Jesus came into the world to save sinners! *It cost God His Son!* Think it over, Jack."

Those five words, he said later, engraved themselves on his mind.

Then back came McNulty.

He opened the conversation with his good news, "I'm going to be married." He worked around to the felt need of a "little widow" who "needs the money." Having explained the lady's plight, he suggested that Jack could meet her need by an act of kindness that would benefit the three of them. He simply asked Jack to rent his room in the woman's home.

McNulty's conscience was clear. He could go marry with no concern for the woman who now had a renter and an assured income. And Jack could leave the YMCA, where he had had to share a room, and now have a room of his own.

"That was fine with me," he said. The boy from South Shields was "always ready" to help a friend and always ready to meet a need.

He moved in on a Saturday but found himself obligated to go hear McNulty preach on Sunday, which he didn't want to do. At some time, during the following week, he picked a book up off McNulty's desk as he was looking for something to read. It turned out to be a book of sermons preached at the prophetic conference of the Moody Bible Institute in 1914.

I started to read it, and then I said to him after a while, "Mac, do you believe what is in this book?"

And he said, "Yes."

I said, "Do you mean to tell me you believe that Jesus Christ is coming back to the earth again?"

He said, "Yes."

"*Well,*" I said, "*that's what Innes believed.*" Innes was a fellow in Brandon College, another preacher. I said, "*He believed that and do you know what I called him?*"

He said, "*What?*"

"*I called him crazy.*" I said, "*It's a crazy idea for people to believe that Jesus Christ is going to come back to the earth again. What does He want to come here for? They crucified Him before. What will they do to Him now?*" This was my attitude, of course, not knowing Him.

"*Well,*" he said, "*how much do you know about it?*"

"*Well, nothing,*" I said.

Then McNulty went off to be married. But before he left, he made Jack promise that he would go to his church—which was about three blocks away from where they lived—and hear a man who ran a plumbing store in the same area. He had preached for McNulty every once in a while and had consented to take the ministry for the month he was to be gone. Jack said later that if he had known what was in store he would have rebelled against it. The man preached every morning for four Sunday mornings on Romans chapter one.

And if you know Romans one, you know it's not a very good picture of the human heart. And I declare that he accused me of doing 90 percent of what was in Romans chapter one and that made me mad because I wouldn't think of being guilty of such things.

Then one night, Jack, having nothing else to do, again picked up the little book on the prophetic conference at Moody in 1914. He read it to the end; and then, intrigued, sat there and read it through again and again.

"For some reason or other," he said later, "it just began to captivate my heart and mind."

Then the alarm clock went off and startled him. It was 5:30 in the morning and he was still reading the book. He decided not to go to work but to keep on reading the book.

"I must have read it through four or five or six times. I was fascinated with the idea that Jesus Christ was coming back to the earth again."

The plumber chose Luke chapter 10 for his last sermon.

I don't know all he said about the story of the Good Samaritan. But I know one thing. Something happened to this man Mitchell.

I didn't know what happened, but I knew that something had happened. It seemed as though God Himself was asking, "But what answer do you have to My love?" I was deeply conscious of the love and mercy of God and of the Saviour who shed His blood for me.

In fact, this man told me afterwards because we became quite friendly, "I knew what was happening to you. You sat on the edge of your seat, and your face was like a moonbeam."

"What's a moonbeam got to do with it?"

"Man, you were saved last Sunday night."

And I said, "Was I?"

He said, "You sat on your chair with your mouth wide open, drinking in every word."

"Oh," I said, "is that the reason I picked up Mac's Bible and read it last night?"

So Jack started reading the Bible every night, smoking a cigar and eating Macintosh apples until 2 or 3 o'clock in the morning.

And then, when McNulty came back the next week, he said, "Mac, do you know what's the matter with you?"

And he said, "What?"

"You haven't enough meetings in your church."

He said, "What in the world has happened to you?"

That confirmed, Jack said later, that something real had indeed happened. But soon after that, some people in the church told him he should now tarry to receive the Holy Spirit—the baptism of the Spirit.

I didn't know much about the Bible and what God said on the subject, but I didn't have any peace about it. Of course, I learned later that it is something God does at regeneration. We're not told to seek it. We're not told to pray for it. We're not told to tarry for it. Unfortunately, it's become a doctrine today that is greatly misused and greatly misunderstood.

But another way Jack knew that something had happened in his heart was that he no longer had any interest in doing some of the things he had been doing with the three fellows at the YMCA.

"Nobody asked me to give them up, but I just automatically did."

He went over to the YMCA and gave his testimony to the three young men as they were playing poker one Saturday afternoon.

I found out that I had some pride. Unbelievers don't have to think twice to give up on people who become Christians. But it was kind of tough when they gave up on me and wouldn't talk to me. They spurned me. I felt like being a good Irishman and clipping them one. You know. You've felt that way. After all, they had taken my money before. Why shouldn't they acknowledge what had happened to me now?

He tried the men in his little machine shop. One of them, a die maker, listened skeptically to the testimony Jack said he now had in Christ.

I tried to speak to him the best I knew how—how God can come into our lives and transform us.

And, when I got through, he said to me, "Now, listen to me, Jack Mitchell. No use giving that to me. I couldn't do that in this shop. Why, a saint couldn't work in this shop."

"Oh?" I said. "There are some saints in this shop."

"I'd like to see just one."

"Well," I said, "there's one talking to you now."

You ought to have seen his face and heard the explosion that followed.

"You a saint?"

Now, it's true that just a few weeks before that—at the outside just two or three months—I had been swearing and cussing along with the rest of them.

A saint in the shop?

Yes.

And then he added this. "And are you going to be like that fellow outside? Barney? Are you going to be like him?"

He was an Irishman, a toolsman who was tempering the dies. He went to church in the morning with a Bible under his arm, but he had one of the filthiest tongues I had ever heard in my life. He had no testimony at all among the men.

"Are you going to be like him?"

And I said, "I trust not. I know one thing though—that I have received some good news from God. And I know that Jesus Christ is my Saviour, and I know He calls me a saint."

Another man in the shop—a foul-mouthed boilermaker who used to come over to Jack's bench for the expanding reamers and taps Jack made for him—came in one day and asked, "Could I borrow one of your little tools?"

He said, "Which one do you want?"

He told him.

Jack said, "You'll find it in the top drawer of my tool chest."

He went over to the chest and pulled one of the drawers open.

I had moved all the tools out of that little drawer and had put a Testament in there. I could just barely close it. So when he pulled this little drawer open, instead of the one he should have pulled open, here was my Testament open.

He looked at it and said, "Well, Mitchell, are you turning religious?"

Jack said, "It's true I have accepted the Saviour." And he gave him his testimony.

The man listened for a while and then said, "Now, if you're going to be a Christian, you be a good one."

Jack was 24 when he received Christ as his Saviour. He remembered having memorized Scriptures with other children in his South Shields neighborhood; but as far as having any real knowledge of the Word of God, he didn't have any. Now, he found he had a tremendous hunger to know the

Bible. He would come home from work, take a shower, have dinner, and then read it sometimes until the alarm went off in the morning at 5:30. He'd leave at 6 o'clock for breakfast and catch a 6:30 bus for work and be at work at 7 o'clock. In those days, a man worked from 7 to 5:30.

Along with his appetite for the Word of God, he loved to witness.

"A friend of mine was a brilliant mechanic," he said of Charlie with whom Jack had at one time roomed and boarded for a number of months. The man had a church background, and Jack was sure he would be interested in his new life in Christ.

He laughed at me. Ridiculed me. He said this to me, "Do you believe that God loves me?"

I said, "Yeah."

"You believe He is love?"

I said, "Yeah."

"I'm born in sin?"

"Yeah."

"You really believe I'm a sinner?"

"Yep, I believe that. You're not only a born sinner, but you're a cultivated sinner."

He said, "You really believe that God loves me?"

"Yes."

"And He's gonna damn me because I'm a sinner?"

"Yes."

"I don't want your God."

Jack went home, back to his room.

"I didn't know much about the Bible," he would later say. "I wasn't raised in a Christian home like he was. But I went home and read my Bible all night long, trying to find answers for this fellow.

"I knew he was a sinner. I knew God is love. He's not going to damn men eternally because they were born in sin and were naturally sinners. See? It doesn't sound logical, does it?"

Jack knew there was an answer somewhere in Scripture,

and he read until he came across I Corinthians 5:18-19: "God was in Christ, reconciling the world unto himself, not charging unto them their trespasses."

He took that verse to Charlie.

"I kind of laid it on about him being a sinner and needing a Saviour. I told him that he could only be saved through what Christ did on the cross. And he got quite furious. He said some things he shouldn't have said.

And he said to me, "Then the Lord is not charging me with my sins."

And I said, "That's what it says."

"Then I'm all right."

I said, "No, you're not all right."

You see, I was so naive. I didn't know what a concordance was then, you know. I just had a Bible. So every time I had a question, I would start reading in Matthew and read right on through until I found the answer. I'd stay up all night—two nights, if necessary—to find the answer.

The next night, on his way through the gospels, Jack came across John 16:8-9: "And when he is come, he will reprove the world of sin. . . . Of sin, because they believe not on me."

"Charlie," I said the next day, "God is not holding sin against you today. He is holding against you your unbelief in the Lord Jesus Christ."

He said a few things that I'm not going to repeat. But one thing he did call it was "d___ foolishness."

And I said to him, "Charlie, do you know what you've just done?"

And he said, "What?"

"You've just told me that you belong to those who perish. The Bible says 'The preaching of the cross is to them that perish foolishness.'"

I took out my Testament and showed it to him.

Our fellowship was broken from there on. He wouldn't even talk to me. He called me all kinds of names—a few names I'm not going to accept by any means.

That experience—a watershed—set the direction and tone of this young believer's life for more than 70 years to come. Convinced that God's Word reveals God's truth, he searched for answers to meet the need of a friend; and he spent the rest of his life doing just that for his friends, his congregations and his students. The early actions and choices of young believers often have consequences more far-reaching than any they might expect.

The men in the machine shop watched closely to see if Jack's conversion would stick. He soon found there was an awful lot of difference between him and them. They would laugh at him and scorn him and do everything they could think of to try to make him mad. One of them magnetized his files. Another, while Jack was grinding a tool and his back was turned, eased the chock on his milling machine when he was working on a die. He returned to his machine and bent over to put the next cut on the die. The action removed the chock and the die fell out of the brace to the floor.

You just had to put a zipper on your mouth. You had to keep your hands on your tool but keep them on the machine.

You know what you want to do? Clean the shop up.

Well, eventually—eventually—they succeeded. They got me mad and it all just boiled up. I'd been saved about three months and I didn't know much about walking with the Lord.

But that morning—I felt like saying, "Lord, give me five minutes vacation to serve the devil and I'll clean these fellas up." You know! You've felt just like that—about ready to clean the shop up. And they knew it, too—I wanna tell ya. They knew it, too. I went over and threw one man outside in the snow. He was six foot two!

You can destroy three months of testimony in just five seconds.

Boy, I was ready to wipe the floor with all of them.

In his anger, he said unkind things. But, when he asked the men to forgive him for acting in such an unchristian way, his apology helped to break down barriers that had risen against him in the shop. They had never seen anyone so broken up over an outburst of anger.

But his temper was not his biggest problem.

My big problem was smoking. I smoked cigars from the time I was 16 years of age. I used to smoke cigars and play poker in my own home.

But it's no use talking to the world about the Saviour when you're doing certain things—because you defeat the very thing you want.

It was that realization that helped him get rid of his cigars. He was testifying to two men on a train, one after the other. He noticed that neither one listened very closely to what he was saying. Instead their eyes were riveted on the cigars that were sticking out of his pocket.

To them it was inconsistent for a man to talk about the Saviour, puffing on a cigar. So I looked at the cigar and looked at myself and said, "Mitchell, are you going to let that thing hinder you talking to men about the Lord?"

Without another thought, he took the cigars out of his pocket and threw them out of the train window.

That was the end of it for me—just like that. It boils down to—do I love the Saviour, do I love people more than some dirty old habit? Then let me get rid of the habit if it's going to affect my testimony for the Lord, if it's going to hinder somebody coming to the Saviour.

Jack had been saved about three or four weeks when he was invited to a Bible conference in Weyburn. It was his first experience of a meeting of this kind, and the preacher said one thing that locked on his heart.

He said, "If I were a young Christian, I would exhort you to take one little wee book of the Bible, read it through and read it through and master it."

And I had heard that there was a book in the Bible called "Jonah" about a man who in some way had got into a fish. That was all I knew about it.

So I went and got a hold of the book of Jonah. You know how many chapters there are in Jonah? The first three are the book and the fourth is an appendix.

I read and reread until I fell in love with the reading of the book of Jonah. I still like to preach on Jonah. I'll never forget it. You take a small book and master it. You get into your Bible. That's what that preacher was after.

Shortly after that, Jack came into contact again with the same little bald-headed barber in Calgary who had witnessed to him earlier. The man had never gone to school in his life. He had been saved out of a life of alcoholism and had moved from New York to Calgary to get away from his old habits and friends. The Lord, Jack said later, wonderfully transformed him.

All he knew and all I heard for the six months I was with him was Romans 3:21-31.

I said to him one day, "Heddy, don't you know any other Scripture besides this?"

He said, "I know a few. I've learned to read a few. But I'm not gonna give you up until you know Romans 3!"

"Well," I said, "I know it backwards and forwards."

"Yes," he said, "you know the Scripture, but you don't know its truth."

Jack was in his room reading the Bible one day when he came across I John 4:17: "We have boldness in the day of judgment: because as he is, so are we in this world."

He jumped up and ran the three or four blocks to the barbershop. It was past closing time, so he knocked. When Heddy saw who it was, he opened the door and let Jack in.

He was stropping his razor, about to give a fellow a shave.

I said, "Listen to this." And I read him the verse.

He just kept on stropping his razor, as if to say, "Well, what of it?"

I said, "Man, don't you see it?"

And he said, "Oh, yes, I've known all about that truth for a long time."

"Do you mean to tell me that you've known this for a long time and you didn't tell me?"

He kind of laughed and said, *"Son, there are so many things in the Word of God that you've never seen. But as you grow in the grace of God, you'll come to them."*

He pricked my bubble, to be frank with you.

Jack sneaked out of the shop and returned to his room, discouraged and chagrined. He felt his barber friend was unwise in dealing with him like that because he was a babe in Christ and didn't know much.

"Instead of encouraging me, he discouraged me."

Years later, Jack credited much of the success of his ministry with that saturation in Romans.

When I became a Christian, I had no doctrine to undo. The Lord just saved me and dropped me right into the grace of God—into the wonderful position that I have in Christ as given to us in the Book of Romans.

In fact, somebody asked me one time if that was the only book I had in my Bible because I reveled so much in the marvelous truth in it.

But I had nothing to undo. When people have been raised from the time they were children in certain doctrines, my friend, you can't expect them to get rid of that in ten minutes.

He felt the experience of concentrating on the Epistle to the Romans made him what he later called "heresy proof," and it gave him a subject to teach as God called him out into gospel work on the prairies of Canada.

Chapter Four

Called to Preach

Many years ago, I worked in the machine shops. Sometimes we had to make bearings for some of the farmers' machinery; and we would take old babbitt, put it in a pot, and put the pot in the forge.

We would melt the babbitt down and begin to skim it. We wanted to make a good bearing; we didn't want any refuse in it.

So, as the metal came to a boil, on the top of the metal would be all the stuff you couldn't use—stuff that would hinder a good bearing. We kept skimming it off until we saw the blues and the greens and the yellows on top of the metal. There was no more scum there. Then we poured out the metal, and we had a good bearing.

Now, faith is put in the crucible, not to be destroyed but to skim off the stuff that you don't want, stuff that is a hindrance to your walk with God or to your service or to your growth in the grace of God.

We are down here in school, and our faith must be tested and tried and purified. I found that out—early on—when the Lord sent me out to preach.

—John G. Mitchell

After he'd been studying with Heddy, the barber, for a year, Jack started to do some preaching on his own. But no one was more surprised than he.

A week of meetings had been announced, and one of his friends—the preacher who had announced the meetings—asked him to go along. Their destination, a small town out in the prairies, responded so overwhelmingly to the meetings that another week was arranged. The preacher readily agreed. But, when Jack got to the rented store building at the scheduled time, he found he was the scheduled event. The preacher had hopped the train and left.

"But I'm not a preacher," he protested. "I'm a machinist! A tool and die maker!"

"You'll do. Get up there!" they told him.

He looked out at the 20 to 25 people—if there were that many—and opened his mouth. He didn't know what to say—out loud. Inside, he was crying, "Lord, I can't talk. I stutter. I'm shy. Send somebody else." But no one stepped forward and he couldn't get away.

His first message, he related later, was four minutes long:

I said, "Well, friends—" and I guess I gave my testimony. When I was done, I dismissed the meeting with prayer.

But nobody moved.

I went to the door.

They were still sitting there.

I said, "The meeting's over. Come back at seven o'clock tonight and we'll give you some more."

I didn't know what I was gonna give them, but I was gonna give them "some more."

An old farmer said to me, "I've driven my team 20 miles to hear somebody preach!"

"Well," I said, "Tell you what. You come on and we'll give you some coffee and sandwiches. They're having it in the house here. Everybody's going to have some coffee and sandwiches and then we'll have the next meeting."

And then Jack hightailed it upstairs to his little room in the attic. Here, he'd agreed to have another meeting but he didn't know what he would say.

"Lord, what am I gonna do?"

As he prayed on his knees, he heard voices coming up from the kitchen downstairs right under him.

In those days, poor people used soft coal they could get right on the prairies—surface coal. In the wintertime, they used a coal stove; and a pipe would go right up through the house, through the bedroom above the kitchen and out through the roof. The bedroom was heated by the hot air that came up through the chimney. In the summer, they pulled the chimney down and used an unvented coal oil stove. Anything said below went upstairs through the hole in the floor or through the pipe in winter.

It was not his intention to eavesdrop; but, as he prayed, he heard them talking.

And one said to the other, "Did you understand what that young fellow said?"

"Never a word. Never a word."

"Do you think he'll ever make a preacher?"

"Never in this world. Never in this world."

Well, I was ready to pull my suitcase out and beat it.

But he felt no freedom to leave. The Lord reminded him that he'd been studying Romans for a year with the barber in Calgary and that was more than these people knew. So he began to teach the book of Romans, studying a chapter a day and keeping "one jump ahead of the people." It wasn't until he got to Romans 3 that he met any opposition:

When I got to Romans 3, I spent all day and night reading passages on justification and righteousness. And when I stood up to speak on Sunday afternoon, I declared that I have a righteousness that is the righteousness of God.

There was another preacher in the audience, and he walked out and announced all over town that this young fellow Mitchell was declaring that he was God.

But I didn't say that.

The look on the face of the man in charge of the Lord's

work in that town stayed with Jack through the years. "He was sitting on the front seat with his mouth open. He was horrified."

Jack looked at him and said, "Did I say something wrong? When I say that I have the righteousness of God, am I wrong?"

And out of his mouth came Scripture reference after Scripture reference on justification and righteousness, the verses he had poured over getting ready for his sermon.

He said to the people, "Please don't judge until you read them all."

He closed the meeting and walked out.

I didn't stay because I was scared stiff. I didn't know what I had done. I was in my innocence. I wasn't a preacher. I wasn't raised in churches. I didn't know anything about it except what I was reading in the book of Romans.

The next Sunday afternoon in the middle of a testimony meeting, the local elder rose to his feet and said, "Last Sunday afternoon, when our young brother spoke about justification and righteousness, I thought something had gone wrong with his head. He was making some drastic statements. But—it's true!"

Jack didn't have a chance to preach that afternoon. The man spoke a whole hour on the righteousness of God which believers in Jesus Christ have.

Jack returned to Calgary, assuring himself that he would never get in that kind of pickle again. Given another invitation to preach, he would turn it down flat. He told the Lord he'd give Him half his wages if he didn't have to preach. He said he fought the thing over in his mind for three weeks and told the Lord that he simply would not go out to preach again.

But he couldn't get away from it. He often said, later, that the Lord obviously had other thoughts and used an accident in the machine shop to convince Jack he was to go out and tell other people what he knew of Christ.

I destroyed $1,000 worth of machinery in two seconds.

"All right, Lord, You win," I said.
I went and told my boss.
"I'm a Jonah," I said.
"What do you mean by that?"
"I've been fighting God. He wants me to go out in the prairies preaching."
"You a preacher?"
"Well, I'm not a preacher, but the Lord wants me to go out and give my testimony."
"But you stutter. You've got a brogue nobody understands."
"Well, the Lord wants me to go."
"Mitchell," he said, "you'll never make a preacher, but go on. Get it off your head. You'll be back pretty soon. Your job's always open."

Jack tried to return to the machine shop another time. He was on his way back when he got caught with a friend in a terrible blizzard in Saskatchewan. They were lost outside from 6 o'clock at night until 3 o'clock the next morning. They finally found a shack to get into, but they couldn't go out for the next three weeks because their faces and hands and feet were so swollen.

I went back to my own place and started preaching some more. To get over my stuttering and my shorthand English, I walked the prairies and read my Bible and newspapers out loud. That kept me from talking too fast. It made me articulate. It helped me lose my brogue—at least I think it did. I don't hear it, you know.

Those early days marked the lifelong ministry of John G. Mitchell. He always felt it was "a wonderful experience" to talk to someone who had never heard the gospel of Christ. He took such pleasure in watching the Spirit of God take the Word of God and make it live in a person's heart. "And then you have the joy of building that person up in Christ Jesus," he said. "There is nothing comparable."

In my early ministry I had the joy of preaching the Word of God on the prairies where no one else had been with the gospel.

They hadn't had a gospel message for some 20 or 30 years. Believe me, I love to stand in a schoolhouse and bring to people the precious Word of God.

And, after preaching for an hour, to have them say, "What are you stopping for? Give us the rest of it."

I preached until 11 or 12 o'clock at night, three or four hours, to hungry people who for the first time were hearing the wonderful grace of God. What a joy to see them accept the Saviour, to see the transformation of their lives and to build them up in the holy faith.

Chapter Five

The Prairie Years

The young preacher learned quickly: Not everyone wanted to hear.

It was only when you stayed in a particular town for a while, giving them a series of meetings, that the opposition would begin to get together.

Like at Radville.

They threatened that they would put the fire hose on me if I ever went down to the roundhouse at the railroad.

So, of course, I went down to the roundhouse at the railroad and talked to them—the boilermakers and the machinists and those down there.

And, having worked in the shops, you know, I was quite well acquainted with the situation.

So I went in and talked to them and they sheepishly grinned, you know.

They never did put the hose on me.

—John G. Mitchell

Jack spent the early years of his ministry on the prairies of western Canada. His first church was in the small town of Radville, Saskatchewan, and, again, no one was more surprised than he.

He had heard of a special Bible conference held annually in a small community 20 miles away from Calgary in the city of Weyburn. Traveling there by train, he listened eagerly and was unusually attentive to those teaching that summer.

He became acquainted with many friends (among whom was Miss Mary Eby, who later became his wife), and he demonstrated a gift for preaching although he did not speak much.

After the conference ended, he returned to Calgary to his position in the machine shop. But soon he received warm invitations to hold meetings in several places. On his return to Weyburn, he asked about Radville and was told it was another 30 miles away. He and a friend, a Mr. Pringe, decided they would travel there to see the Eby family whom he remembered from the earlier conference.

The two men were asked to conduct a Sunday meeting there. Mr. Pringe took the opening and, after singing and prayer, he said, "Now Mr. Mitchell will bring our message."

This took Jack completely by surprise, but he responded.

Later in the day, Mr. Pringe asked some of the leading men if they would like to have a week of meetings. They readily agreed.

In the evening service, Jack took the opening songs and prayer and announced with a twinkle that his friend would speak.

The next morning they both packed their bags and went to take the train. A Mr. Bean, one of the men from the church, saw them at the station.

He said, "Where are you going?"

They answered, "Back to Weyburn."

"But you announced meetings."

Mr. Pringe said, "Oh, I did that for Jack."

"Well, I don't know who, but one of you will have to stay."

When the train pulled in, Mr. Pringe hopped on it before it stopped. As it pulled away, Mr. Bean turned to Jack and said, "We didn't want him anyway."

So Jack started his week of meetings and stayed there two years.

From the beginning of his Christian life, he had evidenced a consuming desire to know the Scriptures; and his years in Radville, his wife Mary Mitchell later recalled, were years of diligent study. Her aunt, who could see the window of his room above the Eby General Store from her home, would report to the family, "I believe that young man often studies all night."

One time, when called to breakfast, he said, "I am not ready for my next meeting so I must study."

His hostess said, "The Lord will bring all things to your remembrance."

He said, "Yes, I know, but it must be there first."

His study was helped when he got hold of a copy of Cruden's Concordance. Someone gave him Dr. C. I. Scofield's book, *Rightly Dividing the Word of Truth*, and *Romans Verse by Verse* by W. R. Newell. But he continued to make it a habit to search the Scriptures to find the answers he needed.

I was troubled because pressure was being put on me concerning the matter of tongues. So I went to my room, and I got out my little old drawing board, and I wrote longhand every verse in the Bible on tongues. And, when I got through examining the thing, I had my answer; and I haven't changed my conviction from that day to this.

His congregation grew with him, Mrs. Mitchell later wrote. Many truths they had not known or completely understood he explained as he studied the book of Romans with them. Many of the folk rightly believed that, when they accepted the Saviour, they became God's children and received eternal life; yet they thought they could still sin and be lost.

"As Jack taught the truth of the wonderful fullness of the grace of God, they rejoiced in the fact of a full and complete salvation," Mary said. He reminded them that, just like their salvation, their hope of heaven was based on what Christ had done on the cross, not on what they themselves had done or could do.

During those years, his ministry was not confined to Radville. He traveled widely across the prairies, holding Bible classes and meetings in many places. He particularly liked to have tent meetings. "You could always get a good crowd in a tent," he said.

He would rig up the tent, first, and then go to a lumber yard and order two by ten boards for benches. He would drill holes in them and cut down a few little saplings for short round legs. Then he would go out to some farmer and get a load of straw. He would strew this around the benches and be all set. When the meetings were over, he would take the timber to the lumber yard and sell it back to the owner. He did this in each town he touched.

One time, during a meeting in southern Saskatchewan with between 150 and 200 people in the tent, eight or ten roughnecks swaggered in and sat on the last two rows of benches. Everyone knew they had come to make mischief. Meetings were often disturbed this way.

And, when we were on the platform, somebody lifted up the tent and said to me, "When you get through, you better come out this way. Those fellows are waiting for you to fix you up."

Well, I've got enough Irish in me that I don't like that sort of a thing.

And so, when we got through and the meeting was dismissed, those fellows were still sitting there. Everybody else had left the tent.

Well, shall we go out the back or shall we go down there?

You can't be asking a man to sneak away after he's preached the gospel just because some fellows were laying for you. Nothing doing. If there was going to be any roughhouse, we'd meet them halfway and throw them off balance and go right through.

So I said to my friend, "Okay, let's go out. Let's go right through them." So we went down the straw aisle between the two sides.

And then, to my utter amazement, when we got about two-thirds of the way down the aisle and were only about 15 or 20 feet from the fellows, my partner shouted at the top of his voice, "The weapons of our warfare are not carnal, but are MIGHTY through God. Now beat it!"

And those fellows got up and—psshhht!—they were out of the tent like a shot.

I just stood there.

I said, "What in the world did you do that for?"

He said, "I don't know. It just popped in my head and I did it."

"Well," I said, "it sure worked." You couldn't see them for the smoke.

You know, it's an amazing thing how the Lord cares for you.

At a meeting in a rented store building in another town, some railroad laborers came in. "They were gonna have some fun with us," Jack said later.

But during the meeting, one of them got up and went out and the rest of them followed.

So Jack and the congregation thought that ended that.

Then, while the preaching was going on, they heard some hammering on the building. The men had gotten some long spikes and were driving them through the door into the door-jam so the people inside couldn't open the door and get out.

But they forgot something. There was a back door. We all— the congregation, everybody—just went out the back door.

Somebody said, "You better go round to your room. Don't go down the street because they're all standing around the front, waiting for you." Small town, you know. Here's about 20 fellows. They worked on the railroad, and they were the ones who nailed the door. To them it was a joke.

So, instead of me going on the opposite side of the street, I went right down through them.

I said, "Good night, fellows," and I kept on going and nothing was said. Oh, it's great to be a preacher of the gospel, I tell ya.

Pranksters tried all kinds of things—all the time. He'd go out of meetings to find the wheels off his car. "And they religiously took the engine out twice a year," he said. "Or they would take the shims out." But that came with the territory.

One of the most memorable experiences came from an invitation he received through the mail. A woman asked that if he ever came to her part of the province would he give them a meeting. They hadn't had one in nearly 20 years. He wrote back and said, "I'll be glad to do that." He gave her a date.

She wrote back with directions: "When you get to a certain town, you can follow the road out four or five miles. You'll find three prairie trails. You take the left one. After two or three miles, you'll come to a gate. Go through that and you'll find my boy waiting for you."

A little skeptical, he drove his old Chevrolet out into the country and found her directions more exact than he had expected. At the last town, he went to the local telephone operator and asked her to put in a general call to each party line. It cost a nickel a call.

When there was a general call, everybody would run to the phone.

That was the way they used to announce things. The only touch they had with civilization was that little old wire, you know. And you could hear the other fellow whenever he had a call. You had so many rings, and your neighbor had a different number of rings. And oftentimes some of these people used to listen in and see what the other neighbors were talking about.

There was always a warm response to my invitation and often to my message. The place was always filled. I had no trouble in getting a crowd. There's nothing else for them to do to hold their interest, unless they'd go into town and get drunk or go to a show.

On this particular occasion, he got back in his car and took the left trail. Sure enough, he found the gate and a little boy beyond it who opened the gate and jumped on the runningboard for the first ride of his life in a car. He loved it.

"Boy-oh-boy-oh-boy," he squealed.

The two of them drove up to the little homestead and the woman came out. She had three little boys, a husband and a hired man. They had dinner and then drove to the schoolhouse three or four miles away.

I preached there until it was dark. That was the place where they had no lights. I asked if I should stop, and someone said, "Go ahead. We don't mind the dark."

And, when I asked them, "How many would like to accept the Saviour?" I said, "Now, I can't see you. And it's no use raising your hand. But you can shout out your name."

And this fella—this old boy from across the Saskatchewan River—he'd driven down half-a-day to get to the meeting because he'd heard about it on the party line—well, he said, "You all know who I am." And he gave his name. And he said, "I'm taking Jesus Christ as my Saviour."

Quite a few did that night.

And on the way back to the house, I led the hired man to the Lord.

The adults were so excited, they sat up until 2 or 3 o'clock in the morning talking. They put the children to bed in the granary. Jack had to sleep in a little bedroom off the kitchen. It had no door, and the bed was a boy's. When his feet were in the bed, Jack's head was out. He could touch the wall every way he turned. He empathized with Isaiah 28:20: "For the bed is shorter than that a man can stretch himself on it: and the covering narrower than that he can wrap himself in it."

He told his hosts they shouldn't bother getting up in the morning because he had a meeting in Saskatoon that night and needed to get on his way. After three hours' sleep, he got up about 6 o'clock and dressed. The woman had the fire on, and she was making breakfast. So the three of them had breakfast and devotions together.

He got his things together and went out to his car. The woman was there, but her husband was not. Jack wanted to say goodbye to him, too.

I said to her, "Where's your husband?"

"Oh, he'll be back in a minute," she said. "Don't go before he comes back."

And, when he came back, he was carrying a milk bucket. He had taken about a gallon of gasoline out of his tractor and he said, "You know, I'm sorry, Mr. Mitchell, but we have no money."

I said, "I don't need any money."

"Well, I want to do something." And he poured the gasoline into my car so I'd have enough gas to get to Saskatoon. I got very good mileage with that little old car, by the way. I'm sure that sometimes it even ran without gas.

He stopped one night for gas at a country store and said, "Fill 'er up." The proprietor's boy came back in surprise. "It's already full," he said.

Telling these stories when he was in his nineties, John G. Mitchell would stop, sigh and say, "You know. I long for those days again." He loved that life.

Really, to be frank with you, it was a simple life. I fed well. Some places, I'd have chicken three times a day. Some other places, I'd just have the eggs. You just had to trust the Lord when it came to some of the things you had to eat. You wondered sometimes.

And, occasionally, the accommodations were nothing to be desired. One place in Saskatchewan, when everybody went to bed, he slipped outside after he saw the condition of the bed and the bedroom they offered him. He preferred hay in the hayloft to dirt and bugs.

One time, to help a friend, he had to do the cooking.

A blizzard had come up in the fall, and the man's entire harvesting crew had quit. This was the same blizzard and the same man with whom he had become lost in the snow and had suffered frostbite on his hands and feet.

When the weather cleared in the spring, his friend tried to hire a new crew.

He came to Jack in distress. He hadn't had any trouble finding men to work. He couldn't find a cook.

He said, "Mitchell, you'll have to cook."

That's when I got the cookbook out.

And I remembered my mother making a rice dish in with the roast. I had a roast and I put it in the oven.

And I filled that big pan with rice and milk, and I beat the eggs in the milk and put 'em on and put some nutmeg on top as my mother did. And then I let it cook.

But, when I peeked in, I had the surprise of my life.

The rice had swelled up.

It had filled that entire stove!

Whether as preacher, teacher, cook, machinist, or friend, Jack felt the Lord had placed him in Radville to serve. One time, miles away, his assistance in repairing a tractor led to the conversion of a man who had no time for the gospel.

He had gone 20 miles out of Radville to see a Swede, named Joe Erickson, whose parents had homesteaded the place and whose younger brother was running it. Jack called Joe, "Old Man Erickson," and his brother, "Young Erickson." Their old parents still lived with them on the farm.

Joe had given himself to the ministry with no background, no schooling at all. But he loved the Lord.

On this particular occasion, Jack had driven out to see how Joe was coming along spiritually.

When he got there, he found the younger brother really discouraged.

He was down in the dumps, you know. He was ready to cut his grave. It was all over his Rumley oil cutter—that's a big tractor truck, by the way. You start it with gasoline, and you push it over to coal oil when it gets warm.

And he said, "I can't run my tractor. I've broken a bearing."

I said, "Let's go look at it."

So we went out and I said, "Well, let's fix it up."

And he said, "I went downtown but they won't help me. They can't take me for two weeks."

"Well, let's do it ourselves. You go downtown and get me some old babbitt wherever you can find it. By the way, bring a rough file and a mill file, and we'll pick the scores out of the crank shaft."

He stayed with the Ericksons several days while he and the younger brother repaired the tractor. On the day he was finishing up, he heard a pig squealing in desperation.

He ran over a small hill and discovered a Poland China sow—a large pregnant white hog with a big black band around its belly—cornered in a slough by a band of six or eight hounds. They were circling tightly around her and slashing at her flanks with their fangs.

And not knowing what I was getting into, I yelled blue murder for help. I threw a lot of mud at the dogs, and I shouted at them. They'd slashed her ears and carved a chunk out of the ham. You could have put your fist in.

But then Old Man Erickson came over the hill. When he came, of course, the dogs moved back, still circling. Then they began moving in closer. I kept throwing stuff at them. I thought the hounds were gonna take me, too.

Erickson got behind the pig with a stick and poked at it, and he and Jack pushed it out of the slough and into the barn. They put some nice clean straw down and called for the veterinarian to come out.

When he got there, he put bluestone—copper sulphate—in the wound. When Jack asked him if the pig would live, he said that he wasn't too sure.

"The hog may live. It's pretty badly damaged, but it may live. But don't expect any of those little ones. I'm sure they're all dead." And then he left.

Well, this younger brother—he and his wife professed to be saved, but they were not walking with the Lord by any means— he just wept. These fellas—these homesteaders—were broke, you know. They were counting on those pigs for the winter.

I looked at Young Erickson and I said, "You know, the vet can't do anything, but we've got a God who can. I think it would be time for us to get on our knees and pray for the pig. It means so much to you and the family."

I said, "The Lord loves us."

And I said, "Let's get down and pray for her."

They got down on their knees in the straw, and Young Erickson just wept like a boy. The three of them put their hands on the hog and prayed that not only the hog would live but that it would give birth to the little ones.

About 2:30 or 3 o'clock in the morning, Jack was awakened by a knock on the door and Young Erickson said to him, "Come on. I wanna show you something."

So he got out of bed, pulled some pants on and went out to the barn to see the pig. She had given birth to 12 little pigs. "Twelve little butterballs," Jack called them.

Young Erickson was all smiles at breakfast the next morning because the little pigs and the sow were fine.

As he was getting ready to go back to Radville, having finished fixing the tractor engine, Jack said to him, "She can't take care of all those 12, can she? You'll have to give them milk in a bottle in the kitchen, won't you?"

And he said, "I guess so. I'll take a couple of them away from her—two or three of them."

"Well, let me save you that job. Give me two of them," Jack said. "I've got an Irish family over here near Radville—the Murphys. Six kids. And one's a cripple. They don't have any meat for the winter."

And I said, "They're as poor as you are, and I want to give one of those pigs to the cripple, and I want to give the other one to Murphy." This was the father. The whole family was saved except the father. They had all been saved in my meetings. I led them all to the Lord, but I couldn't get him to the meeting.

So I said, "You give me two little pigs and you'll have ten left to raise for next winter."

Jack took the sack with the two little pigs Young Erickson brought him and drove the 25 miles to Murphy's house. All six children flocked around his car to welcome him.

I said to the cripple girl—she walked on her toes and heels—her legs never straightened out. I said—the girl was about 12 or 13—I said, "I got a little present for you." And they all got around my little old car and I pulled out the sack and a little pig jumped out of the sack. They screamed after it, you know. The little pig was running around in circles. It was only a day old, you know—a little butterball.

Jack walked toward the house, calling, "Old Murphy, come on. I got something for you, too." He took him out to the car and gave him the sack with the other pig in it. That kindness changed the way Old Murphy thought about the gospel. He saw that someone actually cared for him. The next Sunday night, he was in the meeting and came to know the Lord.

Jack said Murphy had "a struggle" giving up. "He drank quite heavily, but the Lord delivered him. The whole family went on with the Lord."

Jack saw deliverance take another form when he went home with a man for dinner after a meeting in a little town. His host was farming and ranching out in the country on a homestead he had built himself. He had six daughters. He told Jack to go on into the house and that "Mom and the girls will take care of you." But Jack wasn't married, and there was no way he was going to go into a house with six girls. He decided to wait for his host.

The man didn't see Jack waiting. As he got out of the buggy to take the traces off, he pulled a plug of tobacco out of his pocket and bit off a chunk. Just as he did that, he saw Jack standing on the other side of the buggy.

He began apologizing to him for the tobacco.

"Well," Jack said, "it's okay with me if you want it. I don't want it. Thank God, I've been delivered from it. You go ahead. It's up to you."

The man took the traces off and put the horses away. As he and Jack walked to the house, he said, "When I was a boy, we lived in Virginia and we raised tobacco. On the way to school every day, we kids would take a leaf of the tobacco plant and chew it. I've done this all my life."

I said, "Well, do you know the Saviour?"

"Oh, yes," he said. "I've been saved and I've been sanctified. But I can't get rid of it."

I said, "I think you better trust the Lord to deliver you. You've been struggling to get rid of it and you can't."

Jack learned later that the man had been so embarrassed by having someone discover his secret that he went out into the woods to fast and pray for two or three days. But the moment he got back home, he made for the tobacco can again.

Finally, in desperation, he got on his knees and said, "Lord, I'm going to heaven trusting the blood of Jesus Christ, tobacco or no tobacco."

When he got up from his knees, he became violently sick; and from that day on, he wasn't able to even stand the smell of tobacco.

As with so many of his stories, Jack used this one in his later preaching when he was giving an exposition of Romans chapter six:

"I tell you that story for a reason," he'd say. "This man had tried everything including praying and fasting, but he was trusting what he was doing for deliverance instead of trusting the Lord. Paul tells us to yield ourselves to God. Let God do the delivering. Let God have the victory. You can't win the victory; God wins the victory, and we enjoy the deliverance."

Jack found, soon enough, that not everyone welcomed his ministry on the western prairies. Invited to a "wee town" way up in Northern Saskatchewan to hold some meetings in the second year of his ministry in Radville, he was accosted on the street by a local pastor "of So-and-So United Church" who recognized a stranger when he saw one.

Jack introduced himself and pointed to the little store building on the main street where he was holding gospel meetings.

"Oh," he said, "you're that preacher." And then he said, "I understand that you preach that sinners can only be redeemed

through the blood of Jesus Christ, a Jew who died 2000 years ago."

I said, "That's right, sir. That's the only way sinners can be saved—through faith in the Lord Jesus Christ who died that we might live."

He said, "I'm going to tell you, if I had my way, I would liquidate every one of you preachers who preach such a doctrine. I would liquidate you because you are a hindrance to civilization."

Jack recognized that, if he had been an investor or in most any other line of work, the man would have welcomed him into the village with a "Glad to have you with us, sir. Anything I can do to help you? What can I do to make your stay more enjoyable?" But as a preacher of the gospel of Jesus Christ, murder was too good for Jack. Only "liquidation" would do.

This is not a separate case. How would you like to have written on your sidewalk in front of your house: "We give you so many hours to get out of town?"

What would you do?

You'd stay, of course.

"These things I have spoken unto you, that in Me ye might have—" What? Fear? *That in Me you'll get scared that, if you stick to Me, you'll lose your head?*

No, I tell you! "That in Me ye might have peace. In the world ye shall have tribulation, but be of good cheer; I have overcome the world."

Even in Radville, two men in the church made life difficult for Jack by stirring up opposition to his ministry. He got together with the elders and prayed for God's very real help in the situation. Subsequently, one of the men fell off the back of his tractor and the other fell off a ladder in his store. Both were seriously injured.

During a flu epidemic that ravaged the prairies, Jack stayed up every night for three weeks nursing a man and his wife and six children. Cattle were breaking down fences because people were so sick no one was tending them.

Doctors and nurses were simply not available.

When the little baby, the little wee one, took sick, the mother said to me, "Mr. Mitchell, if God heals my baby, I'll believe."

God was very gracious in healing her baby.

And then she said to me, "But I thought He would do it in a minute."

I said, "Mrs. So-and-So, you remind me of what Jesus said: 'If they believe not the prophets, neither will they be persuaded though one be raised from the dead.' "

In the face of that kind of unbelief, Jack would go out, he said later, to walk the prairies and pray all night, pleading with God for people to be saved.

But more than pagans lived on those prairies.

Some of the most wonderful truths I ever learned as a young Christian, I learned not in seminary, not in school, but in some old sod shacks way up in northern Canada, sitting on an earthen floor with a homesteader telling me what he or she knew of the Saviour.

It's true.

I didn't know much in those days, and these homesteaders were not men of the schools. They were not scholars.

But don't tell me they didn't know the things of God.

There was a sweetness, an aroma about them in the things of Christ that stirred in me a tremendous yearning: "This is what I want. This is real—not something to tickle my intellect, but something to reach the need of my heart."

I saw the reality of life in Christ.

Chapter Six

Mary

Four little sentences, tucked in a record of events Mary Mitchell left, must not be overlooked.

She wrote:

After the conference ended, he returned to Calgary to his position in the machine shop. But soon he received a warm invitation to hold meetings in several places.

On his return to Weyburn, he asked about Radville and was told it was another 30 miles away.

He and a friend, a Mr. Pringe, decided they would travel there to see the Eby family whom he remembered from the earlier conference.

She phrased it that he wanted to see the Eby "family" and that he had remembered them from an earlier conference.

She gave no indication that he might have even the remotest interest in the fact that the Eby family had a lovely young daughter as one of its members.

Could such a thought have ever entered his mind?

Or hers?

Surely not.

Mary Eby always felt she was especially blessed as a child because she was born into a loving, caring Christian family. Her mother made the Lord very real to her children. She hung a motto on her wall that reminded them at every meal that "Christ is the Head of this house, the unseen Guest at every meal, the silent Listener to every conversation."

Mary said, later, "She made the Lord so real to me that I wouldn't have been surprised if He had opened the door and come in and sat down at the table with us."

The family included John Henry and Elizabeth Pyke Eby with daughters Mary (born on April 7, 1900) and Marguerite and sons Oliver Edge, John Rodgers Herbert, and Percy (who later changed his name to Don). Another son, Oswald, died at 18 months of age. The Ebys lived on the prairie in Saskatchewan where winters would get really cold and where terrible blizzards would sweep down from the Arctic. The blizzard that stamped itself on her memory was the one in which she almost got lost. As the storm was rising, her father came home from the general store he owned.

Her mother turned to him and said, "Where's Don?"

Her dad said, "I didn't see Don." So he put his coat on quickly and started out to go back to see if he could find him.

Mary, who later called herself "a very impulsive person," put on her coat and cap, said, "Mother, I'm going to see if he is at Auntie Mary's," and was out the door before she could stop her.

The Eby home was one of a cluster of houses a little outside of Radville town. Auntie Mary lived across the open prairie about three or four blocks beyond the Ebys. Mary went down the walk and out to the road, turned and started out for Auntie Mary's.

She walked until she thought she should be there.

I couldn't see anything. There were no buildings. And I went on a little more and still nothing, a little more and again nothing. Finally I realized I was lost in that terrible storm.

I didn't know at that time which direction I should go and I just stood still, praying, "Lord, please show me which way to go."

And then I heard my father's voice. He had found Don.

I had come full circle, right back, not far from home near the path that he would come. Well, I ran over to him, of course. And he scolded me when he found I was out. But he put his arm around me and took me in.

And that was a real lesson to me.

Mary accepted the Lord "the first time" when she was nine. Her people were Arminian in doctrine, and they believed a person could lose his salvation if he disobeyed or displeased the Lord.

I remember as a child I knew I wasn't all I should be, and I used to get up in the night sometimes and go into my parents' room to be sure the Lord hadn't come and taken them away and left me behind. It was just that real to me.

At age 12, she went up to the altar again; but she didn't experience heart rest in the matter until several years later when a young new pastor, Jack Mitchell, entered his first ministry in her church.

Mary graduated from high school and went off when she was 16 for a year at Regina College in Regina, Saskatchewan, to prepare for a career in teaching. When she came home the next summer, she found things in Radville had changed. Even though it was a small town where she knew everyone, she felt very much alone. All her close friends had left. In fact, most of the young people she'd gone to school with were gone. The only ones still there didn't know the Lord. She remembered that they used to try to draw her into the things they were doing, things she felt she as a Christian couldn't do. She said that for her it was a difficult year.

I remember we had a woman staying with us at the time, and she said to me one day, "Mary, what's the matter? You just don't seem happy."

And I said, "I just feel as if I don't have a friend in the world. And these friends have all turned against me because I don't do the things they do."

And she said, "Well, if you give up friends for the Lord,
He'll give you better ones."

And how true that has been.

But she was the one who brought me to the place of really
committing my life to the Lord and making me understand what
it meant.

Interestingly enough, it was the same summer that she
first met Jack. He had just been saved and someone had
advised him to come to the same Bible conference the Eby
family was attending. As folk got acquainted, Jack joined
some of the men who were helping Mr. Eby construct a cabin
there on the grounds. One evening, Mrs. Eby told Mary that
the men who were building the cabin were coming over for
refreshments after the meeting that night.

And I said, "Oh, Mother, I haven't seen Lilly (my best
friend) for a whole year, and we wanted to visit tonight."

And she said, "All right, you go along and see Lilly."

John loves to tell that the first time we met I walked out on
him.

Mary went away again to school the following fall, finished her schooling, and then started to teach on the prairie
eight miles from home in a little one-room schoolhouse. The
government had a rule that every new teacher had to teach in
the country for two years before she could teach in town. That
seemed to be the only way it could staff its country schools.

And about that time John decided to have a class in another
schoolhouse out beyond where I was teaching, and so he used to
pick me up every Friday night to go out and play a little pump
organ he brought with him. And then he would take me home.
We did that for quite a while.

Surely, his decision to have a class "out beyond where I
was teaching" had only spiritual motivations, prompted simply by his love for souls and his desire to teach people the
Word. Would Jack have ever thought of creating an opportunity to spend time alone with Mary out of eyesight and
earshot of the ubiquitous four—her three younger brothers
and sister?

You can almost hear him saying, "You can count on it, brother."

Mary came into assurance of salvation about this time. She recalled that he must have been teaching Ephesians.

I remember he said we are "accepted in the Beloved in whom we have redemption through His blood, the forgiveness of sins. By grace are ye saved."

I remembered all these words. And then John 10:27, "I give unto them eternal life and they shall never perish." It was made very real to me that I had something that I couldn't lose.

A romance really did begin on those Friday night excursions. Jack and Mary began going together during the year and were engaged that fall when she was 18. They decided not to marry soon because the senior Ebys thought Mary was too young—even though Jack was seven years older than she.

Some have wondered what attracted the heart of a gentle young woman, daughter of a prosperous merchant, to a blustering machinist, newly saved, newly hired to preach and teach in the church at Radville.

Members of the Eby family answer that it was his love for the Lord Jesus and his delight in preaching his heart out to the simple country folk on the prairies that drew her to him. She called him "John." She didn't particularly like it when his friends called him "Jack."

But, soon, it began to look as if he was too busy for romance. His ministry on the prairies took him all across the province. When he finally went to Tacoma to minister in the First Presbyterian Church there, Mary broke off the engagement, feeling that the two of them had just drawn apart. She wrote him a "Dear John" letter.

We just didn't go on right. I finally said there's no point in just continuing to write, and so let's just drop it.

Mary went on teaching and altogether taught for three more years. She found the experience strenuous and difficult because she still had to go out on that cold prairie. Sometimes it would be 40 below. The big boys were supposed to light the schoolroom fire in the mornings, but they didn't always do it. Sometimes she'd arrive to find the school bone cold, and she would have to light the fire herself. She also had to teach several grades, including the eighth grade. This added additional strain because eighth graders had to take government exams and that demanded extra tutoring times before and after school.

I really worked very, very hard. But it was the last day of my last year that I became very sick while I was teaching. I was determined to get through the day, and so I would teach a while and then I would go and put my head down on my desk in the back. Then I'd go up and try again.

Finally, I had to call my father and say, "I'm just too sick. I have to come home."

He came and got her, and the next day she was delirious. The doctor came right away and said she had scarlet fever. There had been a very light epidemic in town, and she was already run down. She was very, very sick and almost didn't pull through.

Mother said I taught school all the time I was delirious. I didn't get any rest.

When Mary finally came to, she opened her eyes and and saw her mother standing at the window talking to someone outside and crying.

The first thought that came to me was "Oh, I must have died. Wouldn't it be wonderful to be with the Lord?" That's the way it seemed to me. And then I thought, "I've always wanted to do something for the Lord, but I've done so very, very little. I don't think I want to die yet."

And it just seemed as if the Lord said, "Well, yes, I think I have something for you to do."

Mary began to improve, but it took her a year to regain her strength. There was nothing, though, to indicate what the Lord would have her do until she heard a missionary teacher from Venezuela speak. She thought, "That's what I'd like to do. I'd like to go down with her and be a teacher in that school. I love teaching."

So she began to think about going to Moody. But one day, a friend who had just come from the Bible Institute of Los Angeles came for a visit. Just at that time, the family doctor told Mrs. Eby, "I don't see Mary staying in this climate for another winter. I think you should send her to a warmer climate or she never will be better."

Her mother said, "Why don't you go to Biola?"

Mary sent in her application but received no answer. Winter was coming and her parents decided she couldn't wait any longer. She had to leave before it got cold again.

We had to go to another town to get a train. My mother went with me and I'll never forget—I was the most homesick person in the world. She almost had to take me home. It was night, and the berths were made up on the train. When Mother finally left me, I was so forlorn and homesick that I got on my knees right there in the berth and opened my Bible.

My eyes fell on a verse; and, oh, it was so good of the Lord to give me that verse just then.

It said, "Lo, I am with you always."

Chapter Seven

Tacoma

After the death of his sister Isobel in Portland, John's parents moved to Tacoma. John visited them in 1919 and decided to get work there the following year so that he could spend more time with them.

When he attempted to talk with them about the Scriptures, they did not care to hear. They thought he was very foolish to go into the gospel ministry.

His mother said, "John, we are happy to have you home, but we do not want to hear anything about your religion."

—Mary Mitchell

Soon after his parents moved to Tacoma, Jack took Mary Eby's brother Edge along with him and drove down to visit them. They continued to resist his attempts to talk to them about the Saviour so he left tracts and books and a New Testament around the house for them to read. Sometimes, on entering a room, he would find them reading and talking about them.

On the Lord's day, he attended the First Presbyterian Church, pastored by Dr. Clarence Weyer. In identifying himself to Dr. Weyer, he explained that the Lord had called him to preach the gospel across the prairies of Western Canada and that he had been doing that since 1917.

Dr. Weyer asked him if he would have a week of meetings in one of the chapels his church had begun in a neighboring suburb.

"But you don't know anything about me, Dr. Weyer," Jack said.

"You believe the Bible, don't you?"

"Yes."

"You believe that Jesus is Saviour and Lord?"

"Yes."

"You believe He is coming again?"

"Yes."

"You believe people are lost?"

"Yes."

"Well, that's all I need to know."

And with no more of a catechism than that, he qualified Jack to preach for him, not only in the suburb but also in the downtown church.

Naturally, Jack told his parents about his experience; and he invited them to come hear Dr. Weyer and see the new million-dollar church that had just been built.

One evening, as Jack was helping Dr. Weyer in a service, he saw his parents in the congregation. That visit seemed to be a turning point in their spiritual experience. Later, after Jack had returned to the Canadian prairies, they wrote that they both had accepted the Saviour and were attending the First Presbyterian Church.

The following year, Jack was called back to Tacoma. His mother had undergone surgery.

The next Sunday, in her hospital room, she said to her son and her husband, "Now you men go to church. I am fine." But when they returned home after the service, they received a call that she had gone to be with her Saviour.

Jack had already been planning to move to Tacoma so he stayed with his father and looked for work. He had thoughts of returning to the shops as a machinist, but Dr. Weyer asked him to take some meetings in his chapels.

Jack said he would be glad to do that after he had fulfilled a commitment in southern Oregon. He had promised to have meetings with friends, some woodcutters, who lived at Garden Valley, near Roseburg.

While he was preaching there, some men from Cleveland Rapids, just across the Umpqua River from Garden Valley, came over and asked him if he would give them some meetings.

And I said, "I don't know. I've got to go home for Christmas with my family in Tacoma, but maybe I can work a couple of weeks with you."

The arrangements were made. Jack stayed in his lodgings in Garden Valley and crossed the river each day in a boat paddled by an Indian. They went up the river between two rapids and then cut across. He then climbed 200 yards up the bank to an old schoolhouse where the meetings were held. One day, his boat was almost swept into the rapids by the swift current. He was saved when someone on shore acted quickly and threw him a rope.

The meetings in Cleveland Rapids were packed out for two solid weeks. People came by horseback and buggy from all the country around.

I came into the schoolhouse, and all the women were sitting in the seats and little desks. The men were all outside, smoking and chatting. Their horses and buggies were standing in among the trees.

When I started to sing, I had no books. So I sang solos, believe it or not. You don't believe that, do you. But I sang every night. I sang choruses, and I did what I could with them. But when I sang, the men used to come in and sit down near their wives. Night after night they came for two solid weeks, but there was not a sign of a movement of the Spirit of God.

Then, the last meeting on the third Sunday afternoon, I hadn't sung the first song when a man got up. He was about six feet two. He had rubber boots up to his knees, and he marched up to the platform. You know, it was a teacher's platform about this high. And his eyes were level with mine.

And I said, "Yes, sir, what do you want?"

And he said, "I want God!"

And I said, "Pardon me, folks, will ya, for a minute?"

He got on his knees, and I led him to the Saviour.

"Anybody else who would like to be saved?"

And a woman got up and she came forward. She'd been in Christian Science, and she accepted the Saviour.

"Anybody else?"

There was nobody else.

So I told these two to go back to their seats, and we went on with the meeting.

Before he started preaching, Jack asked how many of the people would like to have another week of meetings. He said he'd be glad to give them another week. "I'll have to go back to the prairies of Canada where it's 40 degrees below zero. I'd just as soon have a week with you down here," he said.

The people put their hands up and voted for another week of meetings; but Monday, Tuesday, Wednesday, and Thursday his congregation was made up of John Jakeman, the man who was saved, his wife, his crippled mother, the Christian Science woman who was saved and her husband, her little boy and the Indian.

Jack thought it was his fault.

And I said, "John, what's the matter? Here we've had a jammed house for two weeks and now we've got half a dozen."

He said, "Don't worry. They're all outside, watching. They'll be back."

And, sure enough, on Friday night, they were all back. And I was up till midnight leading people to the Saviour.

It turned out that John Jakeman had headed a booze ring and all the men were in it together. They had an illegal still hidden in the hills. This was during Prohibition when making and selling alcohol was a crime punishable by law.

When he had gone home after accepting the Saviour, John Jakeman found that his telephone wires were cut. Two men took turns, 12 hours each, patrolling his farm. When he went out to get some fallen apples to feed his pigs, 20 paces behind him walked a man with a 30-30 rifle. They watched his every move for 24 hours, Sunday night, Monday, Tuesday, Wednesday, Thursday.

Friday morning, the two men came to him and said, "Well, John, what are you going to do?"

He said, "About what?"

"Well, you know what we've been in. Are you gonna call the sheriff?"

"What would I call the sheriff for?"

"Well, you know what we've been in."

"Oh," he said, "you're talking about the old John. He's gone. This is the new John. He's left his past life forever."

The change in the man was dramatic. He was transformed. He'd been born of the Spirit. He'd been joined to the living God with a new life, a new prospect and new hopes.

He'd been known for his brutality to his crippled mother. But now he picked up his mother in his arms, carried her down to the front and gently laid her down on the seat night after night. The people saw this transformation, and that's what had brought them back on Friday night.

If I ever saw a movement of the Spirit of God, it was then. There was real conviction of sin. As I said, I was up till midnight dealing with these people. They were transformed! And one of the last ones was a young lady.

And I said, "Mary, don't you want to know the Lord?"

"Yes, I do," she said.

And so I led her to the Saviour.

And I learned later that at five o'clock the next morning, she was up and saddling a pony.

And her mother said to her, "Honey, where are you going?"

"Well, you know, Mommy, we have announced a dance tonight—Saturday night. And I put the dance on. And I've got to

go tell everyone that there's going to be no more dance."

And she'd just been saved the middle of the night before!
Talk about new life! New prospects!

When Jack returned to Tacoma, Dr. Weyer asked him to
become the assistant pastor of the First Presbyterian Church.
In that capacity, he could develop Bible classes in neighboring
towns and begin a work among high school students, drawing
from the nearby Stadium High school and also from Lincoln
High.

"Besides the work at the chapels and Bible classes in different areas, he had large classes at the church," Mary
Mitchell recounted later. "There were between eight and nine
hundred in his young peoples' classes, with three hundred in
the junior high class. He also had a business girls' class of over
two hundred."

Without doubt, God was working. Bob Churchill, who
kept up with the Mitchells through the years, remembered
that "Jack Mitchell was the assistant pastor though he had not
been to seminary at that time. I remember one of the nights
he led mid-week prayer meeting in the absence of the pastor.
The Word of God was very precious to us that night, and the
glory of God came down. I can't recall now just what the lesson was, but I can remember the stirring of the soul. I walked
home that night very full indeed."

Often Jack would take several of the young people with
him to share in his ministry when he went to neighboring
towns for Bible studies.

Willard Aldrich, a high school boy then but later Jack's
co-worker at Multnomah, found Jack's memory of those
times remarkable: "Jack remembered when he first met me,
but I don't remember when I first met him. He said I was riding horseback. That was my principal life at that time. He
had a very good memory. We always joked about his memory
because he could say, 'Oh, yes, it was February 13 at 3 o'clock
in the afternoon. The sun was shining bright.'"

On one occasion, a Volunteers of America convention

conflicted with meetings Jack was expecting to hold at the Eleventh Street Chapel, a small offshoot of the First Presbyterian Church. A famous matriarch of the Volunteers of America movement was scheduled to speak. Jack decided to postpone his meetings but to remain in the neighborhood to do personal work among the many thousands who would come to the meetings.

Willard remembers that "in the process of talking with people after the meeting, he came to one of the elders of the First Presbyterian Church and the owner of one of the larger department stores in Tacoma. Jack didn't recognize him and asked him if he knew the Lord.

"The next day, an indignant elder came to Dr. Weyer, complaining, 'Who is this man Mitchell that wants to know if I know the Lord!'

"It tickled Dr. Weyer—I remember how he rubbed his hands with glee—that Jack had hit up the elder and wanted to know whether he was saved or not."

In 1923, Dr. G. Campbell Morgan, the great British preacher, had meetings in the Presbyterian church and his command of the Scriptures impressed Jack, who told about it later:

I asked him how in the world he went about his study of the Bible and he said to me, "Young man, if I were to tell you, you wouldn't do it."

"Well," I said, "try me."

And he said, "Well, I'll tell you. Before I start to study a book, I read it through 40 or 50 times in the English text. And I might read it through once in the Greek, but I always read it through 40 or 50 times in the English text."

Jack took that lesson to heart and began to do just that. He read his Bible so much that he memorized much of it. He would draw on passages from cover to cover to support and illustrate the points he was making. He would tell his students, "You've got to study the Book. Get your mind jammed through with the text so that you can begin to think it through." He claimed that he never sat down and tried to memorize Scripture. "I've retained it in my memory by reading and reading and reading again and again," he would say.

He also told students what W. R. Newell, author of *Romans, Verse by Verse,* said when they were together one time at a Bible conference:

I said to him, "W. R., how often have you taught the book of Romans?"

He looked at me with those deep-set eyes and said, "John, I have taught the book of Romans some 80 times and the pastures are still green."

And if our Saviour in the first Psalm could say that He did meditate day and night upon the Word of God, shall we do less?

When he was exhorting his listeners to saturate their mind with the text at hand, Jack liked to tell another W. R. Newell story that illustrated the point:

I do not want to do what W. R. Newell did one time when he was teaching the book of Romans in Chicago.

You had to be there at six o'clock in the evening to get a seat in the First Presbyterian Church of Inglewood. The church seated between 1,500 and 1,600 people. Many others couldn't even get into the building.

At six, the people went from downtown with their suppers and ate in the church while they waited for the class at eight o'clock. Because they had to sit so long, Mr. Newell decided to have the Sunday School lesson taught at seven o'clock. At eight, he came on the platform and taught for an hour to an hour-and-a-half on the Book of Romans.

But if the atmosphere was not saturated with the book of Romans when he would walk on the platform, he would just turn around and say, "When you decide to read the book, I'll come back and teach you."

And he would walk off the platform.

He was more courageous than I would dare be. But I do encourage you to read the book through as a whole and then read the portion we shall be taking every day.

To show the importance of the exact wording of Scripture, Jack liked to refer to another G. Campbell Morgan story:

You know, someone said to G. Campbell Morgan one time, "Isn't it wonderful that God counts the hairs of our head."

And Morgan said, "You can't find that in the Bible."

"Oh, yes, it's in the Bible."

"No, it isn't. It's better than that. He's got them all numbered."

He's interested in every detail of our lives—where you live, what you do, with whom you live, where you work, and so on. He never leaves you for a minute.

It was also in Tacoma where Jack met Dr. Louis Sperry Chafer for the first time. Dr. Chafer came to the First Presbyterian Church for a Bible conference every year and was so impressed with Jack's ministry that in the spring of 1924 he wrote, asking him to take his pulpit at the Scofield Memorial Church in Dallas, Texas, while he made a trip to Scotland. Jack told his Multnomah students about it later when he was tracing how the Lord had led in his life:

I had at the time come to the conclusion that my work in Tacoma was through. In fact, I was thinking of going with Roy Aldrich, Willard's oldest brother, to Princeton Seminary. So (when I decided), I was way up in Saskatchewan the end of June having conferences; and then I took the train all the way down to Dallas where it was 100 degrees in the shade and no shade.

I went from way up north in Saskatchewan where you were sleeping under blankets to Dallas where for six weeks in a hotel I had no air conditioning—just a big fan. I never even got under a sheet.

The next five years, he ministered in and around Dallas, serving Dr. Chafer as an assistant in the church and becoming a member of the first class of what eventually became Dallas Theological Seminary.

Chapter Eight

Dallas

It was not easy for John to go back to school. It had been eight years since his college days.

At the time of his graduation, he said to Roy Aldrich, who was his roommate, "There were many times when I wanted to leave my desk and do something else; but I would look at you, so diligently studying, and think—if he can do it, I can do it."

Roy laughed and said, "Oh, how often I have looked across at you and thought the same thing."

—Mary Mitchell

The plans of Dr. Louis Sperry Chafer to set up the Evangelical Theological College (which later became Dallas Theological Seminary) kept Jack in Dallas. Dr. Chafer, who was still abroad, wrote and asked Jack to remain permanently at the church and to help at the college which his brother, R. T. Chafer, was setting up. Jack would teach Greek, continue as associate pastor in Scofield Memorial Church and take classes in the college.

Jack called Roy Aldrich in Tacoma, saying, "Roy, Dr. Chafer is starting a seminary down here to teach men how to preach and teach the Word of God. How about coming down here instead of going to Princeton Seminary."

And he said, "What are you going to do?"

Jack said, "Well, if you come down, I'll stay."

So both enrolled in the first class. Dr. Roy Aldrich, the last surviving member of that class, recalls, "Jack and I were roommates for the three years of seminary from 1924 to 1927. We studied together, prayed together, attended church together, played handball together and sometimes even dated girls together.

"The dormitory students would study until they were tired or about finished, and someone would yell—so those in other rooms could hear—'It's time to take a vote!'

"All of us would collect in one room—usually the one that Jack and I occupied.

"Someone would say, 'The question is: Do we admit we're good? All in favor say: Aye.'

"Then we would all yell 'Aye' so loud any of the absent ones could hear in other rooms. Then we cheered ourselves up with a sort of mutual admiration society.

"In our early association, I heard my dear friend preach and teach many times. No one has had a greater influence on my own life for blessing and edification. I thank my God upon every remembrance of him."

Dallas social life beckoned now and then. It was not often that a hostess could bring in a covey of eligible bachelors such as those in the first years of the Theological College.

Willard Aldrich, present at a Christmas party where mistletoe was pinned in doorways, remembered: "My dad was a railroad man so I'd get passes to use when I went to Wheaton College. I'd go by way of Dallas so I could see my brother Roy.

"I was at a Christmas party with them in Dallas and there were a number of beautiful Texas maidens there, and Jack responded as any proper gentleman would do. But that was as far as it went."

In his sophomore year, Jack came down with diphtheria. He could breathe in, but he couldn't breathe out. To illustrate that one can take advantage of any event to witness, he told his students later:

I was having quite a time. The doctor came to see me and looked down my throat. He said to my roommate—he took him over to the corner of our room and started to talk to him.

And I said, "Hey, you fellows, come over here. What's the matter? What do you think it is?"

And he said, "I think you've got a case of diphtheria. I'll take a culture and I'll let you know tomorrow."

Well, that night, poor Roy—he had no sleep. I was up half the night, gargling. Sometimes I would crash into the book case. I was just off my head. And, the next day, we got the word, "Take him to the hospital."

Roy took me over. I went to the desk and I said, "You've got a room for a man called Mitchell?"

"Yes. Where is he?"

"I am he."

"Oh, this fellow is very, very sick."

I said, "Don't tell me, girl." I said, "I know what's wrong. You get me to bed before I fall down here."

So they put him in a room in the basement. They called him the "dip patient." Upstairs there was a whole floor of children with diphtheria. It had become an epidemic. So they put him down in the basement all by himself.

He was there for half-an-hour when two doctors came in. They turned on a little light and looked down his throat.

"Say awhhhh."

And one of them said, "Isn't that a bonny case?"

Here I'm going—"awhhhhhh"—and he says, "Isn't that a bonny case?" Why didn't they do something?

And so one of them gave a nurse instructions, and she came in with a hypodermic. It looked like an alamite grease-gun. Boy, it was a big one.

She says to me, "Are you right-handed or left-handed?"

I said, "I'm ambidextrous. I use both my hands."

So she stuck it in here. All that stuff went in there—35,000 of antitoxin. All those bugs going in—35,000. They gave me a pill and told me to go to sleep.

The next morning, the doctor inquired about his health, and Jack said, "I feel fine."

The doctor went to the end of the bed. He picked up the chart and he said, "You're not fine. You're under an opiate. The chart says you're not too good."

Jack said, "I feel all right."

He said, "The chart says you're not so good."

That night, the doctor came in and said, "How do you feel?"

Jack said, "I feel fine," and added, "I have a time breathing, of course. But other than that, I feel pretty good."

The doctor picked up the chart and called for the nurse. She came in with another big hypodermic syringe; and, despite Jack's complaints, put 25,000 more "bugs" in.

"So now I've got about 60,000 bugs in me," he moaned.

The next morning the doctor said, "Well, how are you feeling this morning?"

I said, "Fine except I've got appendicitis on the wrong side."

Did he take my word for it?

He never took my word for it. He went to the end of the bed, picked up the chart and he said, "Well, you're going to be all right."

He told Jack to go back to his dormitory room and "just lie around." He was not to go to classes because "the most dangerous time for you is *now*, not when you're lying in the hospital."

The doctor knew that Jack was preaching at the Scofield Memorial Church and teaching at the seminary, but he claimed to have a scientific mind. The Bible was not for him. During the course of a discussion, he said, "You know, I'd like to come and join your church."

Jack said, "You couldn't get in if you wanted to. You've

got to be saved to get in there." He invited the doctor to come when he could. They had become very good friends.

The following spring, as Jack was preparing to leave town for some itinerant preaching, his doctor friend sent for him.

He called me into his office and said, "If you need a friend, if you get into trouble, will you give me a ring?"

I said, "I'm not going to get into trouble."

"You never know, you fellows. You might be sick. You may need some money. You get stuck. Why don't you call me up? You promise?"

I said, "I promise. I don't know that I'll keep the promise, but I'll promise you."

And then I said to him, "Will you make a promise to me?"

He immediately got suspicious, you know, and he said, "What's your promise? What do you want me to do?"

I said, "Read your Bible. Read your chart!" I said, "Did you know you have an incurable disease?"

He said, "I have?"

"You sure do."

"Why," he said, "I'm feeling pretty good. What's wrong with me?"

I said, "You're under the opiate of sin." I said, "The chart says you're dead in trespasses and sin. The chart says you're guilty before God."

"Oh," he said, "I don't feel badly like that."

"But," I said, "I'm going to go by the chart." I said, "You came to me when I was sick and you pushed all those bugs into me. Why didn't I say—talk about your scientific mind—when you came with that great big old hypodermic—I should have said, 'Wait a minute, brother. You're not going to push that stuff into me. Bring your microscope. I want to make sure that every bug is the same kind of a bug. I'm not going to let you push all that stuff in.'"

"Oh, but," he said, "I'm the doctor."

"Well," I said, "I'm the doctor now and the chart says, sir, you're a sinner, needing a Saviour."

I had to put him right where he belonged.

You know, a month after I left, one of my other friends led that dear fellow to the Lord and he became the first medical advisor to the Dallas Theological Seminary.

During most of his three years in Dallas, Jack served as interim pastor at Scofield Memorial Church. When he graduated, he was asked to stay as the regular pastor, but he did not feel it was what he should do.

After graduation, he traveled for some time with a quartet of men from the seminary.

During this time, he suffered one of the sharpest disappointments of his life. Jack's dream had been to serve the Lord as a missionary to China.

The Rev. James Braga of the Multnomah faculty remembers the story:

"He was traveling with the quartet from place to place and at one place he met Dr. D. E. Hoste, general director of the China Inland Mission. He asked Dr. Hoste if he could be accepted by the mission.

"'How old are you?'

"'Thirty-four.'

"'You're too old.'

"They met again at another meeting.

"Jack made a point of speaking to him again.

"'Won't you reconsider?'

"'Haven't I told you you are too old?' He made it very clear that he didn't want the matter brought up again."

The disappointment in no way diminished Jack's love for missions or his love for China. All through the years, he maintained contact with the mission, entertained CIM missionaries and led the CIM prayer meetings held in his area.

After his ministry with the quartet, Jack continued in conference work for about two years, mostly in the east and middle west. At one conference, he and Dr. Chafer were going to share the meetings, but Dr. Chafer was called away. His wife had taken very ill in Seattle with a heart condition, and he had to go be with her. Jack would tell about it:

So I had the whole thing for myself—two hours in the morning, two hours in the afternoon and an hour at night. I was in heaven, I'll tell ya. I had five meetings a day—not just sermonettes. That's what you get in church. At a Bible conference, you get a real dose. Wonderful!

He was speaking at that conference on Christ's present ministry, and he was using the book of Hebrews as a background. After the meeting was over, one of the pastors of the city came to him and said, "Mr. Mitchell, according to your belief, my whole denomination is wrong."

I said, "Well, forget what I said. What does the Bible say?" I knew the denomination to which he belonged. I said, "You folk really believe in the work of Christ at the cross and in the resurrection, don't you?"

He said, "We sure do."

"And you believe in the coming of the Lord back to the earth again."

"Yes, sir. We're looking for the coming of the Lord."

"But you don't know a thing about what He's doing now. When He came to the world, He came to do a work for the world. He died for the world. But now He's praying just for believers. He's representing believers before God. He's our Advocate with the Father. That's the epistle of John, chapter 2. And then He's going to return to the world as a Judge and then to reign as Lord of Lords and King of Kings."

Jack also traveled to Portland, Oregon, in the spring of 1928 and 1929 to fill the pulpit both at the Calvary Presbyterian Church and at the Portland Bible Classes while the pastor, Dr. Bernard B. Sutcliffe, gave his visiting lecturer series to the students of Dallas Theological Seminary. On his return to Portland he extended Jack a call to join his staff as his assistant in Portland, but he did not at this time feel led to accept.

While he was ministering at a summer conference in Gull Lake, Michigan, Jack met with representatives from the Open Bible Church in Grand Rapids who asked him to serve as their pastor. After thought and much prayer, he came to the conviction that this was indeed the Lord's call.

And, interestingly, his thoughts at the same time were turning toward Los Angeles, California, where a young woman friend from earlier days was living and working. Never one to forget a friend, Jack started up a correspondence that would eventually have a very material affect upon his life.

Subsequent events did lead him far from Dallas, but the seminary was always there to call him back. For 50 years or better, he had a profound ministry among the students at the Dallas Theological Seminary as a visiting lecturer himself; and, certainly, in the minds of those students he was a minister on par with Harry Ironside, G. Campbell Morgan, William R. Newell, and Carl Armerding—all great men of God.

Chapter Nine

Marriage

At a Multnomah School of the Bible faculty retreat in the late 1980s, the following scenario occurred during an open forum question-and-answer session with school founder John G. Mitchell and his wife Mary:

QUESTIONER: Dr. Mitchell, where did you meet your wife?

MARY MITCHELL: Oh, now, I don't think—

FACULTY: (Laughter)

JACK MITCHELL: Oh, we met on the prairies when I was preaching up there, and she was teaching school, and we got together. And then she went to Biola and I went to Dallas. After which we got together and we married.

SAME QUESTIONER: That doesn't sound very romantic. Tell it like you tell your other stories.

FACULTY: (Laughter)

MARY MITCHELL: No, don't.

FACULTY: (Uproarious laughter)

WILLARD ALDRICH: You can reserve a little right to privacy.

MARY MITCHELL: Yes.

FACULTY: (More laughter)

Mary arrived at Biola a month late for her first semester. Since she had come alone from Radville, the administration admitted her and let her enroll in the classes scheduled for the first semester of the two-year program she was taking. Not wanting the officials to be sorry they had let her in, she worked hard and made up her work in a short time. She kept her grade-point average high and thereby avoided having to take final examinations.

She said later, "I had a wonderful time those years at Biola. I was very, very happy. And I had an intense desire for the Word and for the Lord. I used to sometimes feel like the psalmist who said, 'As the hart panteth after the water brooks, so panteth my soul after thee, O God.'"

She remembered one teacher, Dr. John Hubbard, who would—like no other teacher she had ever had—bring his students into the presence of the Lord.

"I would often feel, when we got out of class, that I wanted to go right to my room," she said. "I didn't even want to talk to anybody. I just wanted to go right to my room and be alone."

Nearing graduation, she had a real disappointment. She had held to her original goal of becoming a missionary teacher and had been corresponding with the missionary she had heard back in Radville. That woman came home on furlough and, on a visit to Biola, asked Mary to have lunch with her.

"I think she probably had talked to others about me," Mary said. "But she told me that day that she didn't think I should apply to the mission.

"She said, 'You just do not have the physical stamina for that.'"

Mary realized that probably was true because she didn't have much strength even then. But it was a terrible disappointment. She did learn later that the Lord had better things for her, but at the time she found it difficult to accept; and, after graduation, she suffered a let-down.

Even though she kept very busy, working in the school office, being a Sunday School teacher, having a girls club, working in her Christian Endeavor young peoples group and taking night school classes at UCLA, she felt something was missing in her life.

"Somehow, I had lost that eagerness for the Lord and for His Word," she said. "I lost that intense desire that I had had. It just seemed to be gone. I sort of felt that I was wasting time. I wasn't doing just what I should.

"And then it seemed as if the Lord spoke to me. You know, it wasn't in a sermon. It wasn't in a Scripture verse. It wasn't anything particular. But it just seemed as if I heard the Lord say, 'You've given Me your life. Now what are you doing about it?'

"So I really got down to business with the Lord, and I told Him I would be willing to do whatever He wanted me to do."

And it was when she really sought God's will that He gave her the assurance that He would lead her where He wanted her to go. And, interestingly, it was not too long after that when she got a letter from Jack. She had lost track of him. She had no idea he was in Dallas at the time. But he knew where she was.

"And so he wrote me," she said. "Well, I didn't answer. I wasn't sure I wanted to start writing to him. But in a little while, an air mail special delivery came.

"'Did you get my letter and why don't you answer?' it said.

"So I finally did."

Mary's brother Herb Eby elaborated on the romance of his sister and John G. Mitchell:

"Mary left Radville in 1921 and went to the Bible Institute of Los Angeles. Somewhere down there, she met a fellow by the name of Kykendahl. Kykendahl went to Princeton Seminary, and he had a picture of Mary on his table in his room at Princeton.

"A mutual friend of Jack's saw this picture of Mary on his dresser, and he said, 'My friend Jack over in Dallas has this same picture on his dresser.'

"He came back to Dallas and told Jack that Kykendahl had the picture of Mary on his dresser.

"So, I guess Jack got busy. He wrote to Mary and took a trip to Los Angeles."

Mary's "adopted daughter," Mrs. Celia Wiebe, one of several younger women who were very close to Mary's heart in later years, says she has the inside story:

"Mary was actually drawn to John because of his Bible fervor. She said it was so appealing when that genuine force came out as he would teach the Bible up in Saskatchewan. When he talked about the Lord the way he did—that's what attracted her to him.

"But she said she was going to let him go. She was kind of thinking about someone else, and Jack didn't maintain her interest by corresponding with her. So their romance simmered and kind of petered out.

"So when Uncle John found that that man had a picture of her on his dresser, it bothered him and he started writing. She said she couldn't understand why it had upset him because he hadn't been writing. So why did he have any business being upset about her picture? That bothered *her*. She didn't answer his first letter right away. She could be feisty, you know—I mean in a sweet way. She had backbone.

"But when he started wooing her intently, she saw the diamond. She saw the man there."

The Rev. James Braga believes that Mary was drawn to John by his love for Christ and to his complete devotion to serving Him.

"I believe his wonderful character and behavior were largely the result of the Word of God living in his life," he says.

Jack's letters and his visits to Los Angeles soon won Mary's heart and on April 20, 1929, they were married in the Angeles Mesa Presbyterian Church, the Rev. Theodore Parker Smith officiating. The license was witnessed by James Mitchell and John Henry Eby, fathers of the bridal couple.

The next "Young Peoples Society Christian Endeavor Bulletin" for May 5, 1929, contained this article about the ceremony:

"With this ring, I do thee wed" or words to that effect were pronounced on the night of April 20th, by John Mitchell to Mary Eby.

The entire affair was conducted smoothly and beautifully, from the moment we were ushered down the aisles, through the opening vocal and violin solos, the marriage ceremony, on to the very exit of the young couple. The alter (sic) was blanketed with a mass of sweet peas. A spirit of subdued joyousness was prevalent (especially in the front part of the church where we C.E.'ers were congregated — we haven't gone to a sufficient number of weddings to have lost the thrill of it, you know).

Of course, at the entrance of the bridal party, instant silence descended upon us. The minister took his place, followed by the big handsome groom and three of his close friends, two of them familiar to us, Edge and Herbert Eby. Then, down the center of the aisle, with slow measured tread, came the bridesmaids, among them Dorothy Wallace and Marguerite Eby. Each of the girls was beautifully dressed in pastel shades of taffeta. The tiny flower girl was really having the best time of all, as she scattered rose leaves for the young bride to walk upon and smiled upon all who could spare a glance from the bride to look at her.

Mary was beautiful. Her dress of pure white satin, her flowing veil, and above all, her look of suppressed excitement and joy made a picture fit for an artist's brush. One could see that she was bringing to the man of her choice a wealth of love.

—And So They Lived Happily Ever After —

John and Mary honeymooned in San Diego and then returned to a reception hosted by the senior Ebys.

Another article in the "Y.P.S.C.E. Bulletin" of May 5 recounted that occasion:

On the 23rd of April we were invited to the Eby house to greet Mr. and Mrs. John Mitchell. We are very grateful for this opportunity to once more see our beloved Mary before she was whisked away to Michignan (sic) where they will make their home for a time. We are also glad to have become acquainted with the man who took Mary from us. Of course, we all went with the idea of being a wee bit jealous of him but his sincerity and charm soon wore away any such foolish feelings and we are now quite satisfied that we have relinquished Mary to a man who will love her to the end of the chapter, just as she deserves to be loved.

After the reception, the couple took John's father and Aunt Sarah Mitchell back home to Tacoma via Portland where another reception was held in their honor.

From Tacoma they proceeded to their new ministry in Grand Rapids, Michigan, at the Open Bible Church.

Chapter Ten

Grand Rapids

The Dutch are very reserved and very conservative and very strict.

You didn't do anything on the sabbath day.

My mother had her dinner cooked the day before.

We just couldn't do anything.

As kids, we couldn't pick up scissors on the Lord's day. And we certainly couldn't go out and play ball or anything like that.

Well, then Jack and Mary came.

I remember one of the first shocks:

They went out and bought ice cream on the first Sunday!

—Mrs. Sadie Custer

One wonders what the Church of the Open Bible in Grand Rapids could offer John G. Mitchell that Louis Sperry Chafer at Scofield Memorial Church in Dallas and B. B. Sutcliffe at the Portland Union Bible Classes could not offer him. They had made him offer after offer, trying to get him to join them in their ministry, and he had refused.

The Open Bible Church, a little mission church, contained a group of people who were unhappy in their denomination. China Inland Mision speakers had preached the second coming and missions in a local Christian Reformed Church and had so moved the congregation that some of them left and started this new work. They rented rooms first in St. Cecelia Hall until they were able to build on Labelle Street.

They supported missions with heart and soul. They sacrificed for missions. But they had no pastor. Jack Mitchell had held special meetings at the church after he finished at Dallas Theological Seminary and so impressed the congregation that the church extended a call which he accepted shortly before he and Mary Eby were married.

Why did he accept this call? Perhaps it was the pioneering spirit of the people. Perhaps it was their love of missions. More than likely, it was their sacrificial spirit and their hunger for the Word of God.

And from the start, he carried on the kind of ministry he had practiced on the prairies. He preached and taught from a central location, Grand Rapids, and then went out of town to teach Bible classes in Chicago, Illinois; Berne, Indiana; and Zeeland, Michigan. In the summers, he taught in Bible conferences in the east and midwest.

Mrs. Dorothy Custer, one of the church young people when the Mitchells came, retains strong memories of the new young pastor:

"He was a very ambitious man and a wonderful Bible teacher. And while he was pastor of our church, he had a Bible class in Byrne, Indiana, on Tuesday nights and prayer meeting at our place on Wednesday night. He also had a Bible class at our church and people from different churches would come to that. We had gone to the Reformed Church; but, when he became pastor of the Open Bible Church, why, that's when we joined."

The Mitchells inherited 15 young people when they

began their ministry, but in no time the congregation began growing in size.

"He was great on learning Scripture," Mrs. Custer says. "And I remember once, when he was teaching Ephesians, that he promised a Scofield Bible to anyone who would learn and recite the Book of Ephesians.

"We had one girl who was around 16 then. Her name was Charity Haddad. She stood up in church one Sunday and recited the whole book of Ephesians. It was really something."

That same Sunday, a young lady who would later become Dorothy Custer's sister-in-law visited the church. She and her family were so struck with the enthusiasm of this congregation for spiritual things that they joined the church.

"Right from the time we were saved, he would have us giving our testimony in young people's meetings," Mrs. Sadie Custer remembered. "My brother had to do it one week and he stood up. He perspired so—the perspiration was dripping off of his chin—and he couldn't say what he wanted to say.

"And so I memorized mine. I reckoned that I had two minutes. But when I stood up, all I could say was 'I—I—I—I thank the Lord I'm saved.' And I sat down. That was my first testimony."

Jack Mitchell didn't bring Sadie to the Lord, but he did bring her into the assurance of her salvation. And she loved going to his church. She speaks of "hilarious times with the Mitchells" and of parties and great times of good, clean fellowship.

Sadie says she was a black sheep in the congregation. All the young people of the church were going to go to Moody Bible Institute when they graduated from high school. She and another girl declared they would never go to Moody.

"But it was through his teaching that I dedicated my life to the Lord and then went to Moody," she says. "The young people all dedicated their lives to the Lord, and everybody was going into missions. It was a very ongoing thing. The people's heart and soul was in missions. I have seen them sacrifice everything for the sake of helping a missionary."

Sadie went from Moody to China in 1936 and worked until 1951 in Shensi Province Northwest as an itinerant Bible teacher, going from church to church in the Mitchell manner. In 1951 she went to Malaysia. In 1972, she moved to Taiwan and then "retired" in 1975. She is currently living in the Overseas Missionary Fellowship retirement home in Lancaster, Pennsylvania, where she is still teaching several Bible classes.

Jack Mitchell met and instantly liked Dr. M. R. DeHaan during those years in Grand Rapids. The medical doctor/radio preacher had left the Dutch Reformed Church and started an independent church. At one time, Dr. DeHaan called Jack to ask if he would baptize him and his people.

Jack said, "I will baptize you, but I think you should baptize your own people."

In the spring of 1930, Jack was asked by a church in Winnipeg, Manitoba, if he would make a survey of churches in Western Canada. He agreed and, with Mary, traveled with Simon and Ann Forsberg through the provinces of Manitoba, Saskatchewan, Alberta and part of British Columbia. He kept a short diary of the trip:

June 17 to 21st: Left Winnipeg Tuesday morning, June 17, for Dauphin, Manitoba.

On the way, passed out tracts and gospels. Spoke personally to two men in Portage hotel about the Lord and gave them a Gospel of John which they promised to read. Also to a young man on the street who had never read the Bible nor known of John's Gospel. He promised to read it.

Testified personally to two men in Neepawa. They had never read the gospel, but halfway promised to read it. Found conditions thus far lamentable. Apparently people are very ignorant of what God's gospel is and they do not receive it in their churches.

Arrived Dauphin about 6:30 p.m. Had a good talk with a traveling man in the King's Hotel by the name of Edwards. His home is in Neepawa. The man, though a church member, did not know much gospel.

He perspired freely when spoken to. He did not carry a Bible with him, though a professing Christian. Gave him John *to carry and read.*

June 18 (Wednesday):

Drove up to Swan River arriving about 12:30.

Had very great joy in giving out tracts and gospels on the way.

Found joy in handing tracts and gospels to the farmers on the road as they drove their teams to and from town. Asked them to read while they were slowly journeying along. Believe this to be a real work and opportunity.

Passed through a great foreign district—French, Finnish, Ukranian, etc. Greek Catholic seems to predominate in these parts. Gave out the Word just the same.

Dr. Cameron of Swan River was interviewed. He loves the Lord and is looking for His appearing. Has practically no fellowship in the things of God. United Church far from the gospel— no clear testimony for Christ.

Drove to Bowsman, north of Swan River. After going through the country, met Rev. E. Pound, the Baptist missionary. A rare soul. Weak in body, strong in spirit. Has a real passion for the things of God. The only man north of Swan River who is really doing much for God. Works among the families, trappers, lumber camps, fishermen, etc. Has broken down his body trying to reach people with the gospel. A very poor speaker, but has a real compassion for souls. Has suffered physically for the gospel (frozen, etc.). Has reached men and women where they have never been told God's way of salvation. (Pray for Pound.) (Great need north of Swan River for a real missionary who is willing to suffer privation for the souls of men.)

    Came back to Swan River.

The diary details his contacts with Christian workers and his opportunities to witness further.

    Arrived Shoal Lake about 10 p.m. (It) reminded one of the days of the open saloon. Dozens of men drinking in the hotel and quite a few drunk in the street. As far as we could find out, Shoal Lake is without a real testimony. (Pray for Shoal Lake country.)

    Perhaps the germ of what eventually became Multnomah School of the Bible originated during this trip. Increasingly, Jack was becoming burdened by the need to train up young men and women to serve the Lord wholeheartedly. He summed up his observations of conditions in the province of Manitoba in the following entry:

Manitoba: Its Condition

    Very little gospel testimony. Very little teaching of the Word. Very few preachers who are true. Some of these are discouraged. Some of these are denominationally bound.

    People are leaving the churches. A growing indifference to the Word of God and the Person of Christ.

    Many hungry for the Word, here and there, but a great apathy on the part of the churches and people.

    Worldliness on every hand.

Manitoba: Its Need

    Preaching and teaching of the Word. Self-sacrificing Bible evangelists and pastors. A compassion for the thousands. Real intercession. Encouraging pastors who are standing true.

    Building up of believers that they might in turn evangelize their own community. A group of young men filled with the Spirit of God and His precious Word. Men who will pray, give, agonize for Manitoba.

    It will mean sacrifice, a slow, sure, solid work and a continual looking to God every moment.

    (In pencil, added later: An indigenous church the answer.)

Entries for succeeding days show that the Mitchells and the Forsbergs often separated so that they could preach far and wide across the provinces. They moved into Saskatchewan and spoke in the monthly Bible conference of the Moose Jaw Bible Institute. "There is a very great possibility for the Institute," he wrote. "God's hand is manifestly upon it and it looks as if God has raised it up to meet Saskatchewan's need."

They held meetings every night in the Moose Jaw Tabernacle.

Had a real time giving forth the Word. God greatly blessed the Word also on the street. The rodeo was in town, causing many to be in the city and many heard the gospel. Some believed and were saved.

On July 7, they drove to Briercrest and found a baseball game in progress. Mr. Forsberg went out on the field between the sixth and seventh innings and announced that a preaching meeting would follow the game.

He spoke first, preaching between first and home base. Quite a few had stayed to listen. We both spoke until dark and had the joy also of personal testimony to those around. Many Gospels of John were given out.

One of the results of that meeting came to Jack's attention nearly 50 years later when D. R. Aikenhead, a Canadian evangelist of his acquaintance, wrote him a letter:

One of the choice young men of that district, Reginald Glenn, a farm lad, was saved and went through Bible school. He spent many years in Africa with the Sudan Interior Mission. Reg's younger sister was saved about this time, and she went through Bible school and headed for Africa where she met up with Dr. Alex Henderson, a wonderful doctor and surgeon. They were married and spent several years in Africa. It is really an endless story—the clash with the two ball teams and the gospel meeting. The final outcome was WONDERFUL.

Entries in Jack's diary indicate that everywhere they went there was a "tremendous dearth" of gospel witness in the territories. He preached in Lestrek, about 85 miles from Moose Jaw, and wrote in his diary:

Found a family loving the Lord, but starved. Had a meeting in the schoolhouse about 13 miles from Lestock. Place was filled. People hungry. A school teacher of that district was saved. Found a whole territory where no Sunday School was ever held and a gospel service so rare it was a real treat to have one. Tremendous need here.

The couples went to Saskatoon and the men held meetings every night. Forsberg went to Elbow and had "two great meetings in the skating rink." Jack went to towns out in the country. He held one meeting 40 miles north of Tisdale where they "had to clean out bears and goats before the meeting could commence."

He wrote, "Had a great day. There is a real work of God going on here. The great need here is teaching."

The last entry in the diary tells that they moved over into Alberta.

Conditions among God's people in Calgary are very poor. Much contention and schism. The saints here need a renewed vision of Christ.

During this time, Dr. Bernard B. Sutcliffe wrote from Portland, asking again if the Mitchells would come and work with him. Finally, he wrote Jack and said he was resigning and that the council of the Portland Union Bible Classes and the board of Calvary Presbyterian Church were extending a call to Jack to take his place.

The Mitchells loved the people at the Open Bible Church, but they decided they could not stay any longer in Grand Rapids. They both found the cold more bitter than they could stand. The call from Portland was received with greater interest this time.

Notes written by Mary provide the transition from Grand Rapids to Portland:

It was not easy to leave the dear ones at the Open Bible Church whom we dearly loved; but finally, on December 12, 1930, we left for Portland, going by way of Texas and California.

First of all, we stopped with friends in Chicago and John spoke on Moody radio. In St. Louis, he had Sunday meetings at the Gospel Hall. Dr. Ironside, who was pastor at Moody Church, urged him to do this.

In Dallas, we stayed with friends and had a good time with Dr. and Mrs. Chafer and others at Dallas Seminary.

We arrived in Los Angeles in time for Christmas with my family.

On Sunday, John preached at the Angeles Mesa Presbyterian Church, where we had been married, and at the Church of the Open Door.

We were back in Portland, ready to begin ministry, on January 4, 1931.

Chapter Eleven

Young Lion

I first heard him way back in 1929 at the old Sunnyside Congregational Church. We weren't attending that church—but there was an announcement that they were having evangelistic meetings and Jack Mitchell would be preaching.

I was just a boy, but I remember the way he taught us and the way he preached.

In fact, before the meetings were through, that church was packed with people and many, many came to the Lord.

Already there was evidence in his life that he knew something of the love of Christ.

—Bill Wecks

A "great and effectual door" had now opened for the Mitchells and they would spend the next 60 years in happy, fruitful work. From Portland their ministry would extend worldwide.

The call Jack and Mary Mitchell answered put them in charge of the Portland Union Bible Classes which had their roots in Portland area ministry that dated back even before the turn of the century when Dr. J. J. Staub, who ministered in the Sunnyside district for 42 years from 1892 to 1934, encouraged every true gospel effort that developed in the city during that time.

In 1905, Dr. J. Wilbur Chapman with Dr. Henry Ostrom, among others, held nightly meetings in nine sections of the city.

In 1910, Dr. W. B. Hinson, a scholarly Englishman and "a great champion of the truth," came to Portland as pastor of the White Temple and subsequently brought many to a saving knowledge of Christ. Staub and Hinson became a strong team for the gospel in the city.

In 1911, Gypsy Smith conducted an evangelistic campaign that reached many for Christ. That same year, E. R. Martin began a 34-year ministry as superintendent of the American Sunday School Union for Oregon, Washington, and Idaho. During those years, more than 2,000 rural Sunday Schools were started. Some 200 of them ultimately became self-supporting churches.

In 1915, the Irish evangelist Walter Duff pastored Calvary Baptist Church and began a Christian Workers Training class, using Dr. Hinson, Dr. Staub, Dr. A. L. Hutchinson of Piedmont Presbyterian and Dr. W. T. Milliken of Oregon City as lecturers.

Also in 1915, Dr. Arno C. Gaebelein held his first of three successive annual Portland Bible Conferences under the auspices of the Evangelistic Committee of the Congregational Conference of Oregon. The popular response to that prompted 25 pastors to form the Portland Bible League with monthly Bible conferences that moved from church to church. They named Dr. Staub, president, and Dr. Hinson, vice president.

In 1917, the class, now known as the Portland Bible Institute, brought in Dr. Harry A. Ironside of Oakland and Dr. Mark Matthews of Seattle as special speakers. In 1920, Moody

Bible Institute sponsored a November Bible Conference in the White Temple and in Dr. Staub's church. Dr. Louis Sperry Chafer, Dr. James M. Gray, Dr. H. A. Ironside and Dr. Harold Munro spoke. The following year, Moody sent Ironside, Chafer, Dr. Bernard B. Sutcliffe and Dr. George Guille, who later taught at Dallas Theological Seminary.

The enthusiastic response to Dr. Sutcliffe's ministry brought him back to conduct Bible classes at Sunnyside Congregational Church on Monday evenings, at the White Temple Tuesday evenings and in the Irvington district on Wednesday afternoons. Churches in other sections of the city—Alberta, Rose City Park, Sellwood, Milwaukie, and elsewhere—asked for meetings.

After the conference, a class of about 100 women from Westminster Presbyterian Church, intent on having more Bible study, talked to Dr. Sutcliffe about continuing Bible classes in the city. They shared the idea with several pastors and many laymen, and all heartily approved. They formed a committee to arrange for the beginning of the work they would call "The Portland Union Bible Classes," and they held the meetings in several churches for about a year.

In 1922, when the Calvary Presbyterian Church at 11th and Clay invited Dr. Sutcliffe to become its pastor, the council asked him to continue the work of the Portland Union Bible Classes at that church. He consented and held the classes at times that did not conflict with the activities of other churches because so many members of those churches attended the meetings. However, as time went on, the attendance began to shrink. Some people felt the close affiliation of the classes with Dr. Sutcliffe's Presbyterian church dimmed the interest of other pastors for the work.

In October 1927, Jack Mitchell accepted an invitation to conduct a Bible teaching evangelistic campaign in Dr. Staub's church in Sunnyside. In 1928 and 1929, he filled the pulpit at Calvary Presbyterian Church when Dr. Sutcliffe went to Dallas as a visiting lecturer at the new seminary; and then in 1930, he accepted the invitation to succeed Dr. B. B. Sutcliffe as teacher of the Portland Union Bible Classes.

When the Mitchells arrived in Portland in January 1931, the governing council of the classes asked Jack to share his vision for the work. He told the men that he wanted to train other men to teach Bible classes that would reach the Pacific Northwest from the California border to Bellingham, Washington, because he felt that the Scriptures could be better taught through Bible study than through evangelistic services.

Soon after Jack took over the teaching of the classes, he began an independent radio ministry that was endorsed by the council later that year. Though the number and the schedule of broadcasts varied for some time, Jack eventually, once he began a Sunday morning service, went from it to the Heathman Hotel where he would broadcast over Station KWJJ.

Mary Mitchell, who always referred to her husband as John, recalls:

In 1932, John's brother Joshua came from Seattle to sing on the program. He had a very fine tenor voice and had sung in opera in England as a younger man. In 1932, Joshua and his wife Nellie and John and I drove to Los Angeles for my sister's wedding. She had asked John to perform the ceremony and for Joshua to sing.

Later, her friends asked her, "Where did you find someone with such a remarkable voice to sing at your wedding?" It was a trip that was most enjoyable and one we shall always cherish.

In 1933, Joshua had a severe brain hemorrhage and went to be with the Lord, whom he loved, when only 42 years of age. This was a grief to Jack. They had been very close.

For many years after that, Otis Smith, one of the Central Bible Church members, sang on the program.

Later, the Sunday evening service was broadcast for some time. It always opened with the hymn, "All Hail the Power of Jesus' Name."

From the start, Jack's week-by-week ministry with the classes prompted so much interest and real growth that the increase in attendance caused problems. Difficulties arose from having both the church congregation and the members of the Portland Union Bible Classes using the one building even though their scheduled meetings occurred at different times. As a result, on October 4, 1931, the council rented the Behnke-Walker Business College building at Tenth and Salmon Streets, and the classes moved there.

In the beginning, Jack followed the same order of meetings Dr. Sutcliffe had devised, having one on Sunday afternoon, one on Tuesday evening and one on Wednesday afternoon. But now, with their own building to use, Jack and the men on the council felt it would be wise to begin a Sunday evening gospel service since there were not many evangelistic churches in the center of downtown Portland. And soon, a regular Thursday night prayer meeting began as well.

By December of 1931, as the classes grew and people received the Lord as their Saviour, the congregation asked for a morning worship service. A number of families did not have a church home. A survey of members showed that 150 of them had no other church connection. Although the suggestion was tabled at the time, pending further study, the matter came up again at the next meeting in January 1932 and carried. The church would have a regular service every Sunday morning and communion once a month.

That decision brought about major changes in the work and began a trend that would eventually turn the Portland Union Bible Classes into a church. Although this was 1932, the organization was not incorporated until 1941. The name was not changed to "Central Bible Church" until 1942.

Another difficulty that arose came from other pastors in the city who accused Jack of "fishing out of their boats." Members of their congregations were removing their membership and were joining the Portland Union Bible Classes. Though he was an avid fisherman who took every opportunity he could to cast a line and hook, this was one kind of fishing of which he was not guilty.

"People did come," Willard Aldrich said. "That is true. But the charge of sheep stealing would not be a fair one because he would not do that."

One striking factor in Jack's appeal as a preacher is that he ignited men. Men flocked to hear him. They liked what he said and how he said it. They filled his congregation and joined him in his work.

One woman testified that her husband always willingly took her to church, but he would never come in. He had an old Ford that he would park out in front. But he would take his boys and go up to the zoo while he waited for church to end and for his wife to come out.

She never missed a service and, eventually, he let the boys go in with her. She urged him time and again to come in, but he would bring his papers and his books and sit in the car and wait.

She said to him one day, "You know, there's a class in here with 80 men in it. This man Mitchell is a man's man. Come in and listen to him."

And he said, "Well, I can try it once."

He slammed down his books and came in. She never had to ask him to come in again. Willard Aldrich put his finger on why Jack Mitchell appealed to men:

He was big. He was strong. He had worked in the world. He had worked among ungodly men, and he had been truly saved. He still had an interest in the world in the proper sense of athletics and an interest in the problems of men in the world. He knew them. But he allowed the Lord to control his life, so that you have a strong man personally but a strong man yielded to the Lord. Women and children responded to him, as well.

He was a man of decision. He had a manner of dealing directly with an issue and not beating around the bush. He had an intuitive way of arriving at right. There was that immediate perception of right and wrong in situations. It may have been simply that he was steeped in the Word of God.

The man carried a heavy load. He would speak three times on Sunday, have the Tuesday afternoon Bible class and the Wednesday night prayer meeting besides funerals and special events. When the school term began, he would teach heavy classes in Bible exposition there. Each Sunday he had a radio broadcast. When that enlarged to a daily schedule, he seemed to take it in stride.

Bill Wecks could be called a "life-time Mitchell watcher." From boyhood, he had known him, seen him, heard him:

He had a zeal that was catching. He was strong physically. He had a big voice. He was forceful. He could really rally the troops. Young men especially were attracted to him. He had so much energy, vigor, and zeal. But he was never jealous when someone else—some other preacher—had more souls saved than he did. That was a thrill to him. He would get so excited. . . .

And humor! He would talk about Jezebel when he was teaching Elijah.

He said, "Elijah ran a hundred miles because he got scared of Jezebel."

He said, "I would have been afraid of that painted woman myself."

He had so much humor you couldn't help but pay attention.

And he always had something fresh from the Word. He was so excited about it. He was as happy to share it with one person as he was with a congregation. He gave a steady diet to his people.

I remember when he taught Abraham. You could go to the

best seminary in the world and you wouldn't get any better than that. He talked about seven different aspects of faith—the courage of faith, the patience of faith. He went all through the life of Abraham. He could see things in the Scriptures that a lot of people couldn't see because he steeped himself in it. He was very much committed to really teaching the Scriptures.

He really believed the Word of God had power. He knew it had power. He had seen it work. He would say the Lord honors His own Word, and he just kept zeroing in on teaching the Word. In fact, I would say, whenever he got up to speak, he would have a Scripture. It wasn't just talk.

Bill's father Charles Wecks in those days had a summer home, east of Portland, out at Blue Lake and sometimes the young people would go out there to swim and fellowship. One time, someone scheduled Jack to have devotions and neglected to inform him of the fact. Bill recalls:

I thought to myself, "Now, he's not prepared for this. We'll just see what he'll say."

And right away, the first thing he did was get into the verse: "I have no man likeminded, for all seek their own, not the things of Christ." And, you know, I've never forgotten that talk. To this day, I've never forgotten that. He was very effective as a teacher. And he was always ready to teach.

Jack would often say that true ministry was the man of God teaching the Word of God in the power of the Spirit of God. He had no doubt in his mind at all that the Bible is the Word of God. If the Bible said it, that was final. There was no argument about it after that.

People were constantly bombarding him with questions about false doctrine. He would tell his classes stories about who said what, and he used those experiences to teach right doctrine:

I remember in a meeting one time, a woman came forward and she said, "I would like to pray to receive the Spirit again."

And I said, "What do you mean? Aren't you a believer?"

"Oh, yes," she said. "I live in the Yakima valley and I've accepted the Saviour, and I had the Spirit. But I've lost the whole business."

There are a lot of folk like that.

As one woman said to me, "Mr. Mitchell, I've been baptized five times, and I'll be baptized the sixth if I ever have to. Bless God!"

How often do you want to get saved?

How often do you want Christ to die for you?

Once is enough.

He came to abide with us forever!

He told another:

One day, a lady said to me, "Brother Mitchell, what would you do if somebody got up in your morning meeting and talked in tongues. What would you do?"

"Why, I'd tell them to sit down. We don't have anybody here with the gift of interpretation."

"But supposing there was somebody there with the gift of interpretation. What would you do?"

"I would take my Bible to see if they were telling the truth."

It's the final court!

And he told another:

Sometimes people get so occupied with their experiences.

In fact, as one man said to me, "Mitchell, if you only had this experience—what a preacher you would be."

"Well," I said to him, "have you had this experience?"

"Oh, yes."

"And are you that kind of preacher that you claim I would be?"

No more word was said.

And Mitchell was willing to take on a roomful, if need be, to stand up for doctrines and principles that he felt were essential to the correct interpretation of Scripture.

He told his classes this story:

I was invited to a luncheon committee meeting one time. We were preparing for some city-wide meeting. By the time I got away from my classes and got over to the luncheon, they were eating their dessert and there was only one seat left.

You know that, when you to go these meetings where you've got all kinds of preachers, you find your Baptists sitting together in a clique over here and your Nazarenes over there. Here will be the Free Methodists and over there are the Presbyterians and the Bible Church people. Talk about birds of a feather flocking together.

Well, there was one seat left right in the middle of the Nazarene, Free Methodist people. Dear, dear people. They love the Lord. And while I was sitting there, one of the fellows across the table said to the man on my left, "What are you giving your people these days?"

And he said, "I'm teaching the Book of Romans."

Well, my ears went up. Anybody talks about the Book of Romans and my ears go up, you know. They're so big.

And this other fellow said, "Why, that's what I'm teaching. The Book of Romans."

And I rubbed my hands and said, "Oh, this is wonderful! You fellows are teaching the Book of Romans?"

And they said to me, "Well, what better book can we teach?"

I said, "You're right! That'll straighten you all out." And I pulled my little Testament out of my pocket and I said, "Let me ask you a question."

And they said, "Mitchell, we don't talk to you on Romans."

At this point, the class would laugh and applaud, proud to be sitting under a teacher who could take on the world. And then he would press home the point:

Now, young people, the difference between us was what does the cross mean? This will determine a whole lot of your doctrine. I know you're going to get it in Doctrine or some of your other classes, but I don't mind. I want you to get the truth. It's a question of what does the cross mean?

As I told these men, "The difference between you fellas and me is not so much eternal security or can I be saved and lost. The issue is what did Christ accomplish for me? That's the main thing. What did Christ do for me on the cross?"

It was a rare person who could match Mitchell on knowledge of the Scriptures. He would make some kind of dogmatic statement to Bill Wecks as they were driving to conduct a funeral somewhere. Bill would say, "Now wait a minute, here."

And then Jack would say, "For example." And he would quote a whole bunch of Scriptures. There was no question. When it came down to it, he was right; and he had a whole string of Scriptures that proved it. When he got through, you were satisfied that what he had said was right.

The Scripture was so much a part of him. He had it all in his head. He was full of it. He was always full of it. The thing that really struck me was that you could tell he had been over those things hundreds of times. But it was still very fresh to him because it was the Word of God.

In the spirit of that, the new name for the church was "Central BIBLE Church." The name for the new school would be "Multnomah School of the BIBLE" (now "Multnomah BIBLE College" and "Multnomah BIBLICAL Seminary," in keeping with Jack's original vision). Jack loved the Word of God, and he wanted others to love it, too. He always felt one of the greatest dangers in the Christian life was for believers to lose interest in Bible truth because it became familiar. He would quote Matthew 22:29: "Ye do err, not knowing the scriptures, nor the power of God." He would warn his classes:

Oh, may the Lord deliver us from coldness of heart, from losing interest in the things we've known all our lives.

You know, one of the first churches I had—when I resigned from the church, I called the session together, the Board of Elders, and I said, "I just trust that the next man you have in your pulpit you will be a little more charitable, a little more patient with him."

And they said, "Why, Mr. Mitchell, we have loved you. We have loved your ministry."

I said, "Yes, I know, but your attitude is this. If I speak on something that I'm giving to babes in Christ or trying to exhort God's people to get into the Word of God or if I'm preaching the gospel to the unsaved, your attitude is this: 'Well, this is not for me. I've known this all my life.'

"So the things that you have known—you've lost the joy of them, the life of them, the blessing of them."

The great desire of Jack's heart was to reach the whole Pacific Northwest with the Word of God. He wanted to bring in teachers and to have classes in different cities. One important area of this outreach was in Shiloh Basin where men from the classes had services for many years.

Jack's need for co-workers prompted him to write to Willard Aldrich and Dexter McClenny at Dallas Theological Seminary, inviting them both to come and share in a program with him. McClenny was not able to come, but Willard did—for what would become a lifelong association.

Looking back, Willard has said, "I had no special gift for young people's work, but that is what he had me do. He knew something about me through the family and my brother Roy, who was his roommate at Dallas. And so there was a matter of general acquaintance."

Jack also gathered a coterie of lay preachers around him. One, a man named Van Brugen, would go with him down to Mist and Berkenfeld and Elsie near the coast where they had preaching points.

Willard says that Jack was a doer as well as a preacher:

He had a real concern for his people that marked him out.

He was not a professional hireling. He had a vision for the Northwest and how to reach it through the teaching of the Word of God.

He tried to implement that alone, to begin with, by taking on midweek classes in Salem and other places. Then he thought to implement it further by bringing Simon Forsberg in. And I was in on that a little although I had come primarily for the young people.

He had a vision, but it was not the vision of a visionary separated from the realities of how to bring it to pass. Some have that type of vision where they don't face the realities of it. But the school, the church, the camp, the children's work, the bus ministries were all a part of his vision though segments of it may have been furnished by some of those who worked with him.

In 1935, Mr. Simon Forsberg had classes in Corvallis, Salem and Cedar Mill. Willard had a class in Ardenwald as well as his work in the church downtown. Jack had classes in Seattle and several other places. He also spent most of his summers ministering in many eastern conference centers as well as abroad. These conferences were always very rewarding, and the Mitchells told many stories of people who came to the Saviour.

Once, when Jack was speaking at a conference at Moody Church in Chicago, he had a call from a Jewish lady who had heard the radio broadcast.

When he answered the phone, she said, "If what you told us on the radio is true, it should be shouted from the housetops."

Jack talked with her a while and later went to see her. She was very gracious and interested and had many questions.

When the Mitchells returned to Portland, she corresponded all fall. At Christmas, they had a telegram from her which read, "You will be glad to know that I have accepted Jesus Christ as my Lord and Saviour."

About this time, Jack began getting letters from young men in Bellingham, Seattle, Everett, and Yakima in Washington, and Corvallis and Salem in Oregon, saying that they wanted Bible classes and they wanted him to be the teacher of them all. Recounting the story later, he said:

Well, I could only be in one place at one time. And just about that time, we had a conference at Lake Sammamish concerning this and a Mr. Rich wanted to start some Bible classes in Seattle. He asked me if I would give a week's conference—which I did—in the Chamber of Commerce building.

When I got home—oh, about two or three months afterward—I received a letter from a bunch of fellows up there—eight or ten fellows—who said that, if they came to Portland, would I teach them the Bible. They would try to get part-time work and would I give the rest of the day to them and teach them the Bible.

And I said to myself—well, if there are that many fellows that are hungry for the Bible, then there must be more. We've already got enough men here to start a Bible school because Willard is a good theologian and Forsberg is a good teacher. Oran Smith had come with me. He was working among the Jewish people. And Dr. Sutcliffe was up in Tacoma.

I said, "We better start a school for them."

So Jack went up to Tacoma to talk to Dr. Sutcliffe and to ask him if he would come down and teach.

Sutcliffe was not impressed. He said, "It is economically impossible to start a school."

Jack said, "Well, there's no school up here. The Christian and Missionary Alliance school in Seattle has moved down to San Francisco. There's a little Bible school in Vancouver with only about 20 to 25 students. There is room for a school."

And he said, "If they really want the Bible, then let them go to Moody or Biola."

"No," Jack said, "I think there's room if you would come

down and be our president. Let's start a school and teach fellows the Word of God."

And so he came down. The Portland Union Bible Classes took care of the Forsbergs, Willard Aldrich, and the Mitchells.

On Valentine's Day in 1936, Jack called a meeting that brought Sutcliffe, Forsberg, Aldrich and himself together with six Christian businessmen of the city—Ross H. Cornell, Thomas Dryden, H. J. Fitts, Thomas Hazlett and Harry West of Portland and Lloyd Garrison of Vancouver. He told of the need in the Northwest for a school on the order of Moody Bible Institute and the Bible Institute of Los Angeles that would teach the "distinctive doctrines of grace." He said he and Sutcliffe were concerned that the centrality of the Word of God was no longer an emphasis of many Christian schools. He wanted to establish a school that would emphasize the Bible and foster a love of the truth in the hearts of young people.

The men set up a committee of Mitchell, Sutcliffe and Forsberg to organize such a school. It appointed a committee of Mitchell, Forsberg, Hazlett and West to search for a suitable building. The committee ran into difficulties because it needed to have a name for the school if it was going to enter any kind of contractual negotiation. Forsberg, thinking of the Multnomah tribe of Indians that at one time had populated the Northwest, suggested the name, "Multnomah School of the Bible."

The committee on organization offered the position of president to Dr. Sutcliffe. He accepted. A Board of Administration to assist him included Jack Mitchell as vice-president, Simon Forsberg as dean of the faculty, Willard Aldrich as registrar and Kenneth Kober as treasurer. Subsequently, the general committee that met on Valentine's Day reorganized itself into a Board of Trustees.

Since at the founding not one red cent sat in any fund or coffer for use in procuring a building, the committee had to ferret out the least expensive site the city would approve to serve as a school. It found an old former mortuary at 703 N.E. Multnomah Street it could rent for $40 a month. The city required improvements. The Trustees decided to employ the students to do the work.

The next problem was to raise the $40. Jack remembered:

Our first job was to clean out the formaldehyde and clean the place up. But to get $40 to pay the rent was something else. But that's how the school started. We had 35 kids in day school, and we also had 30 or 40 in the night school.

Oran Smith had a class for Jewish people. I remember when they would come into the room where he taught, they would look to see where people were sitting. You know, there was a division among the Jews—orthodox, neo-orthodox, liberal or whatever it is. They all sat in a different place.

And Miss Emily Neil opened her home. She owned a restaurant over town; and she took our students in, roomed them and fed them the first year.

The lack of finances continued to plague the school until the war years when giving increased noticeably. Until then, faculty seldom received a full month's pay.

At this time and for many years, Jack served the Dallas Theological Seminary as a visiting teacher for the month of February. The work at the church was growing. He had about 15 classes a week to teach at the new school. But even though he was a strong man, he was not made of steel. Mary Mitchell remembered:

In 1936, we moved from our apartment, where we had lived for some time, to a rented house. Willard lived with us there that winter. It was a very cold winter, and the house was poorly built. I remember how Willard kept a fire in our fireplace going day and night. In the spring and summer of 1937, we planned and built our home on an acre on the west side of Portland near

Garden Home.

On September 14, John and Willard were packing and moving things out of our home when suddenly John had a terrific pain in his head. The doctor did not seem to know what to do for him. It was later, in visiting a doctor in Seattle, that we knew that John had had a brain hemorrhage. He stayed with friends while I moved.

The Mitchells took a year-and-a-half leave of absence for his convalescence. Friends in Seattle who had a summer home in Leavenworth, Washington, invited them to stay there as long as they needed. Mary wrote about his recovery:

Leavenworth was a wonderful place for a quiet time of complete rest. However, John was discouraged because he was not gaining strength.

One day, he said, "I don't think I will ever teach or preach again."

One Sunday morning, we attended a church near where we were staying. We soon realized that the pastor was liberal and did not even believe the Scriptures.

John's reaction was "Well, at least I could do better than that."

One day we had a letter from a Mrs. Bechtel, a dear lady in our congregation. She wrote that she had wakened in the night to pray for us. She sent a page from a "Choice Gleanings" daily calendar with a quotation from a leader among the Plymouth Brethren. He had written, "This is the best thing that could happen to you. If the Lord had anything better, He would give it to you because He loves you."

That seemed to work like a tonic. John immediately brightened and was soon wanting to go home again to his work.

When he returned, he and the men of the council realized that he needed more help. He told his classes in later years that he had forgotten everything he knew about the Scriptures and had had to start all over again. He was very grateful to have Willard with him.

In 1941, Annette Bolhouse and Kay Little came as secretaries and Pauline Winslow helped for a time. Dave Stewart came in 1946 and was with him until 1957. John Van Diest joined the staff and had charge of the young people's ministries.

Mary Mitchell remembered one prank Jack's staff played on him:

"One time he was sitting in his easy chair in his office, and Johnny Van Diest had a list of things he was talking over with him. Johnny looked up to find John sound asleep. He went to the other office to tell the girls not to disturb him.

"John always called me before he left the office. When he did not call by six o'clock, I began to feel concerned. Finally, he called at seven to say he had just wakened and no one was there. Everyone had gone at five and left him asleep."

She loved to tell that story. But it was true—both Mitchells worked hard. One spring, when they were both very tired, David Stewart, through the council, arranged to rent a boat so they could spend two weeks on the water. John loved boats; and, later, a dear friend in Dallas sent a check for him to buy a boat which they enjoyed for several years.

For 35 years, they spent two weeks each summer fishing on Vancouver Island with the Sloan family. John enjoyed golf and played sometimes with Dr. J. Vernon McGee when he was in town.

Mary had always wanted a big garden and, when the Mitchells were settled in their new home, they decided it would be a good time to start one.

"We were very ambitious," she admitted later. "We planted every vegetable we could think of. We had rhubarb and berry bushes and every kind of fruit tree: apple, plum, peach, cherry, pear and even a fig tree. We also had rabbits and chickens. It wasn't long until the real purpose of our lives, the ministry, took precedence over the fun of 'farming.' We were both too busy to care for it all.

"Very soon, the rabbits and chickens were gone. I think perhaps the garden was weeded once that first summer. We did have some things to can and freeze when fall came. However, John and I found that preparing for our classes and visiting and caring for the needs of the church were more important."

The schedule of daily life made this a wise conclusion because Jack was always anxious to meet the needs of his people and never failed to visit those who were sick or needed help. One time, he woke early.

He said, "I somehow feel led to visit Warren Douglas." Warren had for some time been very ill with cancer. When Jack came home hours later, he told Mary that Warren had passed away in his arms.

There were times when he was called home from vacation when someone was very ill or had died. This was so when Dr. Sutcliffe passed away.

Even when ill, Dr. Sutcliffe had a sense of humor. One time, John was sitting with him in the hospital. All at once, Dr. Sutcliffe sank back and closed his eyes. John thought that perhaps he was gone and began to think of calling a nurse.

Suddenly, Dr. Sutcliffe gave a little shudder and opened his eyes.

He said, "Is that you, John?"

When Jack said yes, he answered, "My, oh, my. I am so disappointed. I thought I was going to see the Lord, and all I see is you."

Jack always said that with Sutcliffe's Homegoing, the Body of Christ lost one of the best Bible teachers of the century.

However, by this time, the Lord had given him a very fine faculty at the school and very capable assistants at Central Bible Church. It was time to "lengthen the cords" and develop the ministry along new lines. He talked with Charles Wecks about developing a summer camp for children in the foothills of Mt. Hood east of the city. He talked to his staff about developing the children's ministries to reach more and more youngsters for Christ. He encouraged members of his congregation to go to the mission field. He taught daily at the school and carried on his radio program.

He saw the fields as "white unto harvest," and he moved out to do his part.

Chapter Twelve

Winner of Children

In the early days, Dr. Mitchell would pop in to the camp at Trout Creek. When he did, he would ask us to call all the boys and girls together. If it was a sunny day, we would have them meet outside; and if it was rainy—as it was much of the time in the early weeks of June—we would meet in the lodge. We would have lots of singing, and then he would speak to them.

And I was always amazed to witness the response.

Children would make decisions when I felt that the message was a little bit over their heads, and yet there was a response.

He had a love for children that came through when he spoke—although he never had children of his own. He had a great desire to see them brought to salvation in the Saviour's name.

—Dave Stewart, pastor (retired)
Abbotsford, B.C.

One reason why the Portland Union Bible Classes attracted Jack Mitchell in the first place may well have been its ongoing ministry to neighborhood children in the Portland area. Miss Alma Bailey and then Miss Josephine Neil had joined the staff in 1927 to develop a children's work. Mrs. H. L. Walter joined their "Department of Child Evangelism" in 1930 as a volunteer. By 1931, when the Mitchells came, the women were conducting 19 classes a week.

Jack talked to them about extending the work, but they felt they were doing all they could. So he suggested that Miss Bailey conduct a teacher-training class so that other women attending the Bible Classes could learn to teach the children.

The subsequent growth of the work amazed everyone. The 19 classes in two years increased to 44, enrolling 1,100 children. By 1934, the women were teaching 68 classes a week. Despite Josephine Neil's resignation for health reasons in 1938, the women were teaching 90 home Bible classes a week by 1939. Even later, during the difficult war years, the workers were reaching 2,000 children each week.

Other cities caught Jack's vision of regular weekly Bible classes for children as early as 1934 when Calgary, Alberta, had 15 classes and Seattle, 12. Vancouver, Washington, had seven plus a teacher-training class.

Of note, the Child for Christ Crusade traces its origin to the children's ministry of the Portland Union Bible Classes.

Also in the early days of that congregation, a Sunday evening young people's group formed and grew quickly. Although it had started with only eight or ten, in Jack's first year it grew to about 100.

Kenneth Taylor (later the paraphrast of *The Living Bible*) attended those meetings when he was in high school. Of those years, he says, "My life has been greatly intertwined with Jack Mitchell's because of what his ministry meant to me personally as a teenager and then on through college years and seminary. He sort of sent me down to Dallas Theological Seminary. Under his ministry I became grounded in the Word of God; and, apart from that, I do not see how it would have been possible for the Lord to use me in the various ways that I have had the privilege of being used."

Jack took every opportunity to cultivate a love for the Word of God and missions in the hearts of his young charges. Council minutes indicate that by 1934 the young people were active in a tract distribution ministry. They involved themselves in outside Sunday School work, in prayer meetings once a month, in raising money for missionary support and in occasional banquets and Bible conferences.

Kay Petrie Groenlund, a long-time English teacher at Multnomah, at age 11 was the youngest member of the young people's group. She always said that she felt "a little bit conspicuous, but they were very kind and let me stay. I fell in love with Mary Mitchell from the moment she came. She was cute and friendly, and she didn't make me feel I was out of place. And she did extra things. I remember one time she paid my way to a youth retreat."

As he had done at the Open Bible Church in Grand Rapids, Jack paid attention to the young people like few pastors in that day did, making over each one, making it a point to know everyone by name.

Kay also remembered that Jack "had a very big smile and there was always a greeting. He wasn't a stuffed shirt. And he was such a cut-up. I remember how he pretended to trip over the rocker of a rocking chair while he was carrying a meat platter full of hot biscuits. And he always played in the softball games at our church picnics. He had such a love for people."

Jack taught the young people himself, singing with them in the opening exercises and teaching them the Word. He wanted to make sure that each one really knew what he believed. Week by week he drilled the youngsters to make sure they could defend their trust in the Lord.

One, Bob Bleid, has said he suffered when Jack's finger pointed at him.

"I think that's why I don't speak up much in church," he

says, "because he was one of those guys that would ask a question and, boy, if you didn't answer it right, he was right on top of you. I kind of pulled inside my shell. He would really let you know you answered it wrong, and most of the time I was wrong.

"But he was a neat guy. I think his sincerity and the walk that he showed us himself attracted us. He showed us how a Christian should live, and he was always in the Word."

Jack made it a point to visit the youngsters in their home. Bob remembers his putting on boxing gloves and getting down on his knees to box with the Bleid boys every time he came over.

Jack also took every opportunity to help and to minister to the families where he could. He came at once to the Bleid home one November night when an emergency arose.

Bob's father had had a cerebral hemorrhage in August, and he had taken time off from work to recover. That November morning, he had taken Bob and his brother to Grant High School and then had gone to sit in a dentist's chair for an hour having an impression made for false teeth. After the boys got home from school about 4:30 that afternoon, he fell unconscious. The family called for a physician and for their pastor. Jack got there first.

"He asked my mom if she would like him upstairs in bed, and my mother said yes," Bob remembers. "And just to tell you how strong a fellow Jack was—my folks' bedroom was upstairs. Oh, it must have been 13 or 14 steps up there. My dad was on the davenport on the main floor. He was a dead weight because he was still unconscious.

"Dr. Mitchell just picked my dad up and carried him right up the stairs and laid him on the bed up there. That'll never leave me, I tell you, to see him do that. That was one thing I thought was impressive.

"My dad died that night."

Bill Wecks, Jack's long-time associate in later years, said of him, "I don't care who it was that was in trouble. Jack had time for him. He was so committed himself, so sold on what he believed. He was very, very diligent. There was no halfway with him. I think this may be why the Lord didn't give him any children."

Bill meant to say, "The Lord didn't give him any children of his own" because Jack did have children; and in church he took time for those children. His first year in Portland, he got Sunday School classes going. On October 4, 1931, some 14 teachers and 176 enrollees showed up for the first class. Year by year, the Sunday School grew in size slowly, but steadily. By 1941, it was up to nearly 350. In the 1960s and '70s it numbered nearly 1,000.

Every Sunday morning, Jack had a special mission to perform. He didn't have to appear in the adult class he was teaching until the opening exercises were finished.

Multnomah faculty wife Charlotte Lawrence noted that he "used to personally visit the Sunday School classes, particularly the nursery, picking up and holding and loving the babies as if to give them his blessing. And he blessed the nursery workers, too. He highly valued them."

Many parents in the congregation were surprised to hear their youngsters speak freely of "Dr. Mitchell" because the little ones were always in classes and junior church and training hour and rarely in congregational meetings where he spoke. But their pastor would make the rounds of those classes, singing with the children and encouraging the teachers.

The Rev. L. Dwight Custis, who followed Jack as pastor of Central Bible Church, said of him, "When he would come down to teach at Dallas Seminary, he would talk to us about reaching boys and girls with the gospel. In those years, it surprised me that a man who was an expositor and busy in conference work and going all over the world teaching was so vitally concerned about reaching boys and girls."

But Jack took Luke 9:47-48 seriously: "And Jesus, perceiving the thought of their heart, took a child, and set him by him, And said unto them, Whosoever shall receive this child in my name, receiveth me; and whosoever shall receive me receiveth him that sent me; for he that is least among you all, the same shall be great."

But Jack was not content with classes in church. He wanted to get out into the community and reach children in their own schools and neighborhoods. The work in the Portland public schools began prior to 1939. Classes also met in the Shriners and Doernbecher hospitals and the Fruit and Flower Mission, a nursery for preschool children.

Mrs. Ray McMinn (known as Janie) had a number of released-time religious education classes in west side Portland schools. She also had a daily radio program for children in government housing where on-site Bible classes were not permitted.

Ever on the look-out for young men and women of spirit and gift who could hold the attention of the young and win them, Jack came upon Dave Stewart first in the late 1930s when a half dozen freshman boys clambered past the upperclassmen sitting in the back rows and took their place as close to their teacher as they could. They were hungry for teaching from the Word of God and excited they could sit on the front row.

Dave's first introduction to Dr. Mitchell was either in a Spiritual Life class or in a study on the book of Romans; he doesn't remember. Both classes captivated his heart, he says, and gave him a love for Dr. Mitchell. He responded to Mitchell's love for the Lord Jesus and his clear exposition of the gospel of the grace of God. Dave had grown up among the Plymouth Brethren and so already had a great appreciation of God's grace.

He attended Multnomah when the campus centered around the old mortuary building at Seventh Avenue and

Multnomah Street down where the Lloyd Center now sits. He roomed in the home of Kent and Lucille Douglas on Seventh Avenue north of Broadway. Mary Mitchell's brother Herb Eby and his wife Verna lived next door to them.

Dave remembers that, because Jack Mitchell was a good friend of the Douglases, he would drop by for an evening to play table tennis with the four boys rooming there. They found their Bible teacher was an excellent table tennis player and very competitive. He would take on the fellows one by one and would beat them most of the time even though he held the paddle in what Dave calls the "old-fashioned vertical manner."

Many of the students went to Central Bible Church downtown at 11th and Salmon; but Dave attended Stark Street Gospel Hall, meeting in those days on southeast 28th and Stark Street, and so did not get to know Jack Mitchell as his pastor as some of the other students did.

When World War II began in 1939, he dropped out of school. Low finances and the imminence of being drafted for service kept him home in Canada. When he entered the Armed Forces, he wrote from Camp Borden, Ontario, asking the now "Dr." Mitchell (Wheaton College had conferred an honorary doctorate on him during graduation ceremonies in 1941) about returning to school when the war was over.

"As I reflect on it," Dave said later, "it just seemed automatic to write to him. Dr. Mitchell was synonymous with Multnomah. I didn't think to write to the registrar or to anyone else to make inquiry. The letter was addressed to him, and I got a beautiful letter back (I am sad that I didn't keep it). He encouraged me without hesitation to make application as soon as I was ready, and he would assist in expediting my return to the school. That wasn't to be until the spring of 1946."

At that time, the school was on the quarter system so Dave was able to pick up in just a few months the courses he had not taken his first year at school. He was now 30-plus years of age; and Dr. Mitchell had his eye out for anyone he thought could serve with him in the enlarging ministry of Central Bible. And so he spoke to Dave about working with the camp that summer. However, Dave Weyerhaeuser, the chairman of Student Missionary Council which operated under the sponsorship of the Weyerhaeuser Foundation, had already asked him to work with Bert Rydman that summer in eastern Oregon.

So Dr. Mitchell said, "Well, keep next summer in mind."

As soon as Dave got back to school in late August of that year, 1946, Dr. Mitchell tapped him to work with Mrs. McMinn who was teaching in the Aloha-Huber school, the Reedville school and the Witch Hazel school at that time. Dave worked with Dr. Mitchell from 1946 to 1957.

In those days, released-time teachers went right into the schools to conduct their religious education classes for the children. Dave played the piano to help with the music. Mrs. McMinn taught the little folk and Dave taught the older ones. Near the end of the school year in 1947, she decided to carry on other ministries and so put Dave in charge of all of the released-time work.

In 1948, the McCollum case came before the U.S. Supreme Court and, as a result, the Released Time Program work was forced out of the school buildings. Six months later, Dave conceived the idea that he could use a school bus, parked off school grounds, as a classroom; and thus the school bus ministry was born.

The church board authorized buying a bus and made the funds available. Dave drew up a route and schedule that took him from one school to another throughout the week. The work expanded from that. Dr. Mitchell and the board and the church congregation were very supportive and excited about what was taking place, he says.

In addition to schools in the western suburbs of Portland, the door opened for districts like Milwaukie, Oregon City and Concord in the southeast and Fairview, a big school near the Columbia River by the Interstate Bridge. Then four schools in the West Union area opened. This kept three buses going five days a week. At first, Sally Morris came to work with Dave. Then Bill Snyder joined him, followed by Dave Hazen, John Van Diest, and Bill and Carol Muir.

Dave presented an account of the benefits of the bus ministry to each local school board where he wanted to work. He would tell about the program and what the teachers would be doing. He would explain that there would be no cost to the school and that his staff would maintain the same degree of behavior the school administration required.

He found that school administrators liked the program. They saw a difference in the youngsters who took it seriously. One superintendent told Dave he was called on the phone by unhappy parents complaining about this "mingling of church and state." He said he told them that he was happy with the program, that it was a bonus for the school and that until the board ruled otherwise that was the way it was going to be.

Parents had to sign up for the children to attend the classes; and likewise the children couldn't discontinue the class without their parents' permission. In most of the schools, more than 90 percent of the children participated in the released-time program.

In 1958, Jack Mitchell wrote Lloyd Garrison, a generous benefactor of the children's ministry over the years:

Two weeks ago, one of the men on the buses was led of the Lord to give a message to the children about the Lord's provision for forgiveness and about heaven. He had unusual attention that day and was led at the end to ask the youngsters to tell him about their relationship to the Lord as they were leaving the bus.

During the day in that school, more than 30 youngsters told him they had that day taken the Lord Jesus Christ as their own personal Saviour. Needless to say, our hearts were thrilled for we are sure there are others who also made decisions for the Lord.

In a thank-you note to the Garrisons the following year, Jack revealed that the children's work was not without cost:

Your gift will be a source of real helpfulness to us, especially in the coming months. As you know, there is quite a drain on the church in reaching these boys and girls for Christ; and yet it is one of the most fruitful of our ministries here in the Portland area.

Grace Bolhouse was directing the children's home Bible classes when Dave came on the scene. Eventually, she had about 100 weekly classes meeting throughout the greater Portland area. They were taught by women who attended Dr. Mitchell's teacher-training classes, held on Wednesdays in the downtown church.

In order to reach junior high age children, the church staff developed the "Real Life Clubs" — Dr. Mitchell's name — patterned after the early Young Life clubs. They met in homes in the early evening after school. Clubs were scattered over a wide distance, from Washougal on the Washington side of the Columbia to Milwaukie in the southeast, and from Troutdale on the Columbia River highway to the Eby home on the west side of the Willamette River.

Jack wrote Mr. Garrison in January 1959:

We have been encouraged these past three or four months in the number of boys and girls who have been saved in the home Bible classes. I think that between 100 and 200 youngsters confessed the Lord as their Saviour this fall and they are being taught the things of Christ. Then, of course, there are hundreds of others who have accepted the Saviour who are being built up in the faith and in the Word of God. . . . We believe there is much ground yet to be possessed; for, as we see the thousands of young-

*sters in this city, we realize we have barely scratched the surface in
reaching them for the Lord Jesus.*

In all of these classes, the children were encouraged to
attend regularly, do Bible reading at home, memorize Bible
verses and bring a friend. Credits, earned by these efforts,
counted as scholarship points toward the cost of camp. Over
the years, hundreds of children "earned" a week at camp in
this manner.

In the summers of 1947 and 1948, Marjorie Good and
Dave co-directed the Trout Creek Bible Camp in the Mt. Hood
foothills east of Portland. She had co-directed the year before
with Dick Cochran, whose father had been chairman of the
board of Central Bible Church. Dick ultimately went to the
Near East as a missionary with the Presbyterians. Dave then had
the responsibility of hiring the staff, purchasing the supplies,
managing the camp, as well as directing the boys camps.

It was in this way that the camping ministry at Trout
Creek evolved. Working closely with Mr. Charles Wecks, who
made the camp available to Central Bible Church, Dave was
given a free hand to develop programs and manage the camp.
It was a growing ministry which, together with the Released
Time classes, the Children's Bible Clubs, and the Real Life
Clubs, required a substantial budget.

Dave remembers that "Mr. Wecks was a man with a big
heart. It was his camp and he paid the shot. The church paid
the cost of the camp operation; but the facilities, the buildings, the grounds came out of Wecks Foundation finances.
He was a dear man, and he was happy to submit to Dr.
Mitchell's leadership in the vision they shared in reaching
boys and girls in the city of Portland.

"Dr. Mitchell always stood with me, and the folk of
Central Bible were uncomplaining in their support."

The camp hired Multnomah upperclassmen as counselors and found that many of them brought along ideas from

their previous experiences that the staff was able to utilize.

On Sunday afternoons, as each week's camp was breaking up, Dave and his staff would have a 3 o'clock program, put on by the campers themselves, to which the parents picking up youngsters could come. If 150 campers attended—and that was the lowest number that ever came during those days—then 300 to 400 parents and family would come out. In the early days Dr. Mitchell would speak to them; and the staff would serve tea, coffee and cookies in the lodge and mingle with the parents before they took their children home.

From time to time, Dr. Mitchell would speak to the staff. In the early days the staff conducted a boys camp one week and a girls camp the next week. The camp had 10 cabins, so Dave had 10 male and 10 female counselors. In the off week, the counselors rotated doing the chores, the dishes, and the cleaning.

When eventually another camp was built on the opposite side of the creek, the staff conducted co-educational camps and Dave hired a crew of church kids to do the dishes and the cleanup chores because the counselors were employed all the time with their campers.

Many church families found that the summers away from home in a solidly Christian camp had a profound spiritual effect on their youngsters who worked on the crew. The camaraderie bound the kids together as they grew through high school years. Many became counselors themselves and ultimately fell in love and married others who had worked on the crew with them year by year.

Jack Mitchell loved having the camp.

He wrote Lloyd Garrison:

I was just saying to Mr. Wecks the other day that in the 13 years we have been having the youngsters go to camp, we have averaged over 100 boys and girls definitely saved each year. When we think of the thousands of youngsters who have been edified

and encouraged and come to assurance and dedicated their lives
to Christ, we lift up our hearts in thanksgiving to God for the
privilege of having a part in this ministry.

Dave and Dr. Mitchell, on many Wednesdays when
their schedules allowed, would have supper together. Dr.
Mitchell had a Bible study class on the same Wednesday afternoons he held the teacher-training class for the teachers of the
children's home Bible classes. First, the teachers would gather
at 1 o'clock under Grace Bolhouse's leadership, and Dr.
Mitchell would teach the lesson to them. And then at 2
o'clock he would have his afternoon Bible study, open to anyone in the city. A lot of folk who were not members of
Central Bible Church would come. The church in those days
met downtown and thus was centrally located.

Dave would report back to the church after his afternoon released-time classes to see if he could help Dr. Mitchell
in any way. Some days, Dave would do visitation, and he
would make a number of hospital calls for him.

On Wednesdays, because he had the midweek Bible class
that night, Jack seldom went home. He and Mary were living
out on the west side of town then, and so he'd simply stay in
town and have a bite to eat.

"He probably hadn't had lunch," Dave recalled later.
"He wasn't too interested in meals necessarily. And so, after
the two-to-three o'clock Bible study, we would go over to
Holmans. They had big ovens on the wall and they were
always cooking a roast of beef or a big shank of ham.

"We'd order a ham bun or a roast beef bun, and they
would pull out the big roast and slice off the amount that
was ours and weigh it on a scale. We'd get our coffee and go
way down to the very far end of the restaurant. He never
allowed me to pay his fare or pay my own. He was generous
to a fault.

"And we would sit there for an hour or so and talk more

about the work, and we'd talk about the Scriptures and just talk and talk.

"He would relax, and we would talk about the Saviour and the Scriptures and the work with its problems present and problems past. He seemed to need to unload and, of course, this gave me a closer look at the man."

Jack always took the month of February and went to Dallas Theological Seminary for his annual week of lecture-ship plus other ministries, and he would ask Dr. Aldrich and other faculty members from the school to fill the pulpit.

But one time, he asked Dave to take one of the Sunday evening services. He reports being "scared to say the least."

Dave went into Jack's office and said to him, "Dr. Mitchell, what in the world can I say to your people in that service that has not already been said?"

I'll never forget his reply.

He looked at me and he said, "Dave, you tell them what you know about Jesus."

I don't think there is any statement that I can recall that more aptly describes what Dr. Mitchell was trying to do in his ministry.

There was the criticism in his early days that folk who went to the Portland Union Bible Classes had "Mitchell-itis."

But it wasn't long, however, till I observed, "No, folk don't have Mitchell-itis. This is no cultish attraction." People were not attracted to Mitchell per se. They were attracted to Mitchell's Saviour and the clear exposition of the gospel that he gave.

And so the phrase "Tell them what you know about Jesus" meant much more to me than an instruction covering what I should preach in a Sunday service at Central Bible Church. It was a phrase that crystallized all he stood for and worked for.

It was a phrase that could even be written on his tombstone as the motto of his life.

Chapter Thirteen

Mentor

Jack Mitchell in my judgment was the champion of the underdog. And people who were arrogant or self-sufficient or who had it all together and didn't need any help did not attract him. As you know, he was always gracious; but, when he would tell me about the different individuals who had impressed him negatively in the ministry, it was always on that basis. They were self-confident, very impressed with themselves, believing their press reports. And that was always a turnoff to him.

I think what I remember most about him from his years at the seminary is his compassion. And it really marked him—very obviously. That's what attracted me to him—his warmth, his interest in me a mere student, and his love for people, hungry saint and sinner alike.

Even though he was invited to some of the larger conferences across America, that's not what pumped him up. What really excited him were these little churches, sometimes up in British Columbia or here in the Northwest, where pastors were struggling. He just loved to go in and encourage them and speak to their people.

—*Howard Hendricks*
Professor of Christian Education
Dallas Theological Seminary

Howard Hendricks first met Jack Mitchell in 1946 when, as a student, he enrolled at Dallas Seminary. Four Bible lecturers came every year—two each semester—and Dr. Mitchell immediately became one of his favorites. Their relationship, at first, was nominal; he knew Howard by name. It wasn't until after graduation that they began to run into each other on the conference circuit at Mt. Hermon, at Moody Bible Institute, and other places. When Dr. Hendricks started to come to Multnomah for a variety of events, they became even closer friends.

"My wife and I used to spend time in their home with them," Howard said. "And we spent time up at Qualicum Beach, fishing with them. We always came away with cherished memories. I would consider him a mentor to me, certainly a model."

He saw Jack Mitchell in action teaching at the seminary level. One of Jack's favorite statements, "Don't you men ever read your Bible?" really caught on. Students would try to copy that in their sermons, thinking their listeners (at church) would laugh as they had laughed in the seminary classroom.

"But their people took offense. Only Jack could say that and get away with it," Howard said.

"And I remember on one other occasion when Dr. Mitchell, in getting ready for his Dallas lectures, had prepared to teach the wrong book. He asked the students to turn to whatever book it was, and they informed him it was not the right book.

"That was no problem.

"'Just turn to the other book,' he said. And he started in with the same knowledge and authority as if he had prepared that one."

Jack's knowledge of the Scriptures "just blew us away." The students were convinced Jack could quote virtually the entire Gospel by John from memory.

"He would just go on and on giving references from a variety of sources throughout the Old and the New Testaments; and we used to wonder how in the world could a man master the Scriptures that well. But later, when I spent more time with him, he used to tell me about his early days up in Canada when he really didn't know that much."

Jack had told him how on the prairies he would study the Bible so intensely, every time he got an opportunity—sometimes through the night—because people would ask him questions when he went out preaching, and he found he couldn't answer them.

"But he would tell them that 'we'll take that up the next time' and he'd go back and study the Scriptures in order to come up with the answers," Howard said. "And, of course, he became a master of the book of Romans. I was recently in Canada, and it's amazing what an impact he had across the plains. I met several elderly people—a couple of elderly pastors—who were quite young at the time but who remembered him very, very well as a great teacher of the Word of God."

Jack would often regale his friends with recollections of those days on the prairies. Given good comrades to vacation with him at Qualicum Bay on the inside shore of Victoria Island, British Columbia, he would fish and dig clams by day and Mary would make clam chowder; and then at night they would just sit and talk.

Most of his guests came away wishing they had a recorder because he would tell them all about G. Campbell Morgan and then all about his own early days in Canada.

"But, you know, after a while a lot of that sort of blends itself into you," Howard says. "You're more left with—at least I am—with overall impressions rather than with specific details."

But he likes to tell about the time when Jack and he had both finished speaking at Mt. Hermon at the Dallas Seminary conference and had then flown together from San Jose to Portland. They stayed in the Mitchell home and then drove to Qualicum for a vacation.

While they were still in Washington State, Jack bought a large bag of big, juicy peaches at a roadside stand.

But when they got to the border, the agent said, "You can't take those over."

And Jack said, "What do you mean? I just bought them."

He said, "I'm sorry, but you can't take them over."

Jack said, "What are we gonna do with them?"

"Well," he said, "you have three options. You can throw them away in the trash can over there or you can eat them here or you can take the pits out of them. And then you can take them in."

"We had a whole sack of them, so there was no way we were gonna eat them," Dr. Hendricks recalls. "And these were gorgeous peaches, so there was no way we were gonna trash them."

So Jack searched through his fishing gear and took out two fish knives and the two men sat there slitting peaches and tossing the pits away and putting the peaches in a plastic bag so they wouldn't lose any of them.

While they were up there, Howard's wife, Jeanne, admitted she had never gone fishing and had never had the joy of landing a fish. So that became Jack's big challenge. She had to catch a fish.

"My wife comes from a Scottish background; so, of course, with his background in that area, he really fell in love with her. And the biggest thrill of the whole time we were there was his watching Jeanne catch a salmon. And I mean, he was beside himself. He was so thrilled. And it was so characteristic of him in many ways. He was more excited about somebody else like that catching a fish than he was himself."

But Dr. Hendricks had another observation after that summer vacation at Qualicum Beach:

"On a trip like that, often, what a man is will come out. My wife and I said to each other one day, 'You know, the closer we got to Jack and Mary Mitchell, the more we fell in love with them.'

"And, you know, it's often just the opposite. All of us tend to look good at a distance, but if you get up too close you see the warts. But with the Mitchells, to us it was just the opposite. He was almost like a father to us, although he never treated me that way. He always treated me as a colleague, as if I was in his league—which is kind of ridiculous. But we had an awful lot of wonderful times together."

The last time the Hendricks were in Portland before Jack's death, the Mitchells took them out for a Chinese dinner, Jack's favorite food.

He remembers how Jack had "a lot of so-called Chinese phrases that he would throw around. Oh, how we would laugh."

But the thing that impressed me whenever I spent any time with Jack and Mary, I came away enriched. I came away a better man.

I never came away depressed even though we talked very realistically about conditions in the evangelical church and so forth. But it was never depressing. It was always kind of a challenge type of mentality, you know, a "What-are-we-going-to-do" type of thing. "What's it going to take to turn it around?"

Jack Mitchell also impressed Howard Hendricks as—in the Biblical sense—a peacemaker.

Oh, he would have had problems with people in the World Council, but he was deeply involved in the Presbyterian Church for a while and in the Congregational Church when he was with Chafer. If a controversy arose over the Person of Christ or the inspiration of the Scriptures, he never stuttered a step; but he cut a lot of slack for people who didn't necessarily agree with him in every detail. I would say in that sense he was a lover not a separatist. His idea was, you know, "If you love Christ and you love the Word, I can work with you."

That came out in the Billy Graham situation when he was in Portland for his first campaign. Both Jack and Willard Aldrich were willing to stand with him. And they took a lot of grief for it, particularly from some of the Conservative Baptists of that time who were more separatist and who felt that the two were compromising.

What impressed Howard Hendricks most about Jack Mitchell?

I would say the authority of the Word of God and the Person of Christ were the two things that stand out in my mind as I recall his impression on me. He gave me a love for the Word. He gave me a love for the Saviour. He gave me a love for people.

He saw that love for people expressed whenever the Mitchells went to Dallas. Jack and Mary both had a whole corps of friends they spent time with and really ministered to—people who often were grieving or their kids had not turned out right or they had other serious problems.

"But though the Mitchells had no children of their own, they probably were a mom and a dad to more people than you could imagine," he says.

I'm sure that it was very largely due to Mary that they got along so well in their marriage. I think he loved his wife as few men I have ever seen. He just thought there was nobody like her—and it was obvious all the time. I think she was the perfect counterpart for him. He, admittedly, had some abrasive spots— you know. He was the typical hard-driving-mechanic type of individual and she was so soft. Oftentimes, she would just reach over and tap him and say, "Now, John." And he would crawl back into his hole.

When Jeanne and I were first married, we used to think of

them as something of the ideal couple. That's what they were to us. They were models of people who really got along.

And, you know, it was hard for me to ever think of Mary as old because for so many years you could never tell her age. She really was well preserved; and she had such a sweet, submissive attitude—not in a negative sense. But it didn't seem to be that hard a chore for her to take care of him.

And she never sought the spotlight. We had a hard time even getting her to talk to the wives. She would do it occasionally at the seminary, but it was obvious that was not her first love. She just wanted to be his wife and share in the ministry and pray for him and provide for his needs.

He was very affectionate with her and very, very concerned for her especially if she were sick or tired or anything. That was his first concern.

"Mary, get some rest." It was something of an inside joke to all of us because he would be talking to me about how much she needed to rest when in reality he needed to rest just as much or more than she did.

Hendricks calls Jack Mitchell "a man's man" whose greatest liability became his greatest strength.

The fact that he was brusque and not the smooth, suave type of individual attracted men.

I remember, when I was a student, one of the churches in our area had a men's conference. I was working in the church at the time. Those guys would miss all kinds of things, but they would not miss that conference.

I mean, "Jack Mitchell's gonna be there. Man! We gotta go."

I've often tried to identify it myself, and I don't know that I've been successful. There are certain men who just are magnetic to other men. And it wasn't that the women didn't enjoy him. It's just that men were attracted to him because of his straightforwardness. I mean, he never played around with the truth. He never sugar-coated it. He hit you directly.

Yet, the burden of his ministry was "falling in love with the Saviour." His voice would change; his face would change. Everything about him would change in terms of talking about the Saviour. Men were not turned off, because—at heart—men are looking for an affection. And, frequently, if a man is not in love with his wife, he's in love with his job. He's got to find some object for his affection. And a fine man who is in love with Jesus Christ is, I think, an infinitely attractive thing to a man.

One thing about him—though Jack loved people, lots of people—he had the capacity for individual friendships, for one-on-one. Howard says:

I don't know if I just happened to be in the right place at the right time, but students used to ask me, "Why is he so close to you?" Maybe it was the father in him yearning for a son.

How did some of us get close to him and others not? Part of it was that I took the initiative. If he needed somebody to drive him someplace, I would drive him. If he needed some notes run off, I would get them run off. And I think that often that's what is lost in this kind of mentoring-protege type of relationship. A lot of young people are not willing to take the initiative.

I've seen it with myself in terms of people I've marked, and in every case they hang around. They're available.

One said, "If I have to hang outside your door, I will. I'll walk you to the car." And, of course, usually it ended up, "I'll mow your lawn." They'd come out to the house and work with me.

And I think that really was true of Dr. Jack.

Another factor, he affirmed the younger men around him who showed promise. They posed no threat to him. In fact, he encouraged them to develop their gift even if it meant that they encroached on his territory. He took them and made them his co-workers.

Howard says:

On the Canadian plains he saw the value of someone else

pouring into your life when you don't have it yourself. He got it later through Chafer and his relationship to Sutcliffe and all these individuals who marked him—like Morgan. But he used to say to me, "You know, Howie, it's great to spend time with these younger people coming up." He'd convey to me his heart for the future of people.

He seemed to realize, "I'm not going to be here forever, so the people I mark are going to be the people that are going to be going on after I'm gone."

Jack's great love for missionaries, Howard says, originated in his appreciation for the sacrifice many of these people were willing to make. Coming up the hard way, he never had a silver spoon in his mouth. He would get into their remote places, as Mary and he traveled extensively around the world over the years; and he would see both the conditions under which they labored and their love for the people. He saw the underdog again doing great things for God.

"He resonated with that type of thing," Howard says; and he points out that it serves as a commentary on Jack's life because he considered himself an underdog. Although he had won honors at Brandon College and graduated from Dallas Theological Seminary, he kept a "common-man" touch as part of his life.

He was not a dumdum. He was very, very sharp. He knew a lot that came out of his machinist background and all the sacrifice that he went through in those years. He was of the earth earthy. But I always perceived that underneath that was a very facile, razor-type mind.

It used to intrigue me to ask what would a guy like that have done in terms of a university background—a Ph.D.—whatever. Maybe it would have ruined him. But it was a lack of opportunity, not a lack of ability that would have been his limitation.

What made him a man God could use?

Howard says:

I think he's a classic illustration of the power of the Word of God on the human mind. All the way up to the end of his life— even though occasionally he would forget something that he told me—when we got into the Scriptures, boy! he came on like horse-radish.

He really was with it.

And I think over the coming years he will never be forgotten by those who were exposed to him. I can tell you from just a semi-nary perspective that any student at Dallas who ever had Mitchell has got the Mitchell mark. They will never forget him.

But Dr. Mitchell hated to have anyone build a monu-ment to him.

My fear is that he may be forgotten by the general public because he was never a self-promotor and would never allow oth-ers to promote him. Unless something is written that gives a per-manent residue that someone can go back to and read and unless someone calls attention to the fact that this was one of the great models of our century, he may drop through the cracks.

Dr. Hendricks recognizes that Mitchell was not as well known on the East Coast or in other parts of the country as he was in the West although, whenever he went back there, he had a very effective ministry.

But it is one of my concerns that he won't be forgotten even at Multnomah. I walked by the front of a building on that cam-pus and saw a sign, "B. B. Sutcliffe Building." I wondered how many students in the institution have a clue as to who that indi-vidual is.

Someone in the administration said to me, "I do not think 90 percent of the students could give you a good explanation of who it is."

I feel one of the losses in contemporary society is that those of us who have heroes and heroines and models do not talk enough about them, and therefore we don't have enough of them to talk about.

He wishes young people could have more opportunity to get some kind of exposure to the great men of God.

I was very close, for example, with Dawson Trotman who drowned. Bob Foster wrote a little paperback and Betty Skinner wrote a more complete biography called Daws. *As a member of the board of the Navigators, I tell them, "You ought to get your people to read about these individuals because you are reaping their harvest."*

He admits that it is easy to see the great school that Multnomah School of the Bible has become and to forget that, when Willard Aldrich and Jack Mitchell started it, they used to meet in a funeral home.

"They made progress when they moved out of that into something else," Howard says. "It was a family and a struggle. I think oftentimes it's like our country. We don't appreciate the price that was paid to get the liberty we enjoy."

I wanted to preserve his memory at Dallas, and so my wife and I have endowed an award for John and Mary Mitchell which will be given at every graduation. We knew he would go into fits if he knew we were going to do something to honor him. Most of what we had to do we had to do secretly.

When Jeanne and I set up his award, we never even asked him. We knew what the answer would be. We just did it and sent him a copy with a note telling him what "you and Mary" meant to us. He couldn't do much about it. He appreciated it. But he was so self-effacing. He didn't want any glory for himself.

And yet, I would just love it if people could pick up his love for the Saviour and his love for the Word of God and his love for people.

Will Dr. Mitchell's Homegoing make much difference in the Christian world?

I think his Homegoing is an incalculable loss to the Body of Christ. I really do. I feel like something's missing. I know what it is. I don't mean something in a vague sense. But he was so unique to me that I'm not sure anybody else can take his place.

Every now and then, God puts His hand on a person. And I always sensed that Dr. Jack was a person who just had the hand of God upon him. And that's one of the things that he created in me—a hunger that God's hand would be upon my life and ministry as it was clearly upon his. You could trace the fingerprints of the Lord in his life. And obviously our hope is that God will raise up some others who will have similar characteristics.

But I must confess that you have a lot of people who externally appear to be more brilliant, but I'm not sure they are more insightful.

Did Jack Mitchell mark Howard Hendricks?

He marked my life permanently. I will have to say I will never be the same as a result of my exposure to him.

You know, I've been very fortunate, particularly as a young man because Donald Gray Barnhouse made a permanent impact on my life. So did Merrill Tenney at Wheaton College as a New Testament scholar, as did Louis Sperry Chafer and John Walvoord and all of these men. But Jack Mitchell—

He gave me a deep desire to impact others, particularly students because that's my role. But I want to impact other pastors and Christian workers as he marked me.

You see, I want to be a Jack Mitchell to somebody else. And I know I'm not Jack Mitchell. But I want to have that same kind of impact.

Was Jack Mitchell one of a kind?

God delights in anyone who totally delights in Him. And I think you have it in the statement, "This is my beloved Son in whom I am well pleased." You know the Son found all of his pleasure in doing the Father's will, so the Father found all of his pleasure in the Son.

And that's what Jack did for me. He gave me that passion, and everytime I was around him I would pick up those vibes.

What was the goal of his ministry as you saw it?

When he would talk to me about young men in the ministry and the problems they are facing and the challenge in the society, it was always that God would give these men a heart for Himself. He never tried to clone people. He never tried to make anybody like himself.

When we got through one conference at Mount Hermon, I remember that we got on the airplane and we sat together. He was so appreciative, so responsive, so affirmative of all that I had taught at the conference. It was as if he was saying that this is the kind of preaching and teaching we need.

And through it came the idea, God will use anyone who becomes available and who is willing to be controlled by the Spirit.

What one thing—if you can pin it down to that—made his life unique?

I think that singleness of purpose has as much to do with the uniqueness of his life as anything. You know, he's the true "This-one-thing-I-do." I mean, he was never hung up with materialism. He was very, very generous with what he had. It was almost embarrassing because it was hard—Jeanne and I found it hard—to give to Jack Mitchell. I mean, he almost didn't know what to do with gifts. But he was very comfortable in giving to you—no matter who you were; and this in a nutshell characterized his life.

Though he had the gifts of teaching and preaching, he gave—himself, his means, his Lord and God's Word—with a singleness of heart.

Champion of the underdog? He championed anyone in need. It seemed he had a double portion of the "helping gift," and he freely gave.

Chapter Fourteen

Husband

A missionary who lived with the Mitchells for an extended time made an observation:

I'm very aware that we are all human; and, usually, in the privacy of our own homes, we are not exactly what we appear to be in public.

I lived with them for a year and a half. The house wasn't that big that you didn't hear conversations. I was there all the time, and I can say for a fact that they never in private were not what they appeared to be in public.

There was always that same graciousness with each other in private as in public.

If I had heard people say that, I would have raised an eyebrow. If you're in somebody's house for dinner, you know they're going to be on their good behavior.

But living there a year and a half, that's very different.

From all appearances, one would have thought that Mary Eby of Radville, Saskatchewan, would have had no problem becoming Mary Mitchell of Grand Rapids and Portland.

Daughter of a successful merchant and child of an attentive mother, one would have thought she would metamorphose into the ideal pastor's wife with no effort at all. Such was not the case.

In a testimony she gave to faculty wives at Multnomah one day, she confessed the following:

I want to mention just a little of my experience as a minister's wife. It was not easy, I can tell you. John had been in the ministry for 11 years, but everything was very, very new to me. Although I had graduated from Biola, I was certainly not knowledgeable about what was expected of a minister's wife.

You know that in that day they didn't have courses for Christian leaders' wives as they do at Multnomah today. There were not many books written about it, and there were no seminars about it. And so I was completely on my own, and I didn't have anyone to share this with at that time.

I felt my inabilities very, very keenly. I didn't feel fitted for the place where the Lord had put me. And many times I asked the Lord, "Why did you put me here? I just feel as if I am not able to do these things." And I was discouraged.

And even after I came to Portland, I had constant discouragement although I had much more help then.

But I remember one incident the first year of school. I went to chapel, and I can remember it so well. It was springtime, and I was sitting by an open window. And I could hear the birds singing. I can just picture that day.

I had been discouraged, and I wasn't really listening very well either. Willard was speaking. And I was so preoccupied with myself that I wasn't listening.

And, all at once, I heard him say, "Your labor is not in vain in the Lord."

And I listened, and I heard him repeat it. "Be ye steadfast, unmovable, always abounding in the work of the Lord; forasmuch as ye know that your labor is not in vain in the Lord."

I will never forget that. It was such a lift for me. I still remember how wonderful it was and how many times since it has come to me when I have felt inadequate and discouraged. It would just take hours to tell you what the Lord has done for us.

Over the years, many people stayed in the Mitchell home. Some stayed only a night or two. Others lived there for extended periods of time. Bits and pieces culled from the memories of some indicate that, as a family, John and Mary Mitchell—always abounding in the work of the Lord, steadfast and unmovable—set an example to be followed.

"They discussed things, but there was never ill will," a friend said. "There were never times when they were short with each other; and, in the year and a half I lived with them, I would think I should have heard it. That absolutely amazed me. And what probably impressed me the most about Dr. Mitchell was the way he treated his wife."

At one point, when Mary was thinking about redecorating, a friend looked at John and asked, "What do you think about it?"

And he said, "She is the queen of this home and whatever she wants to do is fine. I know I'll enjoy it. I've given her the permission and full right to do anything she wants."

And that was how he operated.

Friends observed he never told her what to do in the home. He gave her total freedom. She never abused it. But, when she did things, he almost always noticed them; and he was very quick to compliment her.

"He complimented her as much in private as he did in public, and there were times that they didn't know that I could hear," one said.

He would notice something that she had done, and he would say, "That looks so nice, honey. I appreciate that."

And at the dinner table, he was always very quick to compliment her on her cooking, to notice what she had fixed and how she had fixed it.

"I don't think there was ever a meal," one friend said, "that he did not express his appreciation for the dinner. And it was not just habit. He said it with feeling, with meaning, and you could tell he really did appreciate it."

People noticed that he considered Mary a partner and an equal. There was never any thought that he was either more spiritual or he had more rights. There was nothing of that. And many times he was heard saying, privately as well as publicly, "I am who I am and I have the ministry that I have because of my wife. And without her I could not be and could not do what I do and am."

"There was never a time that I ever heard him put her down—even in joking," a friend said. "There were fishing stories where there would be kidding about who had caught more. But there was never any kind of joking where he would give the appearance that she was inferior. Even in jokes, he always built her up. And I learned much and appreciated much from that.

"To me, they were the greatest role models I could ever have had in my life. They were the ones that showed me marriage as God intended it."

Dolt Miller, a long-time Mitchell friend, said, "We would often hear Dr. John say, 'I want you to meet my Mary. You'll love my Mary.' And the look on his face and the message of his voice would convey the emotion of one who longed for the presence of another whom he loved—not sorrowful, but yearning. . . . Tender pictures of his Mary filled his thoughts. . . .

"I had known few strong men, who, after many years of marriage, still treasured tender yearnings for the wife whom God had given to them. . . . I had known many Christian leaders and had wondered at this lack of verification of their message. They spoke of love, but in their own marriage the flame was burning extremely low.

"But listening to and absorbing the private life of this man was different. His love for his Mary was vibrant within him. His Mary was the great goal of his living. In his heart and in his life, she took second place only to the Saviour. What could we conclude but that his Mary must be very special, and that she must be very important in his everyday world?"

With many other couples—in public they're wonderful. When you see them privately in their own home and when you stay with them a week, it's not quite what it looks.

One observer said, "I felt the Mitchells exemplified marriage as God meant it, that it can be heaven on earth. And it wasn't that they didn't have disagreements. Perhaps the greatest disagreement was that she wanted him to slow down and he wanted to keep doing things. But even in that there was never anger, there were never harsh words, there was never ill will. There was a mutual appreciation for each other."

Mary and John would often praise one another in private conversations with friends. They never demeaned one another. The same observer also said, "They fed off of each other, and it was a very positive cycle of building each other up. It gave each of them energy. It was a beautiful, beautiful relationship. He was very loving and very affectionate toward her. He would come in from school. She would greet him at the door, and she would give him a kiss and a hug. And he was quick if he was in the kitchen to put his arm around her or put it on her shoulder or just lay his hand on her hand to say thank you.

"We would have breakfast at the kitchen table, and so they were sitting close to each other. And often he would reach out and take her hand whenever there were devotions in the morning or prayer. They were very quick with each other to express physical affection, and they were not embarrassed by it. You could see it was very natural."

Verna Eby, Mary's sister-in-law, remembers Jack's telling a congregation about devotions at the Mitchell breakfast table. "You didn't know I sing to my Mary?" He often sang hymns to her because he loved her and he loved to sing. "And he had a wonderful voice in those early years," she says.

Those who shared their home often noticed they both had a sense of humor and many things were accomplished through humor—good humor without any putdowns—in matters that most couples might have gotten into arguments over.

For example, when Jack might have wanted to take some extra speaking engagements in the summertime and Mary felt that they should stay longer at Qualicum Beach, she would kiddingly say, "But, Honey, you know how you love to fish. After all, that's not long enough time to fish if you take another engagement."

Then, very often, he would reconsider and say, "Well, Honey, maybe you're right. I probably should say no."

People were amazed that, if she made a suggestion, he immediately considered it. His immediate reaction was not to go on the defensive but to be open and to consider it. He didn't always end up going along with it, but she knew he had considered it and thought it through. She could handle it because she knew she had been considered. She left the final decision to him; but she was not afraid to speak up and make suggestions.

No one ever heard Mary say things many wives say, like "Why do you always do that?" or "Why don't you do that this way?" or "Don't you know . . ." That would have been very out of character for her.

Her approach would have been, "Honey, have you considered—" And she would say it in such a way that he would consider it, knowing that he knew if she ever raised a question there was a reason for it. He never felt threatened by it, but she did very often speak up.

And she would pray about what was on her mind and pray that an opportunity would come up so it could be discussed. Sometimes the conversation would just naturally arise then, and she would follow through. But she didn't abuse that position. She didn't try to boss him or direct him. She was very careful. Both of them were always thinking of the welfare of the other one when they made suggestions. She was thinking of his rest; and, when he invited anybody home to dinner, he always called and cleared it with her first.

Very often, at the dinner table, he would say, "Honey, I've been thinking about so-and-so. Would it be all right if sometime in the next couple of weeks we had them over, and I'll invite them? But I wanted to see what your schedule is."

He never invited anybody without letting her first choose the date and make the arrangements. But he knew she enjoyed entertaining, and so he was not afraid to bring it up. He always considered her.

Many times, they shopped together on Saturdays; but he did all the grocery shopping because she didn't drive. He knew the brands and what they always used, and so it was not a problem for him. Before he left school, he would call and say, "Honey, what do you need at home?" They did their shopping at Kienows, and so he would go and get it.

As with everything else he did, Jack even got stories out of grocery shopping to tell his classes and illustrate his points. He would often tell them to his "Spiritual Life" classes:

I wish we were in that place where we were so in love with the Saviour we couldn't help but talk about Him and have it pop out of our mouth sometime. Maybe some of you have heard my experience.

I like to buy the groceries. I don't like to buy coats and ties and socks and shoes, but I do like to buy the groceries. And, one day, I was coming through the checking line with my cart and a woman came behind me with her cart full of groceries, and sitting on top of the groceries was a little wee girl.

You've seen that, haven't you?

And I said to her, "My." It just popped out. "On what shelf did you get her?"

The lady changed her looks. She said, "They don't get babies on shelves!"

I said, "That's right, lady. And if I want eternal life, I must be related to somebody who is eternal. You can't buy life."

But by that time my goods were waiting to be paid for so I had to move on. But about two weeks afterwards, I was going down on the other side of the store getting some butter and cheese and cottage cheese and so on. And a fellow came along with his cart, and on the top of it he had a little wee boy. And I tell you, it was a wee boy—red cheeks with dimples. Do you ever see them, you know? Just as lovable as can be.

And the father was a great, big—he looked like a longshoreman.

I said, "My, you've got a bonnie lad there."

"Ah," he said, "he's my boy. My boy." His chest went up six inches, you know. "He's my boy."

"Well," I said, "on what shelf did you get him?"

With a smile he said, "Well, Mister, you know. You're just too late. He was the last one on the shelf."

What I'm trying to say is that I had no more to say.

I've never tried that since, by the way, either.

Jack recognized that Mary Mitchell's ministry was a spiritual ministry, and therefore he never wanted her to be tied down with the things of the home. He encouraged her early on to get students to help her with the housework so she could be free to minister as the Lord gave her opportunity.

The Mitchells were quick to open their home even though it probably did intrude on their privacy. They were always very hospitable. And they loved having children come, too—even families with small children who were not well disciplined. It wasn't that Mary could overlook it and say, "I don't care what they do." She was bothered, but she always handled those families in a gracious way.

If she knew there could be problems with the children, then she would try to anticipate how to offset the problem if she had them over again. Sometimes she would invite a teenager to mind the children, choosing to handle matters that way instead of never inviting the family again.

One of those who lived with them said: "I never saw her outwardly, visibly angry. I never saw either of them angry. I know they were angry at times. But they chose to follow Paul's advice. They were angry, but they did not sin. They were human, and anger is a God-given emotion; and there were times they were angry and had a right to be. But the way they chose to handle their anger provided me another very wonderful role model. I knew they were upset. I knew they were angry. But the first thing they always did was pray about it; and then they would make plans together on how they were going to handle the situation in the most appropriate, loving, Christian way."

Sometimes, when John tended to want to ignore an important situation that needed to be dealt with, Mary would be the one to say, "We have prayed about it. We have talked about it. And you do really need to talk to so-and-so." And then he would do it. And so she often prodded him when, if left on his own, he would have ignored some things that should not have been ignored.

When matters that concerned the church and school came up, they would discuss them. If anything had been said to either of them in private, it was never revealed. They would say to each other, "So-and-so needs a lot of prayer. There are deep problems." And if the one did not go into further detail, the other one would not ask. It was understood.

And so they both knew things that were private.

Sometimes, if a person was talking to one of them alone, that one would say, "May I tell Aunt Mary" or "Uncle John." And if the person said, "Yes," then they felt free to share it. And if the answer was "No," they kept it private.

Sometimes Jack would just say, "There's a real problem at the school or the church with such-and-such a situation. It needs a lot of prayer." He might choose to tell her more or he might not.

It really didn't matter to her because all she needed was the knowledge that she should pray about it, and then they would pray together about it. They would spend time in their morning devotions at the breakfast table praying about situations.

They felt deeply. They genuinely cared about people, loved them and felt their pain. The Mitchells were down-to-earth enough to be deeply concerned about problems and to pray a great deal, but they never let it interfere with their own emotional and personal life. It never got them down to the extent that they could not function.

They certainly knew the problems—the deep heartaches of many, many people—but knowing what they knew never limited or crippled them.

A friend said, "Now it isn't as if they didn't make mistakes themselves. They sometimes misread a situation and came up with wrong conclusions. But, what was admirable about them is that when they did make mistakes and they realized it years later, they were not afraid to go to the persons and say, 'We wish to apologize. We were wrong in the conclusions we came to. We were wrong in the things we said, and we are sorry. Will you forgive us?' It takes a lot of grace and humility for a couple of their stature to do that."

When there were moral situations, the Mitchells were careful of how much interaction they had with the people who had fallen into sin because they did not want to give the impression they approved their actions. And, yet, even in those cases, the people never doubted that the Mitchells accepted them and loved them. But they knew clearly that their actions were not approved of.

And Jack was very slow to put someone out of the church if he had fallen into sin.

Kay Petrie Groenlund observed that Jack was very loving with people. He helped patch up a number of marriages and he always kept a confidence. He would point to his heart and say, "This is a graveyard in here for stories that people have told me."

"He loved to have people come to see him—people with broken hearts," she said. "But he would never put the guilty party out of the church. He would go to the people who were in trouble, but his way of doing it was not to punish somebody. He would just try to love them back into the fold. If you put somebody out of the church, how are you ever going to get them back?"

Willard Aldrich confirmed this:

"He used to tell a story on himself in relation to a prominent man in the church in the early days of the Bible classes who later divorced his wife and married someone else. He was asking the Lord if that man should be removed from the congregation.

"And then he would think, 'Well, he might go out to so-and-so's church. No, that pastor is my friend. Don't send him out there. I wouldn't want to wish him on so-and-so.'

"And he'd go on down the line of the different pastors he knew.

"'No, don't send him there because he's a friend of mine.'

"Finally, he said, 'I guess I'll just have to live with him and keep him here.'"

But the Mitchells did not berate people. If they knew

something was wrong, they did not scold. They said it once, and then they let the person make his choice.

Jack was never really bothered when someone did or said something that concerned him personally. But he would be deeply grieved when somebody did something that would grieve the Lord. Over situations where either a person had backslidden and willfully chosen to go into sin or where a person was trying to undermine the work of the Lord—something that would have hurt the heart of the Lord—he would really grieve.

A friend said of him, "He really was in love with the Saviour. There was no doubt about it. And it was a relationship that was real. What grieved the Saviour grieved him. He was a man who would show emotion and he was not ashamed of it. He didn't try to hide it. He was a real man, but a man with a gentle heart."

Both Mitchells considered "in honor preferring one another" a cardinal principle in their lives. Students and friends who came to help with carpentering or gardening were treated like the brethren they were.

Karl Baker, a long-time friend who probably over a period of years renovated their entire house and even built some of their furniture, said, "A lot of times I would be downstairs working, and he would be upstairs reading and studying. She would come down and say, 'Now, you stop working, Karl, and come upstairs. We want to visit.'

"So I'd go upstairs and we'd sit there half an hour and just talk. It was wonderful. I'd always learn something."

Karen Diggins Wheaton, an MSB alumna whose first husband often helped the Mitchells in outside work around the house, said, "Before he died, Dave (Diggins) would work on Dr. Mitchell's yard and mow his lawn. He did a lot of different jobs like weeding and trimming. And once or twice I went over to his house to help. I helped Mrs. Mitchell plant some plants. And I'll never forget it because they treated us like royalty.

"She fixed lamb chops for lunch!

"I had never had dinner for lunch. I guess that's the way they did it in the olden days—you know, where the farmers feed the workers. But, I mean, she put out quite a spread for us, and I thought that was really special.

"I thought, *My, do they do this for all the people that come to their house and work?*"

Celia Wiebe said, "She wasn't just his wife. He wasn't old-fashioned that way. And Willard wasn't either. I loved that about both of their marriages. They were my example of what a marriage should be. I knew the Mitchells the best, but it was such a respectful—you know—horizontal relationship. There was no chasm between them—he here and she there. It was absolutely respectful and equal in their partnership.

"In fact, you remember when all this chain of command was going around? We were talking one day.

"'That's not submission! They don't know what submission is!' she said.

"Uncle John would never go to those seminars. He would say, 'That's not submission. That's not what God ever intended. That's not what the Bible says. You know what a leader does? A leader washes feet.'"

But the Mitchells were not crusaders. They did not search for issues they might correct or stake out a territory to prove a point. They suffered criticism for this. Husband and wife, they trusted the Lord to deal with problems in the church, even when those problems affected them personally. Mary told a gathering of Multnomah faculty wives what she learned to do:

And then, one time, someone told untruths about my husband. They circulated a story that was not at all true, and I was just terribly upset, and I was going to go out and tell him that this was all wrong.

*And we had a precious church visitor at Central Bible that
year, Mrs. Collette, and she said, "Mary, let's pray about it."*

*Well, we prayed about it, and I waited; and I went home
and I got on my knees and I said, "Well, Lord, this is all wrong.
This just isn't right. Somebody should do something about it."*

*But the Lord gave me that verse from I Peter 2:23: "Who,
when he was reviled, reviled not again, but left all things to Him
who judges righteously."*

*And the Lord kept my mouth shut. I didn't talk to anybody
about it. And, you know, it was marvelous the way the Lord took
care of that. They had even gone to our very closest friends, and
people were influenced by it. But, later on, they all realized that
that matter was not so; and we have had just a precious relationship with them. The Lord did undertake because I kept my hands
off.*

In their home, in their church it was the two of them at
work. She was his helpmeet in every way, and she really loved
being in the Lord's work with him at Central Bible and
Multnomah.

Dolt Miller wrote of them: "Though John stood alone
in the pulpit or sat alone with learners at his feet, he was giving out the wisdom and the love of both Mary and himself.
Together they had learned. Together they had bowed at the
feet of the Saviour and determined to spend their lives in service—their response of love for Him.

"Together they had been polished by the grindings of
life. Together they had faced the daunting heights and
climbed to the top. Together they enjoyed their Saviour. And
together they ministered.

"Mary planned, she wrote, she entertained, she spoke,
she counseled, she encouraged, she inspired, she loved, and
she prayed. And Dr. Jack stood tall as he ministered to the
thousands in the power of the Lord, upheld by the prayers of
a devoted, loving wife."

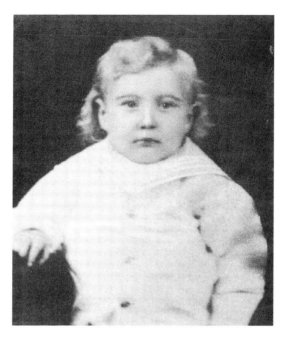

John Greenwood Mitchell, age 3.

Words of warning that her boys stand still seem to hover on Lavinia Mitchell's lips. Her husband James, with Isobel standing between his knees, and Joshua behind him don't move. David smirks. He knows the first to move will be eight-year-old Jack.

In his middle teens, Jack began working in a tool shop as a machinist.

Though Jack looks like he's preaching hell-fire, his wife later insisted that in all his prairie years he never shouted at people.

Seaman Jack had trouble at first steering a giant plow, but he was quick to learn.

Brandon Buddies

Machinist, prairie preacher, now scholar, Jack graduated from the Evangelical Theological College. He returned frequently through the years as a visiting Bible teacher. The name of the school changed to Dallas Theological Seminary.

The old mortuary may have been no thing of beauty, but Jack was delighted to have it for the school. Some did worry, though, that he could come up with the $40 a month rent.

Multnomah's very first class; photo taken in 1937.

Jack (fifth from left) organized a Board of Trustees for Multnomah that included a number of dedicated Christian businessmen. Willard Aldrich (far right) served the school as registrar at that time.

An early 1970's photo shows the gathering of the finest Bible-teaching faculty in the country, a legacy that has singled out Multnomah from its inception to this day. Dick Bohrer, <u>Lion of God</u> author, stands in the back on the right end, just to the right of Dr. Mitchell.

Dr. Mitchell, the beloved teacher, in one of his "Spiritual Life" classes.

The people of Portland responded Sunday after Sunday to Dr. Mitchell's deep exposition of the Word of God. Central Bible Church holds about 1200 people when full.

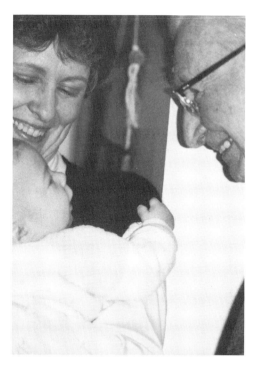

No one in the congregation closed an eye when Dr. Mitchell dedicated babies. He prayed that each one might be gifted to minister to his/her generation. Many babies talked back.

Others slept, peaceful and content under their pastor's doting attention. . . .

He claimed he never memorized a verse. He said his mastery of the Word of God came from reading and rereading it over and over again. Students were convinced he could recite virtually every verse in the Bible—and the one before it and the one after.

Although Wheaton College conferred on him the Doctor of Divinity degree in 1941, Jack always referred to himself as "Mr. Mitchell."

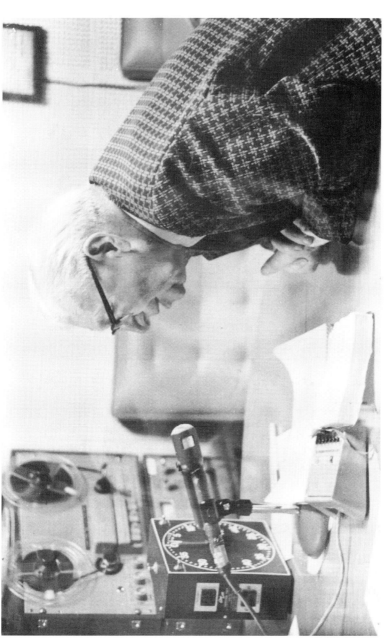

His Bible open and his notes fresh, Jack would tape several hours of his "Know Your Bible Hour" radio program at a time. He preached on the radio for more than 60 years.

The Mitchells, on a world tour in 1969, prepare to board an Ethiopian Airlines plane in Addis Ababa, en route to their next stop in South Africa.

His opportunities to encourage young pastors and their wives, as here in Ethiopia, highlighted his round-the-world trips.

Mary in 1924 on her graduation from the Bible Institute of Los Angeles.

Mary, pastor's wife and poet, also taught for many years a women's Bible class in Central Bible's Sunday School.

Mary, too, enjoyed the outdoor life.

Mary at Carmel, Calif., with Celia in June, 1990—
the one place Mary had never visited with Jack.

Mary and her sister Marguerite kept in close touch through the years.

Shy newlyweds.

Mr. and Mrs. John Greenwood Mitchell

Happy newlyweds kicking up their heels!

Mary stands beside the family car that took them to Grand Rapids after the wedding.

The first year after their marriage, the Mitchells lived in a brick home in Grand Rapids. Their walking to buy ice cream cones on their first Sunday there shocked their old-Dutch congregation.

The Mitchells stopped at Glacier National Park in the summer of 1930 after they surveyed Christian work in Canada's prairies.

Central Bible and Multnomah made much of Mitchell birthdays and anniversaries. A gift of lovely candlesticks pleased Mary on their 25th wedding anniversary in 1954.

Good sports!

The camera shutter snaps an after-dinner picture in the Mitchells' dining room. Mary has no idea what Jack is doing. Fish kiss, anyone?

A joyful portrait touched with Heavenly sunshine . . .

Still the "newlyweds" at one of the many family weddings over which he presided.

Heard often from John Mitchell: "I'm so glad I married Mary Eby Mitchell!"

Always protective of his Mary. This photo, taken in October, 1989, is the last one taken of the Mitchells together.

Wearing his "Do-you-think-I'm-going-to-kiss-you-in-front-of-all-these-people" look, Jack says nothing, does nothing.

The Mitchells' first home on Canby in the Garden Home area.

She loved being an aunt.

He loved being an uncle.

A lover of children and a lover of cars, Jack holds his niece Verna Elizabeth and grins with pride.

Jack and Ruthie developed their own special "fish kiss."

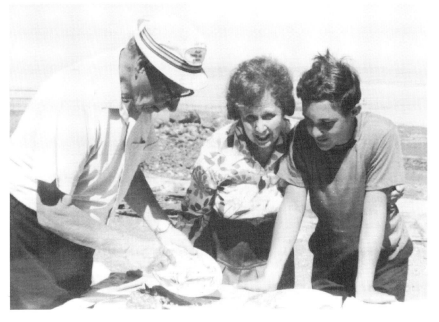

At the beach with one of the numerous grand-nephews.

Willard and John—father and son, brothers, friends.

Jack's "boys" held a special place in his heart. Joe Aldrich, Tony Wiebe, and John Van Diest loved the laughter and the mental and spiritual stretching they got from "Uncle John."

The Mitchells loved being with family. Verna Eby, Herb's wife, played the piano for many years at Central Bible Church. Her husband was on the Board. Edna Remple, Verna's sister, worked in the MSB business office and also typed many of Jack's sermons for his editor.

Let the weather be stormy and the water rough, Jack felt completely at home on the sea.

Whether he reeled them in or weighed them in, Jack found pleasure in everything that had to do with fishing.

The fisherman and his prize. He called it sheer joy when it took two hands to hold up the catch. Especially this one——a 35-lb. ling cod!

"A man's never too old to fish," he would say. He was in his eighties when he posed with this "bonnie" catch.

Fisherman and Fisher Mrs., both Mitchells loved to troll in northern waters.

Mary used a lure Jack scoffed at and hauled in fish after fish.

Famous for his "Uncle John's Fish and Chips" recipe, he enjoyed donning a chef's hat and apron on special occasions.

He loved to host, and he loved to carve.

The Mitchells and the Wiebes often enjoyed dinner together.

Let gray hairs and wrinkles come, the man laughed a good laugh and enjoyed a good joke.

He wasn't above having fun at his own expense, but never, ever, at anyone else's.

The famous Candle Story

John G. Mitchell, D.D.

Multnomah registrar Joyce L. Kehoe said of them: "Mrs. Mitchell was a refined, gracious lady, a beautiful person. I think Dr. Mitchell sometimes seemed more of a rough person though—a gentle, kind, rough person. Some people said she really made the man. I wouldn't know that. I wasn't that intimate with them through the years. But it was obvious that he felt her contribution had really been substantial in his life.

"I know that for years she would accompany him and be a part of what he did when they went to many of their meetings.

"And one thing I especially liked was how he respected her. I can remember years back when he was going to Singapore that he could rightly have said, 'I am making this trip to Singapore and I am going to minister there and do this and that.' But instead of that he said, 'Mary Mitchell and I are going to Singapore.' And that was so characteristic. Wherever he was going, he would say, 'Well, when Mary Mitchell and I are at such and such a place . . .'

"It was as if her part in his ministry was as crucial and key as his own. She was not one who was up front talking. In the church during the years when he was pastor, she was not in the fore although I know she was active with the women in their planning and in their carrying-out ministry. You would not see her in an aggressive capacity at all. But there's no one who doubts the effectiveness of how she worked with him and supported him and prayed for him and gave her counsel and wisdom."

Mary Mitchell summed up their ministry—his and hers—when she told the faculty wives:

There have been so many things that have been encouragements and blessings. The joys of ministry—there is just no way—nothing to compare with it. To have people come with their needs and to point them to the only One that can really help them . . . seeing lives change and being able to teach and being able to counsel and being able to bring people to the Lord.

There is just nothing like it!

Chapter Fifteen

Boss

John Van Diest worked on staff beside Dr. Mitchell for a number of years. Of his boss, he said:

I think faithfulness to family was a John G. Mitchell priority—not only to Mary Mitchell to whom he was unbelievably endeared, but to other families and especially his staff. He had a loyalty to them. There was a loyalty that I experienced. We went through thick and thin together, so to speak. At least, that was my perception of the relationship to the extent where he would protect me from the wolves—and I am a loyal person. So I didn't find it difficult to follow him as a leader.

It was in that context that our relationship grew. I believed him. I didn't ask a lot of theological questions, but I believed Dr. Mitchell's mission because it seemed to mesh with what little I knew about the Scriptures—that we ought to be about the Father's business. He was the leader of the pack and we—as a team—needed to follow him.

John Van Diest experienced a "no-one-ever-spoke-words-like-he-spoke" type reaction to Dr. Mitchell when he attended Multnomah as a student from 1950-53 and sat under his ministry at Central Bible Church. He served as a member of the church staff—in children's ministries and as youth director and director of Trout Creek camp—for several years before he went off to Dallas Theological Seminary for his Master of Theology degree. On his return to Portland, he served as Christian Education director at Central Bible until 1971 when he was given charge of the seven stores of the Christian Supply Center chain, owned by Multnomah. Later, he was named publisher of Multnomah Press and served in that capacity for many years.

As a right-hand-man to Dr. Mitchell, he was able to observe what went on behind the scenes and to note what made the man tick:

"He had six things that he made his priority in his ministry: Jesus Christ, the Word, children, the school, the church, and missions.

"He wanted us to reach as many people as we could. And there was in that a certain mix that I think God blessed. I'm sure there was some flesh in it, too; but God has a way of sifting that out."

When John first joined the church staff, he worked with Dave Stewart, Grace and Annette Bolhouse, and Kay Little Steinhauer. He and Rod Pence joined the staff the same summer.

He remembers: "I was involved with the Real Life Clubs. I think at one time we had as many as 40 to 45 Real Life Clubs. For two or three years, Bill Muir, a few others and myself were involved in Released Time classes. I had about 14 classes a week. I think we estimated that about 10,000 kids a week were being touched by the children's Bible clubs. That whole idea of emphasizing children was very unique in those days."

Actually, the children's ministry at Central Bible got its perspective from a story Harry A. Ironside told about the time he was asked by a deacon, "How many people came to know the Lord at your meeting?"

Ironside said, "Two and a half."

And the deacon said, "Two adults and a child?"

And he said, "No, two children and an adult."

"Ironside said it," John says, "but Mitchell practiced it."

He seemed to be constantly on the watch for ways to "be about the Father's business."

"He was a workaholic," John says. "The only things he enjoyed other than work—I think his life was pretty simply categorized—were Mary Mitchell and the family, his ministry at the church and school (and I would include in that his travels and his teaching lectureship) and fishing.

"He was into fishing, golf and bowling and he swam a bit, but he wasn't big on it. It wasn't a big part of his life. He bowled a lot during the late fifties. I think there was a period of three to five years when we bowled together once a week. Neither of us was a good bowler. He wasn't an especially good golfer either. He reached a level that most people reach if they don't get any special training. He would shoot in the low forties—if he were lucky. He would get 44 for nine holes. He couldn't do 18.

"He had his favorite hill out there on Glendoveer golf course. He called it 'Cardiac Hill' and he'd say, 'Hey, pull me up the hill, John.' So, I'd get ahold of him and pull his cart up. I didn't have enough money to have a cart so I had to carry my clubs.

"I remember J. Vernon McGee and he were teeing off on the back nine of Glendoveer. On the first hole, McGee was on the green in three and was ready to hit a par, which for him was a big deal. He threw his club up in the air and shouted out across the course, 'I love everybody—even the Baptists.'

"Those guys always had something going for one another. They called each other 'The bishop of Los Angeles' and 'The bishop of Portland.' They had a healthy and friendly competitive spirit going way back. They put up with guys like us, but I think they thought of us as 'caddies.' If they hit a ball over too far, it was 'You go get it, will ya? And bring it into the fairlane—oh, yeah, as close in as you can.'

"When we played golf, he would almost always improve his lie if it was raining. The ball would sink in the grass. He'd have to get it out of there and get it up higher. That's not kosher. You shouldn't do that. He knew it. I knew it.

"He'd sometimes shoot more than one ball. The way he got around that was he'd give me another ball, too. If he was in a hurry or if he wasn't having a good game, he would get impatient on the green.

"He would do that with me, but it wasn't limited to me. He'd do it in a foursome. He'd do it with McGee. These were not the driving forces of his life. The competition of the golf game was not the thing that turned him on. It was the fact that he was out there playing. It was part of his exercise program. It was part of what he enjoyed doing—hitting the ball. It wasn't who was winning so much—even though there was some competitive funness to it; but the issue wasn't who won. He just enjoyed being with someone else, doing something together.

"He loved getting a good drive, but he sliced a lot. The same in bowling. He was a worse bowler than he was a golfer. I don't think he cheated on the scoreboard or that sort of thing, but he just loved sports and he loved to have a good time playing."

Johnny went fishing with his boss only once. They went out to sea on Don Brake's boat, fishing for a day. Johnny got sick, and no one seemed to care.

"They seemed insensitive to the fact that I got sick," he says.

The rest of them caught their limit and "we finally got in but I was green—or blue—or whatever color you get."

He didn't resent it, he says. "It still was worth it. I never got over the mystique of being with Dr. Mitchell. Never. I always considered his time more important than mine. I think to the day he went to be with the Lord that would be true. He was God's anointed. No question."

Jack Mitchell was in his late 50s when John first met him about 1950. By then, the Geordie from South Shields had been saturating himself in the Scriptures for more than 30 years.

"I think it's fair to say that he was the most knowledgeable man in the Bible that I've ever met," John says. "He was able to put things into their right perspective. He was able to relate one truth to another truth in the Scripture and come out with a balanced interpretation. He was one of the few men I knew who was able to do it.

"I think Sidlow Baxter was another one who was able to get a grasp on the whole counsel of God; and, therefore, his hermaneutics was sound. He didn't go off on some tangential thing. They both kept central what was central. In Dr. Mitchell's case, Christology was central to what he was. He interpreted everything through a christological kaleidoscope. I don't think very many people reach that level of Biblical integration."

Although students often despaired of finding an outline in Dr. Mitchell's lectures, Johnny's analysis of the man's preaching style has credibility:

"His intimate knowledge of the Scriptures provided tracks to go on when he was speaking. He was always looking for new connections, and he was always taking into account these new connections that relate the totalities of Scripture together.

"Once you moved him into the text of Scripture, he seemed to come alive. He may have had to work—he may have been clumsy in other things—maybe it's unfair to say 'clumsy.' He wasn't good at snow skiing. Right? I never saw him snow ski. He wouldn't have been good at it. But once he got on the skis of Scripture—oh, man—he was the best. And that was because he used it so much. He was in it so much, obviously.

"I think his secret was reading the Word, but I think reading the Word needs to be defined outside its normal simplistic interpretation. A lot of people read the Word and put it down and it has no meaning for them. It's a habitual, word-reciting exercise.

"I think Mitchell generally reached a high level of being able to answer, 'What did the author intend to say to me.' And once one reads Scripture at that level, he's where God intends him to be. He had an intense desire to know what Matthew really said about Jesus Christ, and he read it until he got the answer to that.

"I get to a difficult passage sometimes, and I say, 'Oh, well, I'll look that up some other time.'

"He just hung in there like a tiger. He would have an answer to any question that I ever asked him about the Scriptures, and it was not simplistic. It was usually rather profound. I don't know of anybody who knew the Scriptures like he did. And I knew many of the greats—most of them."

Most great men have at least one foot of clay. Johnny admits there were some things Jack Mitchell could not do well.

"He wasn't the best singer. But I loved to listen to his accent when he sang 'Cheeerr oop ye saints of Gud, there's nothin' to worry aboot, nothin' to make you feel afraid, nothin' to make you doot. Remember Jesus never fails so why not trust Him and shoot. You'll be sorry you worried at all tomorrow morning.' And all those. Some of his favorite songs would be like 'There Is a Fountain Filled with Blood,' maybe 'All Hail the Power of Jesus' Name,' and, maybe 'It Is Well With My Soul.'

"I do think he was shy. I didn't notice him intentionally gravitate toward groups. I think it was something he had to train himself to do. I think he would naturally have preferred to be in his office and away from groups—except when he was speaking. Like I said, that's when he came alive.

"He was not a social-climber or a person out trying to mix. I don't think it was his gift either. But I think he was the center of attention almost everywhere he went. I don't think he was trying to be. I don't think he could escape it. There are certain people who—when they walk into a room—are the center of attention by right of position, size or renown. But I didn't see in Mitchell the desire to have everybody watching him and focusing on him.

"I think some of those kookie responses he had—like speaking Chinese—were examples of his uneasiness, his uncomfortableness. He didn't want people to laugh *at* him. He wanted them to laugh *with* him. Maybe this was why he told the candle story."

But Johnny found Mitchell was not shy as a boss or shy as a leader.

"Oh, he could put you down, particularly in his early years. He didn't have a lot of patience with irrelevance. He wasn't rude, but in the role of a chairman who has to keep things on line he could do that. He knew what to hold on to and what to let go of. It's an art."

Johnny rated him a 10 in the matter of stick-to-it-iveness.

"He was tenacious. He was a bulldog. In most cases, that was a strength. I'm sure he wasn't a seven-star-diary man or that sort of thing, but he did have a plan. I think his view of ecclesiology evolved. He had a council and not a board of elders. They became elders, but he was definitely the lead elder. Even in his older years in his board work at Multnomah, he moved from being a take-charge type person to a leader who was revered. Not that the men were afraid of him, but they revered his person and wealth of Biblical knowledge."

John says Dr. Mitchell never exploited his authority as pastor or as founder of a college, and he never sought to use his position as a platform.

"There's a passage in Psalms that says that God 'made His ways known unto Moses and His acts unto the children of men.' I think Mitchell might be a candidate to include in the number of those to whom 'He made known His ways,' in contrast to most of us. At best, we may get a glimpse once in a while of His ways; but we are mostly involved in His acts.

"I think this comes out in Dr. Mitchell's story about the Senate chaplain who invited him to come to Washington, D.C., to pray and open the Senate.

"And he responded by asking a question: 'Isn't there anybody in Washington who knows how to pray?'

"In him, I could never detect a desire to be out in front, to be Number One. He was always Number One and always in the front. But that was not his driving force. He wasn't interested in popularity. He used to say to me a lot—and he'd say it in his message. He'd say, 'Beware of the error of Balaam.'"

John has an explanation for what he meant by that.

"I've been pursuing some of those comments. I can hear him saying, 'Jude 14—There's the way of Cain, the gainsaying of Korah, and the error of Balaam;' and these, at least—like he said—are the world, the flesh and the devil—three enormous side-tracks that Christians and Christian leaders get off on.

"The work issue with Cain, the authority issue with the Korites, and the morality-greed issue with Balaam are the areas to which he was supersensitive. Probably, a lot of times the areas we are supersensitive to are the areas we have trouble with.

"I think he had those things captive. He was strong on salvation by grace alone, so he had no place for the gainsaying of Korah and the way of Cain.

"In terms of greed, the man was clean. He lived comfortably, but I never saw money to be the motivation for anything he did. He never asked what the fee was when he went out to give a message. I'm not saying it's wrong to ask that, but I'm saying that that was not his style. He was generous with his money. I don't know how much he gave away, but I'm aware he was generous. It wasn't that he asked for a receipt either.

"You know, I'm sure he must have paid an awful lot of extra taxes because of it.

"There was no hint of immorality. I mean zero.

"There was little if any hint of greed. That's the Balaam issue—at least, it's part of it.

"And the authority issue—he was a theocratic leader, and I didn't have any trouble following him. His leadership was very seldom challenged."

His leadership may not have been challenged, but on occasion his tolerance of the beliefs of others was.

Willard Aldrich believes Mitchell "affirmed and stood by truth as he saw it. He was patient with those who didn't have it but who were seeking."

Johnny Van Diest agrees, adding that Mitchell's wide acceptance of other brands of interpretation terminated when it came to error.

"On truth, he seemed to be patient. He had little if any patience with error. In that area he was not a patient person. Perhaps the area he watched most closely was the charismatic movement—charismatic being defined more in the area of second blessing, speaking in tongues, healing in the atonement and the authority of experience over the Word.

"He was a focused, tenacious, hit-the-target type person. He would not step on people to get there, but he would definitely get there. You knew where he stood on most issues. He would make it pretty clear. And he expected you to play ball his way."

Mitchell as an organizer? Van Diest would not consider this his greatest strength.

"As a leader—and there's a difference between a manager

and a leader—he definitely was a visionary. For his day, he was way out in front. Within his purview, he was good because he could control everything. Was he able to push that down and decentralize enough? I'm not sure. Sometimes he had too many handles that he had to control, and sometimes he found it difficult to turn them over."

Mitchell had been a hard driver all his life. Some people wondered how he could live to age 97. Johnny has some explanations:

"He drank carrot juice for a long time. But he consumed more coffee than he should—like most of us. During his latter 20 years, he'd eat a lot of cheese-grill type stuff for lunch.

"He knew that he was getting old. He used to come up to me and plead, 'Will you tell me, John, when I'm getting old?' He wanted me to tell him when he was losing his effectiveness, his cutting edge. He was in his 70s when he asked me to tell him that. But when the time came, he would act like he couldn't hear or he didn't want to talk about it.

"But he was always learning more. He was interested in everything that was going on. As a general rule, he wanted me to report to him about progress, weekly or more. I was with him so much that I felt I was reporting regularly. It would become part of our conversation.

"My work was segmented from his; but it was also integrated in the sense we were dealing with the same families, you know. If we had a family, he was usually working with the adults and I was working with the kids. So there was integration in terms of our ministry. It was perhaps more one ministry than it was segmented. Maybe, I'm implying more speciality. He always showed interest in what I was doing."

Some leaders require that everyone on their staff hold the same opinions on issues as they. Did Jack Mitchell?

"Did he take a position on issues? If we're talking about non-Biblical issues, not very many. Political issues—he pretty well stayed away from politics. Issues like abortion—that wasn't a big issue in those days; but he would not have gotten involved in the abortion issue, generally. He would have preached against it at the appropriate time in the text, but he wouldn't take it as a crusade."

Did he allow other people their right to their own opinion?

"He did me. No question about it. I was not punished if I didn't agree with him. It was hard to disagree with him, however.

"For example, he said to me one day, 'I hear that there are books in the Christian Supply Center that probably shouldn't be there because it is owned by Multnomah School of the Bible.'

"And I said, 'Well, sure. There are a lot of books in the Christian Supply Center that I don't agree with. And you don't either.'

"'In fact,' I said, 'I don't agree with your book on the epistles of John on certain points, and I don't think you're right on those points.'

"I said, 'So, who's going to be the judge on which ones we keep and which ones we put out?'

"Now, that relates to the question of tolerance. Did I feel free to say that? I said it partly in jest, in friendliness. But he knew I meant it. Just because he wrote a book did not mean he was right in all his interpretations, obviously. He was more right than I. But I never felt inhibited to disagree with him in a right spirit."

Was Mitchell not a fighter?

"He stood without compromise for truth, certainly. But he didn't go around looking for molehills he could make mountains out of.

"I organized a Halloween party for our high schoolers when I was on staff, and I arranged to have a hippy-looking guy stop the bus and pretend it was a hold-up. He even took a hostage. The kids were terrified. They wouldn't even believe it when we told them later that it was all a hoax. They said I was just saying that to make them feel better.

"Well, word got to the board of the church. People were out for my throat. But Dr. Mitchell refused to make anything of it. He trusted me. He believed me. He knew when to let something drop. He trusted his staff. We had his complete confidence, and we loved him for it. There wasn't anything that any of us wouldn't do for him."

But not everyone felt that close to Dr. Mitchell. To some he seemed short, at times. Others felt he ignored them or that he was distant. But it wasn't that Dr. Mitchell was rude or didn't want to talk. He just didn't have time to be with everybody.

"Everybody wanted to be with him. There were just a few of us that had the open-door policy with him. That's not untypical of leadership. There are just some people leaders know more closely than others.

"I don't compare myself with Mitchell, but some people walk through my office door without knocking. Others are afraid even to walk down the hall outside the door. That's the way it was with him, too. I never abused that. I wasn't on the phone at night with him, talking. But when I called him, he gave me his undivided attention; and that might have happened once a month or so because I felt the matter couldn't wait. If something was crucial, he needed to know about it. Maybe, somebody had died. But he *was* a very private person."

What appealed to him?

"Nice things."

What bored him?

"The trivial."

What excited him?

"The Scriptures more than anything. And Mary."

What offended him?

"I think some of his greatest disappointments had to do with Central Bible Church, with the inability of the church to stay on course—for which I think he bears a large part of the responsibility indirectly. He wanted to build a building for the youth with a gym and facilities that would draw kids, but he was voted down in favor of retiring the mortgage on the church. I'm sure he wanted to enlarge the missionary budget."

What burdened him?

"He was burdened for the lost. It was the driving force behind his ministry. He wanted to see people come to Christ. I think he had a strong growing concern for missions, that people would get saved and would go out and be supported. He had the respect of mission leaders around the country."

Did he have any unfulfilled ambitions?

"He always wanted to live longer. And he always wished he could join my staff. He'd say, 'If I was any younger, John, I would come and work for you.'

"Well, you and I know that was his way of saying, 'I believe in you and I'm supporting you.' If he had been 30 years younger, he'd be back doing what he did before—preaching.

"Even though he didn't like it that his life was not longer, he had an insatiable desire to see his Lord. I was at his bedside the day before his Homegoing and his longing was part of his makeup."

What about money? How a man handles his money seems to be the best tangible measure of his essential character.

"He didn't hold onto his money. I don't think he ever needed anything. He had several sources of income. I'm guessing he did, just by my observation. He was very generous with us at Christmastime and at other times. I'm sure the 50-dollar bills I got at seminary, unmarked, unsigned were from him. I just know he was a fifty-dollar-bill man. Not for me alone. I think it was his style.

"He was constantly giving money away. I'm guessing that he gave away more money he never recorded for tax purposes than money that he did.

"The Mitchells didn't have kids. They didn't have all the expenses that the rest of us had in raising our children. And sometimes that came out to the disadvantage of those of us who were his employees. I'm not critical, but it's just the fact that the money never seemed to be a major issue with him. I don't believe he ever realized how much month we on the staff had left over after our funds ran out.

"But we didn't hold that against him. We were enamored of him.

"I wanted to give my life to Christian service because of him. I found it a challenge to be a part of and to fulfill the mission and vision that he had. I was not a gifted person. But I think he knew I was committed to him.

"I felt definitely a part of his inner circle. I felt like one of his boys. I don't know whether I was or not, but I sure felt like one. And I will be eternally grateful that I was there at the right time.

"I don't think there's a day goes by that I don't think of him."

Chapter Sixteen

Fisherman

The fisherman in Mitchell kept cropping up. Let something happen at the Sea of Galilee and he would interrupt his Bible lesson, sniff the breeze, and spill out a yearning from his heart of hearts.

"I'm very fond of the sea, you know," he'd say. And that would be enough to get him started:

Have you ever stopped to think of the centuries the sea and the tides have been going back and forth, back and forth?

Whenever I pull my little boat up north to go fishing, one of the first things I get is a tide table. My tide table will tell me how high the tide is going to come up at a certain hour at a certain minute on a certain day and, sure enough, the tide is there. I govern my fishing according to my tide table.

If I want to pick some oysters or dig some clams, I look at my tide table. That tide book was printed a year ahead, and it's always sure. Year in and year out, year in and year out, centuries come and centuries go; and the sea is always right on the exact footage.

Did you ever think of all the rivers that keep running into the ocean? It never gets any fuller. I've seen the old Columbia here pour down like nobody's business, but the ocean didn't get any fuller. While the rivers are rushing down into the ocean, the sun is pulling up by evaporation; and it keeps the whole thing balanced. Now who in the world could work out a thing like that?

I've got a watch and my watch says it's 26 minutes past 9. What's yours say? But yours is wrong. Mine's right. You're wrong.

You say, "No, you're wrong."

How am I going to tell the right time? I look at the heavens. Now, isn't that an amazing thing?

J ack Mitchell balanced the countless hours he spent studying at a desk with hours outdoors fishing. He knew his sea, having been raised on its shores. He knew his fish and his rods and reels. He loved to relax by talking the trade with close friends.

Dr. Joe Aldrich hid a recorder on the table at Holland's Restaurant where the friends would lunch from day to day. A transcription of that lunch, written with Joe as the narrator, captures "Uncle John's" love for hook and line:

"The subject for conversation today is that you give us the A, B, C's of steelhead fishing," I announced to Uncle John over lunch one October day at Holland's Restaurant on Halsey Street.

"I'm not talking to you." He saw my little pocket recorder.

"Well, you talk to Mary then." I pointed at Mary Mangis, my secretary. She and my dad—who didn't talk much that day— made up our foursome.

"Can you catch salmon all year long?" she asked, trying to distract him for me.

"I catch silvers in the fall," he said.

I broke in. "Now, do you use an open face reel or a spinning reel?" I knew he'd think that was a dumb question—which he did. He gave me a disgusted look. "Look," I said, "I want to know—I'm going to buy some equipment."

"Why talk to a steelhead man?"

"Uncle John, you're being a stinker today." I can talk to him like that. I've known him all my life, and he knows I love him.

"No," he said, *"when we started to fish, there wasn't such a thing as a spinning reel."*

"Then what did you use?" I said. *"A regular bait-casting—?"*

"A regular casting reel. The trouble with that was that oftentimes you get a backlash that makes you mad."

"Yeah, a bird's nest," I said. *"Now what was your favorite lure? We used to use these little steel lobbling things. I don't know what they were called."*

"In the early days, we used eggs. Salmon eggs."

"You just let them drift? Down the kern?"

"We used a little bit of pencil lead."

"Pencil lead?" That intrigued Mary.

"Doesn't snag," he said. *"See, you fish the bottom of your river for steelhead."*

That was new to Mary.

"They bump your hook," he explained, *"and you feel the bumps as you walk the line downriver. And then you've gotta— you've gotta develop your sense of touch. When the bump is strong, then the fish is playing with your bait. You pull hard on your line to set the hook."*

I interrupted. "Is it legal to use eggs for steelhead today?"

"I don't know, Joe. We used to get a whole roe of eggs and cut them in pieces and roll them in borax. Some men have a little mash they put the eggs into. I never did that."

"So what kind of a lure would you use?"

"Well, when we started to use lures, I used what Ross Cornell Sr. made in his own basement. He took a piece of—Ross used to fish the Sandy quite a bit. You're not allowed to fish from your boat on the Sandy. With your boat, you go from drift to drift. You get out of your boat to fish."

"That's true in the Deschutes River, too," I said. *"You can't fish from a boat. We were doing it, but a man said, 'I don't mind*

your doing this, but if an outboard comes along, as captain of the boat, I'm the guy who did the fishing.' So we said we better not. We didn't know we weren't supposed to. We got about a 32 inch—30 or 32 incher. It was a beautiful fish."

"Was it black?" he said.

"Hmm—well—how black?"

"When they get up to—after they've spawned they go back to the sea. If you don't catch—as a rule, you don't catch salmon when it's spawned. The steelhead goes back to sea. The salmon doesn't."

"I didn't realize it goes back to sea again."

"Yeah. The steelhead goes back. You see them going down right there. You catch one, you just let it go again because they're just no good after they've spawned. Was it black?"

"The back was black but the rest of it was just a normal—"

"That's Chinook. Yeah. That was okay."

"I haven't been at all on the Oregon coast. Never have been." I wanted to get him talking about the times he went to Nestucca.

"I may have some of those lures that Cornell made years ago in the archives in my basement. If I can find them, I'll be glad to give them to you."

"I'd love to see them if nothing else," I said.

"Well, I'll see if I can find them."

"We're going to get Mary to line up a trip when you get back in July," I said.

"Dan Teeny would take you, I think," she said.

Dan's a master fisherman who practically lives in his boat up on the Deschutes.

Uncle John didn't hear her. The restaurant noise was too loud just then.

"Dan would take you up on the Deschutes," she said again.

"I miss going up on the Deschutes," he said. "When I come back, I'll plan to leave in another day or so and go out again."

"Well, before you go up to The Firs, you have another week, don't you?" she said.

"No, I'm going up into Fort McNeil up on Johnson Straits north of Vancouver. I'm to preach in a little church up there. I go up there to fish—to fish for men and women on Sundays and I fish for fish on Mondays and Tuesday nights. The only trouble was— the last time I was up there—Mary Mitchell caught all the fish."

"Well, we've got to get this Mary catching some of them." I pointed at my secretary. "You see, that's the whole strategy," I said.

"Well, I'll never forget that last day up at Fort McNeil as long as I live. I've told these fellows. You never heard that one, Mary?

"Well, the last night we went out, the four of us—this man and his wife and Mary and I—in about a sixteen-foot boat. And we took two little passes into this place where we generally fish. We'd already caught quite a number in there. And this was the last night we could go.

"They picked us up about 5:15 and we left Telegraph Cove where he lived. He took us to the place that we generally fish and here, right in front of us, not very far over here, were about five or six big seiners—you know what those are. Well, their nets are about half a mile long and they draw about 300 feet. And they would make a circle like this and they'd pull it up into their pocket. And they've got a crew of about eight or ten on board ship and they have a—oh, their boats must be about 60, 75 feet long. Big boats. High up.

"And when we pulled back, I said to my friend, I said— 'You know? Look it, out there. It's no use fishing here. Let's go back through the pass and go on the other side of the island.' We'd fished over there before, too, you know.

"And while we were discussing it, I didn't know that Mary had her line in the water. And before you could say 'Jack Robinson,' she said, 'I've got one on.'

"And between those two women—whenever I got my line out—between taking the fish off either one of their rods, I never got a strike. They got 16 salmon—the two of them. Mary got *nine and the woman got seven. That's the limit for four. We had four each. So we had 16 salmon.*

"And when she was pulling the last one in, one of these great big seiner sailors, waved at us and he hollered over and he said, "Please, lady, leave some down there for me."

We all laughed.

"That's just a woman's touch, Dr. Mitchell," Mary said.

"Now when you fish a drift, you cast upstream?" I asked him. "And won't it come down or does it depend on what kind of a lure you're using?"

"It's what lure you have," he said. "You cast up here and sometimes you walk down, depending on the length of the drift. And as a rule, when you are on a sand bar here, the river is right to the bank. It's steep. It slants out to where the fish are. So you cast up here and it swings down. And, if it's a long drift, you walk along with it. You bump along the bottom.

"And when it swings down this way, oftentimes that means the fish may be following it. And then, when you turn around to come up, they come up, essentially, to grab it.

"Oh." Mary was impressed.

"And as a rule, when they strike—as a rule—they go up straight upstream—which is your salvation. If it's a good big fish and it goes downstream, especially if you're only using an eight-pound test line, it's usually goodbye. Of course, if you come for a fish, you must be fishing in a fast stream. It beats salmon fishing all to pieces. I don't know of any—once a man is hepped up on steelhead, nothing else will satisfy him. Catching trout or salmon is nothing compared to steelhead."

"Well, I could see that, all right," I said, "when Dan was catching that big thing up there. Wow! It was something else!"

"You see, Joe, salmon is salmon. It is big and round. Steelhead is long with a square tail and about this round. They go off the deep end."

"They sure taste good," Mary said.

"A steelhead fisherman, if he is hep on steelhead, he will fish his string from daybreak to sundown until he gets a fish. He's always in anticipation that on the next throw he'll get one. Now in the ocean—"

"Why don't we do that," I cut him off. *"You know, because we could find out where and periodically just schedule a day when we get up early and meet at 5:30 or whenever we need to and get up there and do it because life can get by—"*

"The man who introduced me to steelhead fishing was Lloyd Garrison." Uncle John couldn't drop a subject when that subject was fishing.

"I'd never have believed that," Dad said.

"Right the very first year we were here, he said, 'Come on. You've got a lot of fishing to do.'

"I'd go on down to the river and get my salmon. We used to get a lot of salmon when we went down on the Willamette out of Oregon City. We got a lot of salmon.

"Well, we took a lunch. And—what was her name. Remember the name of those two sisters? She played the organ in the Calvary Church—two sisters. They used to be with Sutcliffe a great deal and, when I came, they used to come with us. We'd go down to the coast and have a picnic—"

"Was that Aquiller and Prisciller?" I piped in.

At least Mary laughed.

"They had a home over on the West Hills," Dad said. *"They gave a piano to the church."*

"No, she never came with us," Uncle John said. *"She stayed with the Calvary Presbyterian Church. There were two sisters. They were really—the one who played the organ—Margaret. She was the one who more or less mothered Peggy Angel before Peggy was married. And the first year here, Peggy Angel was the first one we married in Portland. She was married in our apartment. Peggy and Arnell. He took sick. She worked as the secretary for Mr. Angel. He was in the government."*

"Homer? Homer Angel?" I volunteered.

"He was in the House of Representatives in Washington, D.C. And she took care of the office here while he was there. And he would go East with his wife, and she would handle everything in the Portland office. He was a lawyer, too. Then, Arny died and she gave all her time to that family—to Homer and his wife. Peggy was just with them like a daughter. And, when Mrs. Angel died, Homer Angel married Peggy. And when he was sick, I went to the hospital to be with him—they used to go to the First Presbyterian Church . . ."

That's the way lunches at Holland's were. They'd be full of fishing and reminiscing.

Uncle John, until his later years, never forgot a word anyone said—although he could forget a name—and he loved to retell his stories.

He could even tell you if the sun was shining on April 14, 1934.

What a memory! And what a man!

Mitchell, the fisherman, used fishing whenever he could to illustrate points when he taught or preached.

As he did so, the spume that accompanied the story would often give hints about the life and character of the storyteller himself.

When his class in Acts reached the 28th verse of the 20th chapter, he used it as an opportunity to veer off into a story about his "other love."

We're to feed the flock of God which He purchased for Himself. The King James version says, "Which he purchased with his own blood." And that word "purchase" is an amazing word. It is something that you buy for yourself, you know.

I said a while ago that I don't like to shop except for groceries. But sometimes you see something you want just for yourself. You remember that?

I get ties. A fellow went to Scotland and he brought this

Mitchell tie back with him. I'm not boosting the Mitchell tie. I'm just telling what happened. I wouldn't have bought it. But he did, and he gave it to me.

And I get shirts, socks, handkerchiefs.

But when you want to buy something for yourself—

There's something about that, isn't there?

I wouldn't want to go with you women when you go shopping. You feel this and you feel that and you go around and you feel around and a man stands there, thinking, "When is she gonna get through?"

But when you buy something for yourself, you know exactly what you want.

Let me tell you what happens.

Way back in the 1930s, Portland Bible Class was downtown in what was called the Behnke-Walker building. We were right downtown, only a block from the city library and the Medical Arts building. And just around the corner from where we were—we were on 11th and Clay—on 10th Street was a sports shop.

And I loved to go fishing, you know.

I used to go down to the Nestucker (Nestucca Beach) and cast out there for steelhead. You men know what I'm talking about.

And those old waves, you know. You cast out and all of a sudden—shhhh, you've got a whole nest. You backlash and you reel and you're mad and you pull it out, hoping your hope down there that the water won't get you snagged. But here you are.

And then they came along with a reel called "a spinning reel." It's called a "Mitchell reel." The real name is "Michelle" because it's made in France.

Anyhow, I saw this reel—I heard about this spinning reel— and I said, "What if I get the reel? Well, there'll be no backlash." I saw the rod and the spinning reel in the window.

And so I went into the store and I said, "Is that one of those new-fangled reels?"

And he brought it out and he said, "Here, try it." He had some line on it.

Psssst! Psssst! Psssst!

"Boy! No backlash."

Psssst!

"How much do you want for it?"

"Thirty-four dollars."

I said, "Mister, I'm not buying the store. I'm just asking about this reel."

Well, I went out. And everytime I went by that store, there was the reel still in the window.

What do you think I was doing? I was collecting my nickels and dimes and quarters. Because in the thirties, you know, a dollar was a dollar—in case you didn't know that. You could get a good meal for a dollar, too. Not four and five dollars, but one dollar. I've eaten a meal for fifty cents, twenty-five cents.

Money was scarce, but I was saving my nickels and dimes. And eventually I had thirty-four dollars. And I went back to the sports shop, but it wasn't in the window.

Ahhhh!

So I went in and I said, "Did you sell that spinning reel?"

"Yup." And he reached down under the counter and pulled it out. "There it is. Your name's on it."

He sold that to me the first time I saw it. That was very obvious. I'm a simple fellow and he saw it very clearly, you know.

So I said, "How much do you want for it?"

"Thirty-four dollars."

"Wait a minute! That's a used reel!" I said. "That's a used reel! Everybody's been tryin' that!"

He said, "Thirty-four dollars."

He was as sure as he was standing behind the counter that I was gonna buy it. Why, I must be awfully—simple or something. I don't know. He sure had me. He had the hook in me.

"Well," I said, "it's still a used reel."

"Oh, no, no," he said. "That's it. Thirty-four dollars."

"All right," I said. "You put a new line on, will ya?"

He put a new ten-pound test line on it and I bought it.

I could hardly wait to get my rod and my spinning reel and head out to the Nestucker and try it again on the steelhead without any thought of having a backlash, you know.

Boy! I would try it out.

But, see? I was buying it for myself.

I've oftentimes thought—I look you all over. I don't know whether I would have put you in Christ or not. The Father saw you, your hunger, your desire. And you accepted His precious Son as your Saviour. And He took you and He put you in Christ and He sealed you in Christ. You are His purchased possession.

He bought us, coming back to Acts 20:28—He bought us for Himself. The Greek word there means to buy something for yourself.

He bought you.

Do you think He's gonna let you go?

No, sir! He put you in Christ and He sealed you in Christ.

Divine ownership!

Purchased! Possessed by God Himself!

Getting away to fish was no easy task for a busy preacher/teacher. People wanted his time. If they saw his car on the street and they knew who lived in the house, they would call up to see if he was there. One refuge was the mechanic's garage where Ed Stewart, a Sunday School teacher at the church, worked. Ed remembers the dilemma well:

Dr. Jack was a precious soul, and he and Mary both were giving and giving and giving and giving. But no matter what your attitude is or what your strength is, we all need a time apart. We all need to escape someplace. Occasionally, it was a delight for him to relax and just go out on the river with a fishing buddy.

I was the hiding place for his car when he would go down on the river fishing with Ross Cornell, Sr. He would just leave the car at the filling station where I worked, and I would park it around back. Then I would take him over to Cornells so that if anybody drove by their house to see if his car was there, it was gone.

Willard Aldrich loves to tell this one:

And then there was the story about his being on the boat with Ross Cornell in the river here and they rigged the lines so that a bell would ring when they got a bite. They had the lines set and I think they were praying. And then the bell rang, and he had to excuse himself from the Lord.

A conversation recorded at a Multnomah faculty retreat shows up both Mitchells as devoted fishermen:

Willard Aldrich: I understand that you at one time caught a rather large salmon. I know Mary caught most of them, but you caught a big one one time. How big was that?

Mary Mitchell: Forty-seven-and-a-half pounds.

Willard: Did it grow after it died? (Laughter)

Jack: Well, I don't know whether it grew after it died, but I can tell you one thing. We could hardly get it in the back of the car. We got 38 one-pound cans out of it.

Mary: You didn't tell them that we chased that fish for 45 minutes around the bay. Our line was short, and so we had to put our engine on and follow it for 45 minutes. I didn't dare move.

Jack: I chased that thing all over. We were up at Campbell River on a day hardly anyone was up there. I was scared to gaffe it. I was on the edge of the boat and pulled it in. It pretty nearly knocked the bottom out of the boat.

Bill and Maxine Sloan, long-time friends, vacationed for 35 years with the Mitchells at Qualicum Beach up on Vancouver Island, British Columbia. Bill, a pastor for many years in Yucaipa, California, and an interim pastor at Central Bible Church for a time, covenanted with Jack that they would not talk church business when they went out fishing.

Maxine had learned from a speaker for women at a family

camp how to catch fish in the waters in the Georgia Straits. The following summer, she shared her knowledge:

"I told Mary about the lure. She needed a paring knife and Uncle John had given her $20 to go to the hardware store to get one. She came home with two sets of that tackle for us, one for her and one for me. You just know that our husbands turned up their noses, don't you.

"But it worked. It really worked. But finally, after some years, they deigned to try our tackle, and it did work for them, too."

Jack and Bill Sloan loved to make their own fish and chips and claimed it was especially good when the fish was out of the water no more than 20 minutes. Jack's niece, Mrs. Marty Eby Katcho, provided the Multnomah Family Cookbook with her uncle's favorite recipe:

Uncle John's Fish and Chips
   Potatoes peeled and cut for French fries
   Shortening
   2 pounds fillet of cod
   Batter:
         1 cup flour
         1 pinch salt
         1 teaspoon baking powder
         Water to make thin batter
   Prepare potatoes for frying. Heat shortening until hot enough to sizzle when a drop of water is dropped into it. Deep fry potatoes and place in oven to keep hot. Slice cod 1/4-inch thick, cutting on a slant, into 3-inch pieces. Mix batter and dip cod pieces into the batter. Fry until golden.
   The key to this recipe is to keep the potatoes in the oven once fried; and, as the cod is fried, remove it to a rack in the oven to drain.
   Serve hot.

Jack made it a point to fish for men when he went north. He would keep an eye out for commercial fishermen. He loved to witness to them:

I talked to one about the Lord Jesus. And he said, "Mr. Mitchell"—and he pointed to another commercial fisherman who was a Christian—"I wouldn't trust him as far as I could throw him."

And I said, "Bert, I'm not talking about him. I'm talking about the Saviour. Can you find any fault with the Saviour?"

The only sad note in stories about Jack Mitchell, fisherman, came from an explosion on their boat at a marina on the Columbia River. Spring had come to Portland and he and Mary planned a morning of fishing on the river. They had stored the boat in a shed for the winter.

There were no eyewitnesses, but several friends can recall what they heard Jack talk about it.

Willard M. Aldrich: *I remember his telling me that he had turned on the fan. There's a fan to vent the accumulation of gasses and he thought it was safe. Now, whether he turned it on without opening certain vents, I don't know.*

Ed Stewart: *The only thing I heard was that he hadn't opened the hatch covers before starting it up. You know, when you store a boat, sometimes there's a very small amount of seepage over a couple of months. And you always throw the hatch covers open because just a small amount of fumes confined won't evaporate in the cold. It will just build to the proper volume to explode.*

Tony Wiebe, M.D.: *They had a shed in the boathouse and he was starting up the engines and there were fumes there. Mary had stepped off the boat. I don't think she was injured. At least she wasn't hospitalized. It was scary but he really wasn't burned all that badly. He was in the hospital a day or two and then home.*

If there was anything Jack Mitchell put quickly behind him, it was personal illness or injury. He did not like to draw attention to himself. He did everything he could to keep people from making much of a certain "man named Mitchell," as he often referred to himself. But he treasured stories of fishing and fishermen and reveled in telling them. One of his favorites he shared with a grad class at Multnomah:

Those who are spiritual feed on the Word of God, and that transforms your life.

Whenever I think of that, I think of a dear fisherman. I do a lot of talking about fishermen. You must think that I like to fish, too; and I do.

I was holding a week of meetings with 125 tribal pastors at a place called Princeling up in the mountains in Taiwan. We had a wonderful time together.

But I noticed that after a meeting, when the men were outside chatting about things—talking about the Word of God, on the outside was a fellow with a beard, a Chinese with a beard— a very unusual thing—and he was always listening.

And I said to the man I was partner with at the meetings, Timothy Tsau of Hong Kong, "Timothy, there must be a story attached to that man."

And he said, "Who?"

And I said, "That fellow over there."

And he said, "Oh, you mean Old Whiskers."

"Yeah, what about him?"

He smiled. He said, "You know, he's a fisherman down there in the Pescadore Islands. And one day he was walking down the street and he picked up a piece of paper. It was a page out of a Bible. He'd never seen it before—never seen a Bible. And he read the page, and he was interested. He went and somehow bought a Bible to read, and he came to know the Saviour just by reading the Bible."

God means business, you know. God is accessible. As Hebrews 11:6 says, "He that cometh to God must believe that He's God and that He's a rewarder of them that diligently seek Him."

And this dear old man Whiskers picked it up and eventually bought a Bible. But, you see, he was a fisherman. He touched five places in the Pescadore Islands, one island after the other. And he had a wife on each island. He had five wives.

He would fish all night and sell his catch in the morning and live with that wife that day. He would get in his boat, fish all night and go to the next island and stay that day with his wife there. And so, of the five wives he had, the oldest one was a very sick woman. The last one he married, the fifth one, was a beautiful Chinese girl.

But when he read the Bible, he was transformed. He acknowledged Jesus Christ as the Lord of his life. And every time, when he sold his fish, he would start preaching this new story, the good news about a Saviour.

And the first thing you know, he had five little churches, one on each island.

And then he read that an elder in the church must be the husband of one wife. He was a yielded man.

Now, listen, you fellows. If you had five wives—which you don't—and your first wife was the oldest of the five and she was a sick woman. And the last one was a beautiful Chinese girl. And you find that, having yielded your life to the Lord, you've got to give four of them up. Which one would you keep?

Come on, you fellows. Now you're scared. You'd all say, "Well, I'd like that beautiful girl."

You know what he did? On each island he had a home, and you know what he did? He gave all of his goods to his four wives. Gave all that he had on each island to that wife. He kept the first one who was sick. Transformed? This man was a man who was Spirit-filled.

Although he said little publicly in the meetings, you could just see his face transformed when you talked about the Saviour.

I had a wonderful time with that man—Old Whiskers.

And, surely, Old Whiskers had a wonderful time with him.

Chapter Seventeen

Personal Worker

Warren Yost recalls:

During the hippie generation, I had a lot of trouble with the hippies myself. You know, I just kind of looked down my nose at them. I wasn't sure I wanted to have anything to do with them.

But Dr. Mitchell didn't feel that way at all.

I remember his talking about that. He would stop if he was in a public place like an airport or train station or wherever, and he would talk to them and treat them nicely.

It really opened my eyes to—to loving people. I kind of equated it to our missionary friends going to another culture where the people don't dress as we do and yet God loves them the same.

And that's the impression he gave as he mingled with these kids with their long hair and their different style of living.

He was very loving to them.

Everywhere he went, Jack Mitchell was ready to give an answer to any question about his faith in the atoning work of the Lord Jesus Christ. He had a profound sense of the lostness of mankind.

His remarkable gift of being able to remember "what-he-said" and "what-I-said" allowed him to share his "you-were-there" witnessing stories with his classes and congregations. And he took advantage of every opportunity he could find to work a lesson on witnessing and holy living into his teaching.

He was mid-stride in Romans when he told this story:

I tell you, my friends, when one thinks of the hundreds of people who have just in simple faith said to Him, "Lord Jesus, I take Thee as my own personal Saviour"—why, they have gotten off their knees transformed!

You may not see it immediately, but it's there just the same.

I have in mind now a young man who was forced to come to a meeting, and he came only because he was forced to. He didn't want to offend his friends. He had no intention of becoming a Christian.

At the end of the meeting, he was brought down for me to talk to. He didn't come of his own volition. And I told the folks who brought him to go and sit down and pray for him.

And I said to him, "Bill, you want to talk to me?"

He said, "I don't know."

I said, "I know you came here under duress. Could I ask you a question? Would you allow me to take just two minutes and tell you what the Lord has done for you and for me?"

And in two minutes I explained to him just the simple gospel how God knows our frailty. He knows that we can't do anything to be saved so He has made the provision.

After explaining the gospel of the wonderful grace of God, I said to him, "Would you like to accept Jesus Christ as your Saviour?"

And he said, "You mean I can do it now?"

And I said, "Yes."

And we got down on our knees and I said, "Well, now, Bill, if God gives you a gift, what are you going to say?"

He said, "I'd thank Him."

And very coldly—there wasn't a sign of any emotion, he said, "Jesus, I thank You for Your salvation. Amen."

And he said to me, "That's all I can pray. I don't know how to pray."

"That's OK," I said.

He went out and one of my friends said, "Do you think that fellow was really saved?"

I said, "I don't know. I can't read a man's heart."

Do you know that before that man got out, he became an absolutely transformed man? The beer and the whiskey went down the drain along with other things which I am not going to mention. He was absolutely transformed. In fact, today, he is ministering the Word of God in another part of our country. He just simply came as he was in all his sin and accepted the Saviour.

Listen to it. "If you will confess Jesus Christ as Lord and believe in your heart that God hath raised Him from the dead, you shall be saved." There's no doubt about it.

Not everyone responded to his witness. He told one class:

I've been told to shut up a number of times. Do you know that?

A businessman from Chicago sat beside me as we were coming from Philadelphia to Chicago on the morning plane. As the girl brought our breakfast in, the captain of the plane said, "Good morning, ladies and gentlemen. Welcome to United Air Lines. We're going to be traveling at four hundred and some miles an hour, 32,000 feet above sea level and we're coming into Chicago. There's going to be a snow storm. We may be held up in Chicago."

Well, on my tray and on his tray was a little complimentary package of cigarettes. They don't do that any more, so you know how far back this is. And I took my little package of cigarettes and I set it over on his tray.

For the first time, he sat up and he said, "I was just thinking of putting mine on your tray."

"Oh," I said, "don't you smoke?"

He said, "No, don't you?"

I said, "No, but I used to."

"You used to?"

That opened the door and I gave my testimony.

"Why don't you shut up," he said.

I said, "Why should I shut up? I'm just telling you how I gave up my smoking."

"Ah," he said, "you fellows. All you talk about is faith, faith, faith. I was raised in the Roman church, and I was an altar boy, and I've had problems with preachers coming to my office with a Bible under their arms—("Which I have my own doots about, by the way," Mitchell would insert)—and they're talking about faith, faith, faith. What's faith?"

"Oh," I said, "you're a living example of faith."

He said, "What?"

I said, "You're a living example of faith."

"Whaddya mean?"

"Well," I said, "here we are chatting and eating our breakfast 32,000 feet above sea level, going over 400 miles an hour, calmly eating our breakfast, sitting in a bunch of junk that men have put together and you ask what faith is? The object of my faith is a risen Saviour who upholds all things by the word of His power. I have a risen, glorified Saviour, sir, who loves men and women and who came to seek and to save the lost!"

He got up. "You've got your philosophy, and I have mine."

"Well," I said, "where does your philosophy get you?"

"Oh," he said, "I suppose—to hell. Where does yours get you?"

"Oh, mine gets me to heaven!"

"And what if you don't get there?"

"Well," I said, "I won't be any worse off than you are."

Now I ask you people—do you find it hard to witness for the Lord? Huh? You sit alongside somebody on the plane and you

*pray, "Lord, help me to witness to whoever is sitting with me."
Isn't that right?*

*And so you sit down and there's a businessman sitting along-
side of you and you say, "Good morning." And you say a few little
things and you talk about business. You talk about politics, who's
gonna be the next president. You can talk about football or some
athletic event. And you have perfect freedom. But the moment
you mention Jesus' name, a barrier goes up.*

*And you stutter and you mumble and you don't know what
to say next.*

I know.

*I talked to a businessman on the plane and he said, "Shut
up! I don't want to hear that."*

*And you know what I said to him? "Isn't it strange, you
know. You and I have been talking for the last 10 or 15 minutes,
and we've talked about everything under heaven. Perfect. Good
rapport between the pair of us. But the moment I mention Jesus,
why you stiffen up and tell me to shut up. What's wrong with
Jesus?"*

"I don't want to hear about it."

"Why don't ya? Does it convict ya?"

*But it is true. You can sit down with people. You really
want to witness. But you're tongue-tied. You stutter around.*

*"Why," you say, "Brother Mitchell, you don't have that expe-
rience, do you?"*

I sure do. And I've been told where to go sometimes, too.

And I've told them, "I'm not going there."

*Why is it we're so shy to talk about our wonderful Saviour?
You don't mind talking about Him in your church. You don't
mind doing it in Sunday School or with your Christian friends.
But get down with some of these unsaved people and you're
tongue-tied. Isn't that right?*

What does God do?

In Acts chapter 1: "But you shall receive power with the

Holy Spirit coming upon you. And you shall be my witnesses wherever you go."

We've been called to witness.

At this point in his lesson, Dr. Mitchell would turn on his listeners and apply the message to them:

If you're going to witness, you've got to be real in your confession. You can't fool God. You just can't fool God. And please don't use I John 1:9 as a kind of wand—you know what I mean—where you say, "Oh, well, I John 1:9—I'll just follow that through and I'll be all right again."

You've got to be real in your confession.

When you and I sin and we get down and confess our sin to the Lord, what do we do? Get off our knees or wherever you've confessed your sin and what are you thinking about? You're not thinking about your forgiveness. You're thinking about the sin you've committed. And what do you do? Not very long after that you go and do it again.

And you say, "Well, that's my weakness."

Don't excuse sin. You have within you the Spirit of God who can give you that deliverance. The Word of God can give you that deliverance. And, if I might add this to that statement: Please don't put yourself in the way of temptation.

What do I mean by that?

Let me give you a very crude illustration. I do this because I know you folks won't do this.

But here's a man who was delivered out of alcoholism. He's got a weakness for alcohol. For him to say, "I'm a Christian now and I'm strong and I don't care, I'm going to go into the saloon anyhow with my friends. I don't want to break my fellowship with my friends."

Well, what'll he do? When he gets in there, he'll start to drink. I know this. You can't put yourself back in the situation that tempts you. If you've got a weakness, run away from it.

I had that very clearly set before me with a fella in

Philadelphier. I was having some meetings there. And, after the meeting one Sunday afternoon, this fella stayed behind and sat in his seat; and I went back to him and I said, "You want to see me?"

"Yes. I have a problem."

And, when I sat down, I knew what his problem was. It wasn't beer. It was whiskey. I know the smell of whiskey. And I talked to him about his need for the Saviour.

And he said, "I've already accepted Jesus as my Saviour, but I can't get over my sin. I've been doing this for 32 years. Mr. Mitchell, there's not a morning that I get up but the first thing I do before I get out of bed is take a drink. I have a bottle right alongside the bed.

"When I go down to the office, we stop in a grog shop, two friends of mine. We commute into Philadelphia and we stop at the grog shop and get a drink.

"In the middle of the morning, I slip out and take a flask out of my pocket and take a drink because I'm a certified public accountant and I can't write my figures because I'm shaking— because I need some alcohol. And I go back and take a drink and that will last me till noon.

"At noon I get some more. In the middle of the afternoon, I have another drink. Then we stop at the grog shop after we get through the office. Then we take the train home. Before I go to bed, I drink. Thirty-two years I've been doing it. I can't live without it. The doctor says I'm one of 3 percent incurable."

And I said, "You accepted the Saviour?"

"Yes."

What would you have said to him?

He said, "I've prayed, prayed, prayed. Can you help me, sir?"

You feel kind of helpless because the man said at one time he had already accepted the Saviour.

So I said to him this, "Do you read your Bible?"

"No."

"How long is it ago since you read your Bible?"

He said, "I don't read it."

"When you were led to the Saviour, weren't you told to stay in the Word of God?"

"No."

"Do you have a Bible?"

"Yup. It's in the attic somewhere. And, Mr. Mitchell, my wife has given me two weeks to get over it. I've been doing this for 32 years, and now she gives me two weeks. She's gonna leave me and take my kids with her. I got two children. She's gonna give me two weeks."

And I thought of a verse of Scripture. It just came to my mind. You know how the Spirit of God will do that—in John 8:31-32: "If you continue in my Word, then are you my disciples indeed; and you shall know the truth and the truth shall set you free."

I said, "You go home. Find that Bible. I suggest you close your door, get on your knees and open your Bible and read."

He said, "Where shall I start?"

"I don't care where you start. Just read the Book. But do it on your knees. Close your door and do it on your knees."

"My wife will laugh me to scorn. She'll say, 'Hah, using a religious stunt now to keep with me, huh?'

I said, "Well? So what? You've lost her anyhow. You've got nothing to lose."

I prayed with him, but I made one grave mistake which I learned the next Sunday afternoon.

I didn't see him all week until the next Sunday afternoon. He lived outside of Philadelphier. He came into the meeting just as I was starting to preach. And my heart sank because, when he came in, I knew he was a defeated man.

So, when everybody was gone, I went back and I sat alongside of him and I said, "What happened? Did you do what I asked you to do?"

And he said, "Yes. I went home and got my Bible. My wife laughed me to scorn. I went in the bedroom and shut the door, got on my knees and, Mr. Mitchell, I was shaking so much I couldn't even read."

I said, "What happened?"

And then he made an amazing statement. He said, "Mr. Mitchell, don't blame God. Don't blame God. When I got on my knees, my wife laughing outside. I was shaking so much and I wanted to have that liquor so badly I couldn't even see what page was open. I couldn't see the print.

"So I just knelt there and looked at the Bible," he said, "and there came over me a peace and rest and quietness and I stopped shaking and then I could see the Bible. And I read it, and for the first time in 32 years I went to bed without drinking whiskey. And I slept like a baby.

"And I got up in the morning and I had put my Bible where I used to put the bottle. And when I woke up in the morning, I reached out for the bottle. No bottle. I opened my eyes and here was the Bible. I was shaking so much, I got up on my knees and I had the same experience. A peace just came over me," he said.

"I read it, got dressed, had breakfast and went to work.

"For four days I went through the same experience. Down at the office, instead of reaching for the bottle, I took my Bible with me. I didn't even leave my desk. I opened my Bible, read a verse and I quieted right down. And I went for four days without a drink for the first time in two years."

"What happened?"

By the way, his two buddies were on the train the first day. He said, "I'm not going with you to the grog shop."

"You on the water wagon?"

He said, "Yes, I'm through with it."

They knew his problem. They knew his family situation. They said, "Boy, we're sure happy about that. Now maybe your wife will stay with you."

He said, "Well, I'm on the water wagon and I'm not going to take any more."

And on Friday morning they said to him—listen. "We've been doing this for years. We're so happy you're going on the water wagon. But come on in, Dan. Take a cola. A seven-up. You know. We miss you. We miss being with you."

So he went into the grog shop to get a coke or a seven-up, but the moment he smelled that whiskey he was gone. He was gone!

"Well," I said to him, "Dan, there is only one thing for me to say. The Lord has already given you an experience of deliverance and the deliverance now is the same thing as it was. Get back to your Bible."

And then I apologized to him. I said, "Sir, I should have told you last Sunday not to put yourself in the way of temptation."

I had just learned a lesson.

And I want to say to you folks today, I've dealt with a great many alcoholics through the years, a lot of men. This is the thing I always remember—never to let them go without reminding them, "Don't put yourself in the way of temptation."

If you've got a weakness, if you've got some frailty that affects your relationship with God—I don't care how big or how small it is—don't you put yourself in the way of temptation. Run away from it. Your body is not yet redeemed. Your body has desires. And God wants you to walk with Him, trusting Him. But He's also put a head on your shoulders.

If I put my hand in the fire, I'll be burned. . . .

God's great desire for you is your fellowship. Nothing delights the heart of God more than for you to trust Him. And you can trust Him whatever the frailty or weakness may be. The Lord is sufficient for it. He's El Shaddai—He's "the God who is enough."

I know that.

My biggest problem was not cards—I used to play a lot of poker. When I was saved, that was just coming up. But my big problem was this question of smoking. I smoked cigars from the time I was 16 years of age. I used to smoke cigars and play poker in my own home years ago. When it came to witnessing, the issue was—this is what opened my eyes—am I willing to give up something I enjoy?

You say, "Enjoy that stuff? Pooh!"

All right, "Pooh!" away if you want to. But I'll tell you . . . it smelled good. But that ended. And don't you go out and spill the beans on me now. Now?

The question is—even though you may say, "But I like to do this. But there's no harm in doing this"—I'll accept that. But if it's going to affect your testimony, you better get rid of it.

Do I love the Saviour? Do I love people more than some dirty old habit? Huh? Then let me get rid of the habit. If it's going to affect my testimony for the Lord, it's going to hinder somebody's coming to the Saviour.

Someone was speaking to me just the other day about a fellow who glories in his liberty as a Christian.

I said, "That's not liberty. That's license. He's just flaunting what he calls his liberty. That's license. He's never thought for a moment what effect it's going to make on other people."

You say, "But that's legalism."

No, no, no. A man accused us here at Central Bible of being legalists.

I said, "Just a minute. You get this word 'legalism' right. Legalism has to do with things that affect your salvation. You don't work to be saved. A 'legalist' is a man who is trusting his works for salvation. That's 'legalism.' That's the book of Galatians."

He says, "I'm saved. I can do these things because I'm free. 'Free from the law, oh, happy condition.'"

All right, but he's got a tremendous responsibility to somebody else.

The Apostle Paul could say, "If eating meat will offend my brother, I will not eat another piece of meat as long as the world standeth."

There's nothing wrong with eating meat. But if it's going to cause my brother to stumble, we've got to quit it.

Chapter Eighteen

Brother

Willard M. Aldrich had a unique friendship with John G. Mitchell:

We had a very happy, happy relationship down through the years. The picture we have—the two of us together—is a very appropriate one. Neither one of us would move without the consent of the other. We had no private enterprises or programs that either one or the other stood in the way of. We saw things pretty much together.

He had, certainly, a practical deep submission to the Word of God. His own heart and life were subject to it. It's like D. L. Moody said of the Word of God: "Do we need to defend it? No. It is like a lion. Loose it and let it go." That was characteristic of his life. He had a wise simplicity in his approach to the Scripture. He was not simple; you know that. But he approached it from a practical point of view.

We used to talk and talk about many of the profound issues of life, and he would always evaluate them in light of the principle that the Judge of all the earth will do right. That God IS righteous was basic to his thinking. He would cut the Gordian knot of theological abstractions or contradictions by the assurance that God always does what is right.

On the question of election, he reduced it to simple terms. "If God says 'whosoever will,' He means it. He doesn't mean that 'whosoever will may come if I let him come and that I have a secret agenda that isn't known.'"

Jack Mitchell always came out with boldness and conviction on the things that he believed.

The close association over the years between Willard M. Aldrich and John G. Mitchell has led many observers to look upon them as a David-Jonathan combination, as near to being brothers as two men can be. Their offices, for many years, were side by side in Sutcliffe Hall on the Multnomah School of the Bible campus; and they worked side by side on the faculty, on the Board of Trustees, in public ministry and in private. They even met for lunch each weekday, usually at Holland's Restaurant on Halsey Street. Willard recalls:

There was no Reuben sandwich like Holland's. We'd split one when we got to the place where it was too big a sandwich for us. He would enjoy that.

They had first met in Tacoma when Willard was a teenager. They had met again when Willard, en route to Wheaton College, dropped by Dallas Theological Seminary to see his brother Roy, a classmate, roommate and close friend of Jack's.

It was Willard who responded to a call in 1934 to come and work in Portland for a summer, directing the Portland Union Bible Class's young people's ministry. The letter Jack wrote Willard and Dexter McClenny at that time shows the dimension of this young pastor's spiritual concern for the Pacific Northwest:

My dear Willard and Dexter:

I have just returned from a seven-week trip and, needless to say, all my correspondence is behind time. I had the privilege of having a conference in Seattle, Yakima, Corvallis, and Medford. The latter two places are in Oregon, as you know. This whole country is certainly in need of consistent, consecutive teaching of the Word. A Bible conference is a good thing to stir up new interest; but it takes consistent, consecutive teaching to really build up the people of God.

People are hungry for something, but they do not know what it is they are hungry for. The churches as a whole are not even beginning to meet the need, and I believe that it is up to those who claim to know the truth to give it out. It will call for sacrifice, but that need not prevent any yielded heart from making an attempt in the will of God. Not only is such a thing confined to those who know the truth, but it is narrowed down to those who also have vision of the need.

Believing that God is putting this upon our hearts, there is the great possibility that I shall call a number of men together from Seattle, Yakima Valley, Southern Oregon and other points in the Pacific Northwest to see if we can come to some plan whereby a consistent effort shall be made to reach people with the Word of God. Please join us in prayer that the Lord shall be pre-eminent in all this and that His blessed will shall be accomplished. . . .

Dexter wrote me some time ago about the possibility of work up here this coming summer. I hardly know what to say with respect to this. I could very easily use you both, but economic conditions are such that we could not offer you a thing in that line. I can guarantee you real experience and the possibility would be that you would get along while you are getting the experience. . . .

There is also the possibility that in the near future we would need to use two or three good men who can teach the Word and can follow through on this consistent, consecutive teaching of which I have already spoken. This, of course, is in the formative stage, but I believe there is a great field open.

There would be a weekly class in each town, a union class, the Sunday School lesson taught first, then a popular Bible study

*following. Each night the class would be held in a different town
and thus a whole district would be in the position to get the Word
of God. The teachers would have to be men of tact, vision, and
passion for the Person and Work of Christ. Nothing else is worth-
while. He is the only one worth talking about; so, I say, the need
is for men who have a real passion for HIM.*

*I would like you both to be much in prayer over this matter.
First of all, get the mind of the Lord. "The servant of the Lord
shall not make haste," but when you do get the mind of the Lord
remember, "The king's business requires haste." It pays to move
slowly and when in doubt, just rest in Him—do not move. . . .*

*Above all, wait on the Lord. Be in His will. This is the only
place of blessing and usefulness. I believe the Lord has a place for
you in His work and the thing to do and be is in His will.*

*Do not worry about openings as many do. This is not faith,
nor is it the place of rest and peace. Be content to just wait on
HIM. He is the Lord of HIS vineyard; hence it pays to walk in
close fellowship with HIM.*

*This is the important thing, NOT what men think you
ought to do. No one can tell what God's will for you is. This of
necessity must be for each one to find out. There is no place worth
living apart from His will and, whether it be in a large place of
ministry or small, it is His will that He wants you to be in and I
am glad that He never rewards for greatness, but for faithfulness.*

*There is something that is a great deal more than service,
preaching, or teaching. It is that intimate fellowship with God.
This is the paramount thing for us all; otherwise, how can we
know His will? None of us can afford to live one day out of fellowship with Him.*

*The Lord is blessing the Word to many hearts in these days.
There have been souls saved each week: not only in the meetings,
but especially in the personal work of the men. There have been
souls saved each Sunday night since returning home and this, of
course, makes our hearts rejoice.*

The children's work is going along well. There are about 60 weekly classes being held among children and high school students with rich blessing to many homes. I would estimate that more than 1,500 children are being reached with the Word every week in these home classes. . . .

It looks, however, that the more the Lord blesses the work, the more Satan attacks the work. But "greater is He that is in you than he that is in the world." This opposition comes, as a rule, not from the world as such, but mostly from professing Christians. That need not worry one as the work is the Lord's, not ours.

We are anxious now to spread out beyond Portland to this whole Pacific Coast, as well as send our young people into the lands that are without the real gospel of Christ. Please remember this work before the Throne of Grace. We feel the great need for wisdom and tact and spiritual discernment.

Now may the Lord's richest blessing be the portion for each of you, and may His every blessed Word abound and prevail in your hearts and lives.

Mrs. Mitchell joins me in best love and regards to you both. . . .

Again, the Lord bless you.
Much love as ever,
Yours through His grace,
John G. Mitchell

The door of opportunity certainly attracted Willard. Brought up in Washington State, he knew the need of the Northwest. But he had been working summers at the Rainier (Washington) National Park as an ice cream maker at $120 a month plus room and board; and the line from the letter that said, "Economic conditions are such that we could not offer you a thing in that line," gave him pause. But he knew "Jehovah-Jireh." He knew the Lord would provide.

Looking back on the experience, he has said, "When I came to Portland, I lived in the YMCA at $19 for the month.

Harry West, a member of the Board of Trustees, came to me and said the Board had unitedly decided to call me and they would pay me $60 a month. I didn't rise to that with much enthusiasm, but I lived on it. I got lunch at the Green Lantern for 35 cents."

Willard told another story on himself that occurred when Jack Mitchell was absent from his home one time and W. R. Newell, who wrote the commentary on Romans, was a visiting speaker and a guest for lunch at the Mitchells' home.

"Marian Little and a couple of our friends from our young people's group were also guests. Mary Mitchell called on me to return thanks. And I prayed, 'Dear Lord, we thank You for this food and we ask You to give us strength to eat it.'

"The girls had to bite their lips to keep from laughing out loud. We really didn't need to pray for strength to eat Mary Mitchell's good cooking. I'm afraid that story was retold many times."

When Willard finished his Th.D. studies at Dallas Seminary, Jack asked him to become a permanent member of his staff. He invited him to move into their home for a while. His memories of that experience include the fact that "Mary remembered how cold the house was and that I used to like to make the fires in the fireplace. I remember that once, when I didn't have the key, I had to climb up a drain pipe and get in a second story window. How it happened to be open, I don't know.

"I remember in 1937, I preached in the First Baptist Church in Salem and drove home with another young fellow, Don Misner. Some 27 inches of snow fell that night, and it took us nine hours to drive the 50 miles back to Portland. We arrived at six o'clock the next morning, somewhat to the anxiety of the Mitchells—and Doris Coffin. She and I were beginning to get interested in each other at that time.

"Interestingly, when she became my bride, I brought her home to their home while they were on vacation."

Willard worked closely with Jack as the Multnomah School of the Bible developed, teaching theology and acting as the registrar.

When, later, Dr. Sutcliffe resigned as Multnomah's first president and they were looking for a new one, Dr. Mitchell suggested that Willard be president.

"And I said, 'I'll consider it on the one ground that it's offered to you and you turn it down.' I would far rather have served under him. But he was not interested. He had the church at that time, too.

"Once during my presidency, there was a private meeting of some members of the board to which I was not invited. Floyd Bolich was invited—like some of the guests to one of Absalom's parties. When he found out what it was, he got up and left. And when Dr. Mitchell heard that there was some move to get me out, he just simply said, 'If Will goes, I go.'

"So I guess that illustrates loyalty, friendship, and hopefully there was some reason why I should stay. But that was as far as it got."

A chance remark at lunch one day probably did not help any.

Willard recalls that "four members of Multnomah's faculty were having lunch downtown in the Union Depot—Si Forsberg, Gordon Fraser, Dr. Mitchell and I. I don't know what led up to it, but one of them said, 'Anybody can teach exposition.'

"That was like saying, if you were an eye-ear-nose specialist, that anybody can operate on a limited area like that. I know that hurt Dr. Mitchell because he was the exposition teacher at Multnomah and not anybody could teach exposition—not like he could.

"I'm sure that off-hand remark seemingly aimed at the heart of Dr. Mitchell's ministry was not intended to hurt him as it surely did."

A brother would remember a thing like that.

Willard has also noted that there was a manifest spiritual and moral holiness about Dr. Mitchell which discouraged evil.

"Evil was not at home in his presence," he says. "People would not tell dirty stories in front of Dr. Mitchell. People would not try to engulf him in gossip. Such was his integrity."

The Aldriches spent several summers with the Mitchells up in the San Juan Islands and, in the earlier years, accompanied them on the summer Bible conference circuits.

"But that was before I got too heavily familied with nine children," Willard says. "We did go to Mount Hermon and we did go to The Firs together. But usually I would be included only because I was with him, I'm sure. I was not the popular Bible conference speaker that Dr. Mitchell was, and I recognized that. But then, on the other hand, probably everything that was written—the constitution and all the detail of explicating what Multnomah's ministry was—came pretty much from my pen. And so there was a hand-and-glove relationship between us.

"At events where I spoke, I would give greetings from Dr. Mitchell, the chairman of our board. It was a very natural thing because I was not competing with him at all.

"And he would do the same. He would honor those who were working with him, and he would share the credit. He probably had a half-dozen men who went on to 'call him blessed' as they became successful in other areas of Christian service. There was a closeness, a bond.

"I think it stands as a tribute to him that those who passed through his field of labor were bettered as a result of it."

The salaries at the school were not what they might have been and probably were apportioned on the basis of need. One wag said that, because some families had many children, faculty members were not paid for what they produced at school but for what they produced at home.

"We pretty well went on the unwritten principle that we

wouldn't ask individuals for funds through personal face-to-face solicitation. I could write you a letter, and I could hint subtly or not so subtly or I didn't need to express it. That was the old China Inland Mission principle that their missionaries never appealed for funds. They just told people that there were needs. That was a rather deep principle with Jack."

Even when a millionaire visited at a time when the school was obviously outgrowing the old campus, Jack made no mention of money.

"When are you going to put the bee on me, Jack?" he asked.

"I'm not going to put the bee on you. If the Lord lays this on your heart, then fine. If He doesn't, that's His business."

When another millionaire invited him and Willard to lunch, Jack said, "You know, it's wonderful to be able to have fellowship with you on these occasions and not to be thinking about money."

Willard refers to Jack's "transparent honesty. He would not cultivate friends with the mixed motive of what they could do for him."

At a later date, one man promised a million dollars to pay for the new library on the present campus.

"Oh, the deference we paid him," Willard says with a grin.

The envelope the man presented at a formal occasion turned out to be as empty as the promise.

"I imagine the Lord must have laughed at us over that one," Willard says. "But I mention this because Dr. Mitchell was never involved in fawning over the wealthy. He remembered the widow's mite honored by our Lord.

"I remember when the Jewish community of Portland presented a plaque to Fred Taylor, who was a Multnomah trustee. In commemoration of his service to Israel, they had his name written in the Golden Book in Jerusalem. They gave a banquet in his honor, and Jews and Christians were there together.

Several gave short speeches, and Fred gave his testimony so clearly—why he believed in Jesus as Messiah and Saviour.

"Dr. Mitchell was there, and he made no effort at all to cultivate the interest of these wealthy people in the school. He spoke on 'You people, get into your Bibles.' It was really a very remarkable occasion, and there wasn't a dry eye in the place."

Exaltation of the Word of God was at the heart of Multnomah's founding.

In Willard's words, "The school was going to be one where we were going to put double emphasis on the Word of God. And so we set out to do that; and with that and the simplicity of our appeal that 'If it's Bible you want, then you want Multnomah,' students came. We wanted to be faithful in teaching the Word of God and to get people out to the mission field. We didn't call in outside experts to plan our strategy for us. It was just that simple.

"Dr. Mitchell would be thrilled at commencement and the missionary conference, seeing young people dedicate their lives. For 40 years or more, he always dedicated the graduating classes. And at the close of the missionary conferences, he had the prayer of dedication. I think that was a delight to him to share in that."

The one-year course for college graduates came after World War II with the return of the GIs. Jack had crossed paths with C. Stacey Woods, president of Inter-Varsity Christian Fellowship, who said, "Here's a bunch of guys who are ready to be taught." The course was instituted, and Jack Mitchell really loved his "grads."

Willard says, "He was alert to the opportunities of that sort—like the evening school. When he taught in it, he always had big classes. And I think of our extension schools. We started at least four other schools. They started out as evening schools and later became day schools. We gave the program to John Groenlund of our faculty to draw up its constitution and bylaws and points of severance. These became day schools—no longer our schools—all in perfect, pre-agreed steps of progress."

What motivated Jack Mitchell to keep him going? A love for the young people, an ability to relate to them and a desire to further the work of Christ.

Willard says, "He had that remarkable ability to forget himself and go. He was like a fire horse. As soon as the harness dropped on him, he got out of the barn in nothing flat. And then he would come back and collapse. But teaching the Word here at school was his prime interest.

"Now, I don't mean he couldn't have turned to something else. He could have kept busy as a conference speaker. If it were known that he was available, all our alumni in pulpits would have been more than happy to have him come. He could do supply preaching. But God laid the school on his heart. This was his calling here.

"And he was aiming at his students' hearts. He wasn't wanting them to repeat outlines.

"Some students who didn't know the value of what they were receiving criticized his teaching methods. They wanted a more organized, more academically set up classroom situation. But he had a very direct personal ministry.

"In his later years, this was his parish."

What about John G. Mitchell has marked the heart of Willard M. Aldrich?

"Well, I have mentioned first of all the reality of his relationship to the Lord. That dominated his life. That is, he was not just teaching doctrine. He knew the Lord. He knew Him in experience. And he loved the Lord. He made no attempt at being a scholar in the scholarly sense. He was greatly concerned about knowing the Book, and I think he had a good library. When he was needing help, he would turn to it. But, basically, he was a man of the Book itself.

"But he was not a bookworm. He applied it. He was a doer of the Word and not a hearer only. And then there was a warmth about him that always attracted.

"We could share burdens together, too. We would often kneel at his desk and pray together. And that not as a formality but out of a sense of need—either our personal needs or school needs or individual needs.

"And then, I think the recognition of the Lord's giftedness—that we each recognized that we were not the other person. We never rode each other's necks trying to correct and keep each other in fellowship. It was a matter of knowing each other and knowing strengths and weaknesses and accepting and loving on that basis. And certainly he had to do that as far as I'm concerned.

"Actually, we really didn't need to talk to understand each other.

"He was closer than a brother. Certainly, we've been together more than most brothers.

"And I'll remember his perseverance. He persevered up until his death. That last prayer, the last class he taught would be an example of that.

"He was an example of faithfulness.

"He kept on right to the end."

Chapter Nineteen

Uncle

I hesitated (but not much) to become close friends with them because I knew they didn't need any more friends. But they always had room for one more.

They never tired of the endless round of events in the lives of their friends—marriages, births, deaths, anniversaries, dinners, needs.

How did they ever do it—and right to the last?

I am sure they got very tired at times, but still they graciously gave of themselves.

Of course, they didn't have any children of their own, and that simplified their lives a little. But instead of becoming bitter or unhappy about their lack of children, they just "adopted" a host of others.

Theirs was a legacy of love.

May their tribe increase.

—Charlotte Lawrence
Faculty wife

To all appearances, Jack and Mary Mitchell were childless. And they were.

Celia Wiebe, an intimate friend of Mary Mitchell's and one who knew her heart, has talked about this aspect of the Mitchell's domestic life: "Mary Mitchell wanted a baby so bad. She said, 'I never felt like I've really been completed.' Because I remember telling her how I felt after my Stephen was born. You know how it is after you have your first child. My first reaction was 'this is why I was born.' I felt finished, that my personhood was completed by having had this child.

"When I explained that to her, she said, 'I have never felt finished.'

"That was exactly how she felt. That was a heartache for her. Any woman who hasn't had a child would identify with her. And I know she was able to help women who weren't able to conceive—to help them through it. She was so tender. I just loved the way she cared about them. . . .

"And she loved holding our babies and playing with them. Even when our twin grandbabies were born and Auntie Mary was pretty frail, the kids took them over to see her. And she held them on her lap and she played with them and cuddled them and cooed with them just like a normal grandma would."

Mary wanted to adopt. Jack didn't want to. He felt that, if the Lord didn't give them their own children, there must have been a reason.

Celia says, "We saw the reason. They were the parents of how many people? They had such a parental influence on so many people that they wouldn't have had time for. I don't have time for that with my family—to be that open to that many people the way they were. So I think definitely that was the Lord's plan for their life, and they came to recognize it.

"But it was a terrible, painful time for both of them not to have a child or two. And I don't think people know about it because they didn't talk about it."

To all appearances, they were childless.

But they were not.

Instead, they were surrounded by a coterie of dear young friends who loved them and called them "auntie" and "uncle." Whether or not some were closer than others, who can say? Two couples, Dr. Tony (Jack's physician) and Celia Wiebe, and Norm and Muriel Cook, were among those who were close to the Mitchells' hearts and they can speak for the rest.

Celia says, "For years and years, Johnny (Van Diest) and Joe (Aldrich) and Tony and Uncle John were quite a foursome. We all celebrated our birthdays together with him. And he would get a look on his face—a kind of patriarchal look that showed the kind of ownership feeling he had about these boys who were 'his boys.'

"And he would say to Tony, especially the last two weeks when he was dying, 'I'm so thankful for the family relationship. I don't know why the Lord let me have this.' He would say, 'I will always be grateful that I have this family relationship with you and your children.'

"As if it was something for *him*! It was something for *us*!"

For the Mitchells, love was not just an emotional attachment. It meant embracing support, financial as well as spiritual.

"Uncle John was a generous man," Celia says. "He was tight with his money in some ways, but he wasn't in others. I mean he was careful. They both were careful, and they were good keepers and good budgeters. I wish I could have learned more from them that way. But he was generous, and he would sacrifice his money to help you if you needed it. And I know he did that for lots of people. He would dig down deep in his pocket.

"When we were in medical school, they helped us out so many times with food or a little check for clothes. Nobody knew about that. They didn't talk about it and we didn't, but they helped us financially and also with little extras.

"And they would take our kids home from church once in a while—one at a time. They would take them home just to give us a rest—I had so many babies. They would play with them and feed them and bring them back and tell me all the cute things they'd said or done."

The Mitchells never gossiped, and family secrets never became public knowledge via sermon illustrations. Most people never even knew of the relationships the Mitchells had with the Wiebes and the Cooks, among others.

Celia says, "You would never hear anything private from him. He was kind. His heart and his tongue were full of kindness. His tongue was full of healing. You know that verse in Proverbs? 'The wise tongue gives healing?' That was their tongue. They gave healing with their tongues. They medicated us. They kept us on the right path, and nobody was allowed to get away with gossip. Ever. That was a taboo.

"What did she say? 'Nagging is out and gossip is out. Those were two things we didn't do in our marriage. Don't nag your husband and don't gossip.'

"I remember a lady coming to me and saying something very unkind about Auntie Mary. I turned to her, and I was nice—and this is only because I've been around Auntie Mary so much—and I said, 'But she says the nicest things about you.'

"And that woman just blushed red and felt so bad. She sputtered. But it startled her. That woman never said anything again, and she was extra nice to Auntie Mary from then on.

"But that's the way Auntie Mary was with me. We'd find something good to talk about. If I ever started to complain, she would turn it into a positive thing so that I wouldn't dwell on the negative. That was something she had a special gift for and which he had a special gift for, too. It was not to dwell on the negative.

"It's going to be a long life without them, I tell you. The rest of my days—not to have them? It's really tough. I really miss them. It's like a big hole. I feel like part of my heart has been ripped out. Now I don't have that base any more. They were my base. I *really* miss them.

"I miss Uncle John's smile and loveliness and character."

And being "family" means being a part of crisis times. When he was needed, Jack was there.

Celia says, "I saw Uncle John cry a couple of times. Talking about babies they didn't have, he had tears. And he cried once with me. It was when Tom was born. He had meningitis when he was two weeks old, and we didn't think he was going to live.

"The day the doctor told me Tom wasn't going to make it, he said, 'If I were you, I'd prepare. You know, call your pastor and get the funeral prepared and make arrangements because he's not going to live through the night.'

"And so I called Uncle John. It was a Wednesday. And he came right over. It was like two in the afternoon. He came right over, and he walked into the house. Tony wasn't home yet. And he cried with me over losing my baby. I was that sure I was going to lose my Tommy.

"And he said, 'Oh, Celia.'

"It was such a traumatic time. But he came in and we prayed together and he said, 'You know, I just feel like there's a wall of angels around this room. There's a wall of peace in here.' You could feel that peace.

"And he said, 'The Lord is really here with you.'

"And I said, 'Yes, He is. He's helping me get ready for my little boy.'

"And that's when Uncle John got the tear. Then he prayed, and then he left. He had stayed with me for about an hour to make sure I was okay. And then he went back to church, and he called later and asked how we were doing. And I told him we were waiting.

"And he said, 'It's about time for prayer meeting to start. We're going to have everyone pray for Tommy tonight, and then the women are going to send around sheets; and we're

going to sign up and we're going to pray through the night.
And somebody will pray every half hour. They'll pray for
Tommy.'

"And that was all his doing.

"So about three in the morning, I woke up (I had other
babies at home and so I couldn't be with Tommy in the hospital); and I felt like something had happened. I didn't call
the hospital, but I felt that something had happened. I didn't
know what it was.

"And so, about seven, I called the hospital and I said,
'This is Mrs. Wiebe. Is Tommy still with us?'

"And they said, 'Mrs. Wiebe, we don't know what happened. About three o'clock last night, all of a sudden the
fever went down and the color went into his face. It was just
a miracle.'

"And they said, 'He might make it.'

"And then the doctor called me a little bit later, and he
said, 'Well, we don't want to be too hopeful because there are
still lots of problems.' But he said, 'So far—'

"Tommy had had a fever of 107, and they said he would
be brain damaged, he'd be deaf, be blind.

"And I said, 'Oh, no. He's not going to be—If the Lord
healed him, he's going to be all well.'

"And he said, 'Well, don't be too optimistic, but he *is*
better. He looks like he's going to make it.'

"Well, he did. You know, Tom graduated cum laude and
his brain was fine. He didn't have any hearing or seeing problems, and he's a dear boy. And Uncle John really had a special
heart for Tommy after that.

"I remember, when Tommy was at church—he was about
30 pounds—and Uncle John was swinging him around and
around after church. And Uncle John had just had a heart problem. He had been in bed for it—maybe even hospitalized.

"And I ran over to him and I said, 'Uncle John, will you

quit doing that! You can't swing Tommy around like that.'

"'Don't you tell me what to do, young lady!' And he just kept right on swinging him.

"And I said, 'I want Tommy to have you as a teacher at Multnomah.'

"And he said, 'I'm not going to live that long.'

"This was 1952!"

To all appearances, the Mitchells were childless.

But, again, they were not.

They first met Norm and Muriel Cook, missionaries with Overseas Crusades, on their visit to Taiwan in 1959. Something clicked and the two couples became very close friends. Norm became one of Jack's "boys," and Muriel really loved "Auntie Mary." The women were "prayer pals" for 12 years, praying for each other every day. The birthday celebrations with the Wiebes and Mitchells now included the Cooks.

Jack told Celia that he loved to be with Norm and Tony because they made him laugh.

"They would just—you know—keep him going," she says. "It was stories all night. He really enjoyed it. He was in a revelry, kind of, when he was with those guys. It was fun. He felt he could be himself with them. He didn't have to be on stage. Even though he was like somebody said, 'He was always the same person. He didn't have to put on any facade.' Yet, with the guys, he could be himself. He could let his hair down a little bit."

When the Cooks first met Dr. Mitchell, he was 67 years old. They knew him in that slice of his life until he was 97. He encouraged them for their own enjoyment to enroll in the grad course at Multnomah when they came home on their next furlough, and they did.

Norm says, "He insisted we call him 'Uncle John.' But we saw him more than as just an uncle. We saw his love for the Lord Jesus, his knowledge of His Word, his ability to expound it, his fondness of singing ('The Lion of Juder' and 'Cheer Oop, Ye Saints of God'), his warm relationships with people, his vitality when preaching, his wisdom when counseling, his kindness, his moderation, his balance, caring, selflessness, his pulpit power.

"But, you know, I never saw him wear a red jacket or a yellow one. He always wore dark suits. He was a gentleman. He was a throwback to a previous generation. I think it came from his ministry, his love for the Lord and his desire to minister to people. He was a people person. He tried to smooth out all of his rough edges so that the gospel would flow freely from him. He didn't have a lot of quirks like some of us which separate us off from people. He was sort of a 'man for all seasons' type of person.

"I think he got it from spending time with the Lord and the Word and really taking the Bible seriously. It wasn't just what he studied from Scripture. It wasn't just in his head. It was down in his heart, and it affected his actions and his reactions and his relationships with people. Colossians 3 talks about putting on kindness, courtesy and love.

"He did."

The Cooks feel they were a link for him to his Grand Rapids days and preaching in the Middle West. They had grown up in Winona Lake, Indiana, and he had had some ministry there.

"We often talked about the ministry in Grand Rapids and the old timers we knew—Dr. Harry Ironside, for one," Norm says. "And we talked about the Youth for Christ conventions and the Bible conferences they had had at Winona Lake in the late 1940s. I even have a book, 'Winona Echoes,' which was a printing of messages that were given. Muriel's father and Dr. Mitchell are printed up in the same book—about 1951."

The Cooks also provided a link to the mission field, a great love of both Mitchells.

"We'd had eight years on the mission field," Norm says. "The Mitchells were in Taiwan twice for pastors' conferences that I set up for them. He loved them. They had no time clock there. They sort of went by the calendar. He'd preach for 45 minutes to an hour at a time, and then he would stand around and talk to the men and interact with them. He was just in the height of his glory at those conferences.

"Then he went to Hong Kong and spoke at a 'Spiritual Life' conference there three times a day and loved that as well. He always talked about going back and doing those things again."

Norm would ask the pastors in Taiwan which of the many men who came to minister to them over the years they liked best. Who had been the most effective?

They said, "Dr. John G. Mitchell because he always answers our questions from the Bible. It's not what 'I think.' It's what the Bible says—'Let's see what God's Word says.'"

"He just knew it so well that he didn't have to stop and research," Norm says. "It just came automatically. I think it was a tremendous compliment. They always wanted to have him back. It was such a special time. But, as his health began to fail, he realized he couldn't go. But there was something in him—he wanted to go back. And now I wish we'd just set everything aside and taken him back because he really made an impact."

The Mitchells, the Willard Aldriches and the Cooks would often go to Sunday noon dinners at the Matterhorn Restaurant near Multnomah and Central Bible Church, taking others occasionally.

Norm says, "Six or eight of us would sit around and talk about various things. Uncle John was and liked to be the center of attention. I don't think he realized it. Of course, after his hearing started going bad, it was hard for him to enter into the conversations and react. And so we tried to figure out ways to ask him questions about the Bible or get him to relate some experience. And then he'd come alive and be terrific. But it was hard for him to just be passive in a conversation. We had many, many wonderful noon dinners at the Matterhorn with them."

Often, in such gatherings, Jack Mitchell would remember and share details of his life that filled the picture in. Or he would say and do things that showed his character.

"He used to tell us," Norm says, "about when he first started preaching in Oregon and he would drive down to different places and preach for a weekend or a week or start a meeting for Friday, Saturday, Sunday and extend it over the next Sunday and then he'd go for another week. And the meetings would grow and wonderful things would happen.

"Just before he died, we went off on our sabbatical. The Mitchells took us out for dinner to the Matterhorn again. And we talked about the forthcoming trip and visiting various places. And when we finished eating, we battled over the bill.

"I wanted to pay it and he said, 'No, I'm gonna pay it.'

"And I said, 'No, I'm gonna pay it.'

"And he said, 'No, I'm gonna pay it.'

"And, finally, he said, 'Well, Norman, this may be the last time I'll be able to do something like this for you.'

"And so we let him pay for the bill. And then he gave us a check for $150 to help to cover our expenses to South America. He knew that it was going to cost us something to go, and he wanted to help us on that. It was an indication of the generous heart that he had."

Just as Jack Mitchell loved to relax and laugh with "his boys," he was as willing to share his sorrows and disappointments.

"I never saw Uncle John discouraged," Norm says, "except once when his hearing was going and students would try to ask questions. For a while he wore a device on his ears that would receive the sound and magnify it through his ears. It was kind of a silly thing. Then the students worked out a system where a person in the back of the room would ask a question and a student in the front would pick it up and repeat it to Dr. Mitchell in a loud voice, and he would respond to it.

"But one day I walked by his class and he was standing outside the door. His face was down and his head was down, and he said, 'They don't want me any more.'

"I said, 'What do you mean?'

"He said, 'I've got 13 students absent in my class. They don't want to come. They don't want to hear the Word.'

"That was the only time I ever heard him when he was discouraged. He was tired a lot at the end, but the discouragement didn't seem to bother him except that one particular time. I tried to assure him about that."

Another thing that surprised Norm was that Dr. Mitchell didn't want to write books. Asked why, he said, "If you write, you write it down, and everybody refers back to that. Maybe you change your views on something."

Norm says, "I sensed he didn't want to sit down and take the time. He didn't want to attach himself to the written page. He was grateful for the books that were made from his sermons on the Gospel and epistles of John and on Romans, but it was the preaching of the Word that was important to him."

Norm has tried to put his finger on what was different about "Uncle" John:

"There was an aura about him. You just felt comfortable in his presence. I think that's a definition of grace. A gracious person makes another person feel comfortable. Mitchell did that.

"There was a fatherliness about him that the students responded to. He wasn't austere and judgmental. He was kind.

"There was one guy, a very obnoxious guy, who was a leech, who befriended the Mitchells and vice versa and I couldn't stand him. I wanted to cut him off, but Dr. Mitchell didn't. He listened to him and allowed him to enter into his life, and I wouldn't have been surprised if the guy probably even got some money from him. I wanted to protect Dr. Mitchell from him, but Uncle John opened his door and had him in his home. And after three or four months, the guy disappeared.

"But I would have said, 'Hey, buddy, go out and get a job and start making some money.' But Dr. Mitchell didn't. He was never critical. He was very careful about what he ever said about other people."

Muriel Cook says she appreciated about Jack that he was always such a grateful person, that he knew how to say "Thank you," that he was humble. He didn't expect anything. "I think that's not easy for men," she says. "It's not easy for anybody, but men often forget to do that."

Norm really startled Dr. Mitchell one time. It was an introduction he gave. In fact, it brought down the house. Norm was presenting him as the guest speaker at a Junior-Senior banquet.

"I've never seen him so flabbergasted," he says.

"I mentioned in my intro that Dr. Mitchell was a Bible teacher, and he was a radio minister. I said, 'It reminds me of that passage in John 11 at Lazarus' tomb.'

"I said, 'Not where it says, "Behold he stinketh," but— "Loose him and let him go."'

"The place exploded. He was speechless and he was tickled. He stood there for a long time before he could get going. People could not stop laughing. He loved it."

Norm discovered Jack Mitchell had one pet peeve:

"One time he said, 'I don't mind it when people say I'm older, but I'm NOT old.' He said that very emphatically when he was in his 90s. He didn't like it when people thought he was old. He did not want to be referred to as old.

"He was something of a Barnabas—a good man, full of the Holy Spirit and largeness of soul. Tony, Johnny and I were sort of his boys. We felt that, although he never was 'father' as such. He never tried to portray that."

What brought one into that family of close friends?

Muriel understands: "It was his confidence in you, his love for you. He didn't smother anybody, you know. If Norman would show up at his office, he would be delighted. The Mitchells were very loving."

The Mitchells?

Childless?

They were not.

Chapter Twenty

Pastor

Jack Mitchell in his pulpit on a Sunday morning is introducing a new series of messages he will be delivering on the Book of Romans. He is explaining the relationship of the epistles to one another and their bearing on the Book of Romans:

The books of I and II Corinthians guard the practice of Romans, and Galatians guards its doctrine. We get the revelation of the righteousness of God in Romans where the grace of God makes it possible for unrighteous people to be fitted to come into the presence of a righteous God. The practice of that sort of life is found in Corinthians.

Someone has said that Romans is "Christ, My Righteousness" and Corinthians is "Christ, My Sanctifier." Then, when you come to the book of Galatians, it is "Christ, My Liberator." Galatians guards the doctrine of justification set forth in Romans. These three books make one package.

When you come to Ephesians, Philippians and Colossians, you have another package. Ephesians reveals the church, the Body of Christ. Philippians guards the practice of Ephesians—"for to me to live is Christ." To have the mind of Christ operating in you, to know Christ, to do all things through Christ—this is to be the practice of the church and this is Philippians in four chapters.

Colossians guards the doctrine of Ephesians, especially the head-ship of Christ over the Body which is the Church. So Ephesians is "Christ, my Life;" Philippians is "Christ, my Joy;" and Colossians is "Christ, my Head."

Now, when you come to the books of Thessalonians, I Thessalonians is the coming of the Lord for His own. Each chapter of the book ends with the coming of the Lord. II Thessalonians deals with the coming of the Lord to earth with His saints. He is going to come in judgment, as it says in the first chapter. He is going to come in flaming fire, taking vengeance on those who know not God and obey not the gospel of our Lord Jesus Christ.

Now, these are the Pauline letters to the churches. God gave Paul a two-fold revelation: in Romans, the revelation of the grace of God; and in Ephesians, the revelation of the Church, the Body of Christ.

If you want to know something about the sweetness, the loveliness of Christ and the claims of Christ, then you'll go to Matthew, Mark, Luke and John where these four men report what they saw and heard. They were not fabricators. Each one wrote with a definite point in view. Dr. Griffith Thomas has given the following outline: Matthew wrote of the coming of a promised Saviour; Mark wrote of the life of a powerful Saviour; Luke wrote of the grace of a perfect Saviour; and John wrote of the possession of a personal Saviour. We need all four gospels to give us a full picture of our Saviour as a Man in the midst of men.

The book of Acts deals with the ministry of the Spirit of God through the early Church. What the Lord Jesus began as He walked among men is continued by the Spirit of God in the Church as He gathers out "a people for His name." In the epistles, we see Paul as the apostle who declares the meaning of faith in Christ Jesus; we see Peter, the apostle of hope; and we see John as the apostle of love.

Romans starts with man corrupt and fit for hell; and, in Thessalonians, man is translated and glorified. The epistles between Romans and Thessalonians reveal to us how God changes sinners and fits them for His presence.

In the epistles of Timothy and Titus, we have instructions to young preachers concerning conduct in the house of God. Philemon is a wonderful story of grace. Hebrews declares the superiority of the person and work of Christ over the Old Testament priesthood and the sacrifices. James informs us how the godly should walk. I and II Peter relate the sufferings of the people of God and the opposition they meet. In I Peter the opposition is from the world. In II Peter it is from false teachers.

The epistles of John speak of the believer's fellowship with God. In the first epistle, we have fellowship with the One who is Light, who is Righteousness, who is Love. II John tells who are to be excluded from the fellowship and III John tells who are to be included in the fellowship. Jude is a book of the last days. In Revelation, we see Christ as Judge in the midst of the churches, in the midst of Israel and in the midst of the nations. We also see the final revelation of a new heaven and a new earth.

What's the Lord doing now? He's doing a job for you, for believers. When He came to the world, He came to do a work for the world. He died for the world. But now He's praying just for believers. He's representing believers before God. He is our Advocate with the Father. That's the epistle of John, chapter 2.

And then He's going to return to the world as a Judge and then to reign as Lord of Lords and King of Kings.

Did you ever realize the Bible starts with creation and ends with creation? It starts with man in the Garden of Eden and it ends with man in Paradise in the presence of God.

Follow it through in the contrasts between Genesis 1, 2 and 3 and the last three chapters of the Bible. Just compare them. In between, you have the whole purpose of God for the earth.

It's high time we Christians got to know something about God's purpose for the earth, for man on the earth, and for you and me.

No one who ever heard him will dispute that John G. Mitchell was a great man in his pulpit. He knew the Bible "like the back of his hand," a close friend said. He knew the Lord and the power of the Word of God like few men in his generation. Congregations gathered in the thousands to hear him when he spoke—and they went away fed. His radio audience numbered in the hundreds of thousands.

People he had never met wrote him soaring letters of congratulation and praise because his ministry had meant so much to them. His love for his Saviour struck a resounding chord in the hearts of people starved for the eternal truth of the Word, people whose own pastors fell far short of having Mitchell's mastery of the Book.

Members of his congregation sent him little letters of genuine pride that he was their pastor. One, Elizabeth Potter, sent him a note his wife kept with her special letters. She wrote:

Knowing that you have so many people's troubles and problems always before you, I thought this excerpt from the letter of a friend of mine in Detroit might be like a tiny gleam of sunshine through the clouds.

My friend is a fine Christian woman, very active in things of the Lord. I "met" her through the Christian Pen Pal Club advertised in King's Business.

This is what she wrote me, "We had an especially good speaker from your city, Dr. John Mitchell. My, he was fine! He has been to Founders' Week before, several years ago. This year he spoke each morning on 'Faith,' the same time each morning and so many said, 'Now we're filled up. We can go home for the day.' Many of the following speakers were overshadowed by his wonderful message."

I am sure you can understand the pride with which I wrote her, "Dr. Mitchell is my pastor, so I can understand fully how much his message meant to all at the conference."

John G. Mitchell did have a pastor's heart. He yearned, Sunday by Sunday, to be instrumental in feeding the flock of God. His sermons, filled with gold, silver and precious stones from his hours of Bible study, fed the hundreds who congregated at Central Bible Church. One never left his service at 12 noon. His "now, just one wee minute more" often extended the hour to 12:30 and even 12:45. He knew the Book, and people went out from there longing to be—not more like John G. Mitchell but more like the Saviour he exalted.

On his return from his trip to the Orient, he preached on "I speak this to your shame that there are many without Christ."

His niece Marty Eby Katcho never forgot her impression of that sermon:

I think he was just amazed at how many people there were in the Orient without the Lord, and the burden of their need filled his heart. Here we all were, sitting in church and there to take in another sermon, while millions in the Orient went to hell without Christ. His heart came across in that sermon more than many I can remember. It wasn't just vain words. It was his whole heart just yearning for those people to come to know the Lord. He had the real heart of an evangelist.

He also had a shepherd's heart and found great personal satisfaction in having a part in people's lives in good times and bad.

Mrs. Joyce Scott, a dorm mother at Multnomah for many years, remembered how Jack comforted her grieving heart:

My younger brother was dying of cancer in the Portland Veterans Hospital in October 1944. He was young, only 26 and the father of two small children. He had been drafted into the army one day before his 26th birthday, which was the cut-off line. Now, four months later, he had been moved here as his case was terminal. He was in Portland one week.

Our family responded to a call from the hospital that the end was near. We gathered around his bed, and I experienced seeing death for the first time. I was awed as I actually saw the moment the spirit left the body. The doctor entered the room, as I pondered this, and pronounced the fact that my brother was dead.

As the doctor took hold of the inside door knob, Dr. Mitchell took hold of the other side. He had been on the way to another call and had been prompted by the Spirit of God to turn around and come to Don's room. What timing!

Then, within five minutes, the family was asked to assemble in a lower floor room. It was a large, bare room—stark, really. Chairs lined the walls. A huge desk with a chair beside it was at one end.

My young, grieving sister-in-law was ushered to that chair as we took chairs along the wall. The uniformed gentleman at the desk, without a word of greeting or consolation, turned to her and in a brusque tone asked, "What do you want done with the body?"

At that point, I fell apart. Almost blinded by tears, I jumped up and ran out of the room, slamming the door. Dr. Mitchell was standing in the hall. When he saw my condition, he opened his arms wide and I rushed into them. I finally was able to sob out my hurt.

"How could he say that to her! He's only been gone five minutes. He's cruel! He's cruel!"

I was devastated.

He held me and allowed me to cry. Then in a soft, comforting voice, he said, "That's the way of the world."

What a true statement. And, as a babe in Christ, I understood the contrast.

I've recalled those words many times in the past years. They have helped me cope with living in this sin-cursed world.

Dr. Mitchell was used of God to exemplify the heart of God

for His hurting children. The challenge of those words, over the years, has been that I might in like manner portray to a suffering world God's loving heart.

Wes and Alice Kent, who sat under Jack's ministry for years, remember his love and concern for people—"from wee babies," as Alice put it, "to those who were nearing the time to say 'Goodbye, earth; good morning, Glory.'"

She remembered that to those who were anxious for that day to come, he would encourage them with this remark, "The very fact that you are still here is proof that God has a job for you to do."

As a pastor, Jack took time for anybody. He left his study desk, when this author was a Multnomah grad student, to come and kneel with me and pray over my present and future. Ruth M. Hanson of the congregation found him willing to pray not only for her primary request but for needs related to it:

When my son Eric's wife was pregnant with their first-born, the child's heartbeat became so low and slow the doctor did not expect her to hold a live fetus. My son called and asked me to pray, and I called Dr. Mitchell and asked him to pray for my son and the baby his wife was carrying.

He said he would and added, "I'll pray for his wife, too."

The heartbeat came up and she in due time had a son. Some time later, I told Dr. Mitchell in church the child was born and is very healthy and active.

He smiled and said, "Isn't that just like the Saviour!"

I had considered my son and his son Shane, the baby, who would probably not have been born; but I never even considered his wife who was carrying the child.

But Dr. Mitchell did.

Church missionary Coral Snyder, lying in a bed a thousand miles away from Portland, told of a surprise visit she received:

Dr. and Mrs. Mitchell were ministering at the Church of the Open Door on their way home from a trip to South America in 1969. I had left Zaire, Africa, on a Saturday evening and by noon on Monday was in a bed at the City of Hope hospital in Duarte, California, with a diagnosis of probable cancer.

Some visitors from the Church of the Open Door relayed to Dr. Mitchell that I was there. On Tuesday afternoon, I was astonished and thrilled to be visited by—my own pastor and his dear wife! They had brought me some beautiful pink rosebuds, and Mrs. Mitchell slipped me her own pocket copy of Daily Light *which I still cherish.*

But remembering their presence in that room that day still overwhelms me!

And all the signs and symptoms of the cancer disappeared.

An out-of-town couple, Ed and Glenis Trammell, hosted Jack on one of his speaking tours. They have related the impression he made on them:

In the early 1960s, Dr. Mitchell was invited to speak at our church. It was our privilege to have him to dinner and to stay the night. After dinner, he chatted a bit with us and then asked to be excused to his room as he said he'd like to have some time in prayer before his evening message.

An hour later, he appeared, ready to present the Word of God.

Twenty-five years later, he was staying with us for the same reason. He again excused himself to retire to his room for prayer.

There is no doubt in our minds how much he valued prayer in relation to giving out God's Word.

Eleanor Bower Yost, Central Bible Church soloist, joined him when he went to her hometown of Mossyrock, Washington, to speak in her home church and stay in her brother's home:

My brother was just kind of awestruck. He could hardly believe that Dr. Mitchell was staying in his house. It was a really special weekend. They asked him if he would do an overview of the whole Bible in Sunday School. I don't think Dr. Mitchell had planned to be a part of the Sunday School at all. But he did it. He came up with an overview.

And he said to me, "Oh, you've heard this 100 times."

I don't know for sure if the people appreciated him or not. I really don't know to this day if they really realized who they had speaking, because I've often said to people, "One day we're going to say we knew him."

Men of renown wrote letters of remembrance of blessing on Mitchell anniversary days.

Lorne Sanny of the Navigators wrote:

I was still in my early twenties when I took my first Navigator area responsibility in Seattle, Washington. I remember the first trip I made to Portland. I went to see Dr. Jack at Central Bible Church.

He welcomed me, put aside whatever he was doing and made me feel like I was the most important, if not the only item on his "do" list for that day.

After talking with me for a while, he invited me to a time of prayer. It was like praying with Elijah. He told me, "One of the greatest hindrances to prayer is the misunderstanding of other Christians."

He went on to explain, "If you tell a parishioner you are going to spend a half-day in prayer, he will look surprised and say, 'Why, what's wrong?' as if one would never spend that much time in prayer unless he was in terrible straights."

Cliff Barrows of the Billy Graham Evangelistic Association staff wrote:

Dr. John G. Mitchell was chairman of the follow-up work (of the Billy Graham Portland campaign in 1950) and no one could be better qualified and prepared for this responsibility. In fact, his involvement then and in the way he has taught the Word of God to countless numbers of people not only in Portland and the surrounding states but across the country and around the world has been a great blessing and inspiration and a great encouragement to all the believers to go on in their faith—to grow up in Christ and to develop in Christian maturity.

A monthly highlight of morning services at Central Bible Church brought new parents to the platform with their babies. He would take the infants one by one and pray that God would "gift him (or her) for a special ministry" to that child's generation. Not one of them ever cried in the process, some remember. He would laughingly say it was because they were fascinated by the moles on his face.

"The children would grab hold of them. They thought they were handles," Jack said.

Youngsters he had dedicated to the Lord as infants would return to call him blessed.

Kathy Bleid Lasater did:

I remember him from my entire life. I guess I urped on him from the time I was a baby. I grew up listening to him. I remember him when I was about three or four years old in Sunday School coming down to sing a song with us. He wasn't the greatest of singers, but he'd always come down and sing a song with us toddlers and pre-schoolers.

I remember his commitment, his love for the Saviour, the ability with which he spoke the Scriptures. I remember he would say at the end of prayers in church, "Even so come, Lord Jesus. Come quickly." And his love for songs about the second coming of Christ are vivid in my mind. Every time I sing "Hallelujah! What a Saviour!" I see him.

I was always just a little bit afraid of him. Not really afraid, but, I guess, awestruck or respectful. I was never quite sure I could be totally myself around him. But I was always very attached to him in many ways. He was somebody I knew who would remain the same. He was a constant. He was somebody that was totally dependable.

He was very conscious of the children in his congregation and he often went out of his way to minister to them. Missionary Coral Snyder was particularly grateful for his attention to her daughter Cathy when she was in a Bible school in the States and the Snyders were far off in Africa:

How many little Bible schools did Dr. Mitchell stop at going to or from his yearly visits to Dallas Seminary?

Not many, I imagine.

But for a few years he did stop at little Ozark Bible College in Arkansas. This was probably at the request of Jack Wyrtzen as the school (now defunct) had become a step-child of "Word of Life."

That is in the natural, but it was by divine appointment because at that particular time there was a little MK (missionary kid) attending there, whose parents were in Africa.

Imagine our daughter Cathy's great surprise and delight to have her own Dr. Mitchell on campus, and what joy she had in talking with him and ministering to him in any way she could during those days.

It was because of this association that he consented, several years later, to officiate at her wedding at a time when he was "doing" only family.

Mrs. George Rizor thanked Jack for his ministry to her son in a little note:

We remember first of all that you taught me that I should teach him the Word of God and (you also taught me) how to lead him to the Saviour.

We remember how your prayers saved his daddy. . . and all your wonderful kindness during that trial of illness.

We remember how you stood by little George's unconscious body while the doctors set his leg after he had been run over.

Ready to speak or preach on a moment's notice as a good pastor should, he gave every evidence that "out of the fulness of the heart the mouth speaketh." His associate Bill Wecks recalled how Jack had to shift gears for a funeral when the widow decided she would like him to speak on a certain passage:

I remember one time we had a funeral for Marshall Meloy. Dr. Mitchell was going to speak, and he wanted me to be there too because I represented the church. He said when he got in the car—he'd been teaching at Multnomah for two hours—that he had just learned that the widow wanted him to speak on a specific passage, Psalm 27.

And he started to quote that psalm. He had the whole thing (in his mind). He was thinking and talking to me about it.

And, when he got there and took that Psalm 27, it was awesome to say the least. It was just all there. It was a very, very wonderful talk. It showed the way the Word was just a part of him.

I'm sure that mastery of the Word had some effect on the alertness he had his long life. He was a man of the Word from beginning to end.

Jack was in demand. He was available. His conference speaking schedule was always full.

Eleanor Yost recalled:

He would often do a lot of traveling.

He would go to Dallas and then go out from there. I asked him a question about Mary and how she felt about traveling.

"Oh, Mary," he said, "she has her bags packed before I've even said 'Yes' to an engagement."

His great concern for his flock deeply affected his soul.

Norm Cook said Jack would tell him about his aching heart; that, when he was teaching, preaching, and pastoring at Central Bible and traveling quite a bit to meetings, he would go by train so he could study and pray and look at the scenery and rest.

"And when he'd go away," Norm said, "he'd just have a wonderful ministry. Let him get on the train and start coming back to Portland—there would be a certain place where the train went through a certain pass coming into the Portland area. He said his heart would begin to ache for the school and the church and the people. He carried that aching heart."

But he did not carry a depressed spirit. He knew that a merry heart "doeth good like a medicine." He was quick to laugh and to enjoy something humorous. And he learned to avoid incidental issues. The one great burden of his heart was the message of Christ. He didn't want to interfere in the ministry of the Holy Spirit as He worked in men's hearts.

Norm said:

I don't think I ever heard him run a person down. I heard him criticize another man's teaching; but, when something like this happened, it was not over some petty thing.

He could go into any place and minister. He could minister in a saloon or a very liberal church or a high liturgical group because he had a message to give. It went everywhere. It was effective everywhere.

He never made movies and all that an issue. That isn't what he preached. That isn't what he taught. He could tell you from a Biblical background why you couldn't do such and such. But he could listen to you and not be distraught by what you were saying.

One of the big name missionary speakers of the world was at a conference at The Firs in Washington State, and he chose as his text Matthew 16. He spent 45 minutes and didn't get anywhere close to what Uncle John did in about seven.

It was even being rumored that Dallas Theological Seminary was considering Jack for the position of president. Mrs. Louis Sperry Chafer implied as much in a letter she wrote Mary Mitchell:

My dear Mary: How rejoiced you would be could you know the blessing Jack's ministry has been to every student, to many friends and to all the Seminary family. I have been praying that this intense service he has rendered shall not prove to be too much for his physical strength. God has promised "As thy day, so shall

Thy strength be," and we have been praying much for the fulfil-
ment of this promise. Some day, perhaps, the Lord will lead so
that Jack may have even a larger ministry to the Seminary. For
this we are "waiting on the Lord."

And when Jack Mitchell did resign his pastorate at
Central Bible Church the end of December 1967, telegrams
and letters from evangelical dignitaries around the world
poured in.

Ken Taylor thanked him for his "wonderful ministry
that has meant so much to so many."

Charles Feinberg, Talbot Seminary professor and author,
wired, "Thousands have been edified through your exaltation
of Christ and preaching the Gospel of Grace."

John F. Walvoord, president of Dallas Theological
Seminary, wrote, "All of us at Dallas Theological Seminary
have followed your faithful and effective testimony through
the years with thanksgiving to God for giving such as you to
the body of Christ."

Roy Aikenhead, who had known him since 1918, wrote,
"It is fifty years last July since first meeting you, Jack; we had
known Mary a few short years before that. Those years that you
spent on the prairies cannot be forgotten and hold only happy
memories. Your messages from the Book of Books were always
so soul refreshing and challenging, plus stimulating to faith."

William Culbertson, president of Moody Bible Institute,
wrote, "Our own thoughts and memories go back to the late
1930s and our fellowship beginning at The Firs. Through the
years you have been a tower of strength and a wonderful fel-
low-servant."

Norman L. Cummings, home director of Overseas
Crusades Inc., wrote, "I will never forget one of our days of
prayer at Multnomah when with 'strong crying and tears' you
interceded for the lost in the city of Portland. Such experiences helped fill our hearts with compassion for the lost. Your

faithfulness in the proclamation of the gospel in Portland and your many journeys overseas have challenged us to share the gospel with others."

Dick Hillis of Overseas Crusades Inc. wrote, "Our missionaries in Taiwan, Viet Nam and the Philippines bear testimony to the new touch brought to their lives through your meetings with them. We have seen revival in the churches as you have taught the Word to the dear national Christians."

Hudson T. Armerding, president of Wheaton College, wrote, "I think it is particularly appropriate that I should have the honor of extending these greetings to you, since it was the year that I was graduated from college, Dr. Mitchell, that Wheaton bestowed its doctor of divinity degree upon you. Even after these more than 25 years, I can well recall the occasion."

J. B. Rowell, pastor emeritus of Central Baptist Church in Victoria, B. C., wrote, "I have had the unique pleasure of knowing John G. for more than fifty years. We first met in Brandon College, Manitoba, 1914-16. Because of his happy disposition he was known as 'Happy Mitchell.' He was a leader among students, keen in sports. . . . No society, no gathering of friends could be dull if Jack Mitchell had a part in the program."

Ray C. Stedman, pastor of Peninsula Bible Church of Palo Alto, Calif., wrote, "You are one of the three or four men, Jack, who has vitally shaped and molded my own ministry through the years. I am so grateful to God for your faithfulness to the Word and your obvious love of the Lord Jesus. These have both been a challenge to my own heart, and I hope find some reflection in my own ministry."

Jack received a letter from a very close friend.

Dear Jack:

It has been my happy privilege to know you since seminary days—and that has been a long, long time. You were a great blessing to me in my own preparation and early ministry. Since then I have counted it a high honor to have had fellowship with you in conference after conference.

It was with a feeling of sadness that I heard the news of your resignation from Central Bible Church in Portland. Jack Mitchell and Central Bible have been synonymous terms. However, some of us selfishly anticipate that you will be more at liberty to accept invitations that will give you a wider ministry. As long as I am at the Church of the Open Door, this pulpit is always open to you. However, I am beginning to look longingly at the end of the row. Some of us will be following your footsteps shortly.

— *J. Vernon McGee*

If a man has to have a flaw, he is fortunate if it is a little one. A man can be forgiven for taking on too much when hundreds celebrate his slightest anniversary or celebration and his mail is full of words of praise.

A problem arose when the congregation of Central Bible Church decided to leave its downtown site in the Behnke-Walker building and buy property out near the campus of Multnomah School of the Bible more than 80 blocks away. Dave Stewart, Dr. Mitchell's assistant, found himself in the middle and he became concerned.

He wrote:

It must have been in the fall of 1955 when plans began to take shape for a move. I remember Harold Hall, who was then church treasurer. He was a lawyer by training, and he was the man destined to find the property where the new church now stands.

I was so intrigued that on my own initiative I went to the local library and read all I could on building committees and on getting started and what have you. I drew up a format of things to do and things not to do. Then, when it came time to select a building committee, as being Dr. Mitchell's assistant, I was riding on his coattails so to speak.

They made Dr. Mitchell chairman of the planning commit-

tee. But everything I had read up to that point said, "No way." Not one of the staff persons, including the pastor himself, should be chairman of any of the committees. So I had to speak up against that, and lo and behold they wanted me to be chairman of the building committee.

I was unhappy with this whole arrangement because I had read six manuals and they all said this was a bad move.

But the men said, "Well, you've done the homework and you have the time. You call us and we'll meet with you."

I only mention this to point out the fact that it put me in a bad spot insofar as my relationship to Dr. Mitchell was concerned because, being chairman of the building committee which followed the planning committee, I was at least equal to my boss and that was a bad situation.

I can remember going home one Sunday evening after church and I'd been distressed. We had had a special business meeting on the whole matter of building and what have you. Dr. Mitchell and I had been down to the architect, but we were laymen as far as building a new building was concerned. The men on the Board were more expert, more knowledgeable than we; and it made us feel a little stupid at times.

So, on the way home from church, I gingerly proposed to him that perhaps we should do as the apostles had done in the book of Acts and appoint some deacons. We should stick to the ministry of the Word.

And very softly and gently he said, "Now, Dave, I have this in hand and you just leave it to me."

And that was the end of the whole issue as far as I was concerned. I never raised it again and my position never changed. I still remained a chairman, but it was one of those issues that— oh, I felt so defensive for him.

I felt my hands were tied and I couldn't do anything to get him out of the predicament I found him in.

I was at a meeting one evening when he was not there, and

I really was disappointed about the train of thought that was present and the remarks that were being made.

Here was the man I had idolized all of my life, and I could see him now in their eyes as not the man on the platform who ministered the Word. He was one of their equals—perhaps less than their equal as far as his knowledge of building was concerned. And this distressed me no end; but my hands were tied, and I couldn't do anything about it.

The massive cement block rectangle of a building, constructed at 88th and Glisan streets, came to be known as "Fort Mitchell." Some said it was devoid of ornament because, if the church could not make a go of it there, the building could be sold as a warehouse. Others called it "lovely in its elegant simplicity."

The main auditorium held nearly 1,500 for services and, Sunday by Sunday in ensuing years, was full. Any frustrations in the building of it quickly vanished as the Spirit of the Lord seemed to come upon the place and bless the ministry presented there. Squabbles and intra-church factions never reared their ugly heads. Divorce among the members was rare. The missionary arm of the church was strong.

Jack Mitchell had 11 more years of ministry in the Glisan Street building before he resigned. And, even then, he resigned only because he was afraid his dear assistant pastor, L. Dwight Custis, might move to another church. He loved Dwight and wanted to see him established in the ministry of Central Bible.

He thought he would have to give up the radio program because he knew the Board could no longer sponsor him as pastor of the church. At that point, Multnomah took the program and he carried on.

But leaving the congregation affected him deeply. He dearly loved the flock God had given him. He might leave the church, but the church would always be a part of him. He continued to attend as a member of the congregation, but he did not enter into its decisions or the conduct of its affairs. He had his opinions, but he was not one to hang on to or try to control something when he no longer had a responsibility. He felt his role would now be as an encourager.

Indeed, a story he told may be read as a parable of his own on the matter of letting go and helping other people:

God comes to live in His people. May something of the wonderful, wonderful grace of God flood your heart and my heart—to love one another and to be a channel of blessing and comfort.

You know, when I think of that, I think of an incident here in Portland some years ago that demonstrated divine love and divine grace.

I buried the baby of a woman. It was six months of age.

About three or four months afterward, the baby of a lady down the street from her died. The funeral director came to get the baby, but she wouldn't give it up. She held her baby in her arms as she was sitting in the kitchen. She just sat there, staring at the fire. No tears. Just staring, stunned—with her baby in her arms.

The father couldn't get the baby either. And the preacher couldn't get the baby.

"What are we going to do?"

The woman whose baby I had buried heard about it, and she went down.

She said to the father, "I understand your baby's died."

He said, "Yes."

"Can I see the mother?"

She went to the kitchen and took a chair and just sat alongside of her. She didn't ask for the baby. She just began to talk about her own baby that she had just lost three or four months before.

During the conversation, she said, "My baby is in heaven. I haven't lost my baby. You remember David said about his baby, 'He can't come to me, but I can go to him.' I haven't lost my baby. My baby's just gone ahead of me; and, when the Lord Jesus comes, we're going to be together again for all eternity." And she just talked about the Saviour and how He had comforted her heart.

And the mother put her baby in the lady's arms and burst into tears, a flood of tears.

The lady gave the baby to the husband and went back and sat with the poor woman in the kitchen and put her arms around her and talked about the Saviour.

That's what I'm talking about.

The Spirit of God in that woman knew what this woman was going through. She became a channel for comfort, blessing, and peace. It's a marvelous thing. The living God is living in you. What for? To reveal to the world His character, His love, His grace for men and women.

And, indeed, he did become a channel for comfort, blessing and peace for many in the ensuing years.

But even if it appeared that John G. Mitchell had left active church ministry on his resignation from "C.B.," active ministry never left him. To his last days, he had a shepherd's interest in the flock he had known during his years at Central Bible.

His secretary, Marian O'Connor, made note of this in his latter days when she said:

He had many friends he would try to visit, especially those he knew from his pastorate at Central Bible Church. If he knew someone was in the hospital, he would try to pay at least a brief visit to that person. He had physical limitations near the end, but his heart was large.

He would usually have a hard time finding a parking spot. When he would finally find one, it usually wouldn't be close by the entrance and he would have to walk. He was finding it more and more difficult to walk any real distance.

When he got inside, I know he had to sit down and catch his breath. Then he would visit and pray with his friend. Then to leave, it would take him a while to get through the hospital.

He would have to rest again, get up and go outside and walk the distance to his car.

But he made no complaint. He felt it very important to shepherd the people who had been part of his flock.

That was also something he reiterated in his last years. He was very concerned that Bible colleges and seminaries develop men of God who would be real shepherds for God's people. He felt that lack. He wanted men who would not only have knowledge and teaching ability, but men who would have a heart for God's people, who would carry them through the difficult times and be there for them, committed to them.

I often, when taking his dictation, would hear him ask people to pray that there would be shepherds for God's people.

One final illustration capsulizes the essence of Mitchell, the pastor, who was always the shepherd.

Norm Cook tells the story:

Bruce Wilkinson, when he was teaching at Multnomah, came to Dr. Mitchell and wanted to be discipled.

And Dr. Mitchell said, "I'll have to pray about that." He said, "Come back and see me in a couple of days."

Bruce came back.

Dr. Mitchell said, "Well, Bruce, I decided I would not disciple you."

And Bruce in his testimony says it just "blew me out of my saddle."

He said, "Why wouldn't Dr. Mitchell want to disciple me? I'm going into a nationwide, a worldwide ministry with Walk Thru the Bible. If he disciples me, then I'll disciple them and he'll just multiply himself."

He says he just couldn't figure out why Dr. Mitchell wouldn't disciple him.

Then Dr. Mitchell said to him, "But I have decided that I will teach you how to fall more in love with the Lord Jesus."

Chapter Twenty-One

The Lion in Stride

Mitchell in full stride—a great man of God preaching the Word of God to the people of God—outdid the seven wonders of the world! No wonder his large church was packed. No wonder he had a large radio audience. No wonder his students went far and wide, equipped to do the work of the Lord in the fields of the world.

Hear him on a Sunday morning, preaching Romans 8 at Central Bible Church:

Oh, what a wonderful, wonderful thing—no condemnation, never to come into judgment, and to be eternally free from the law of sin and from the law of death.

Don't you revel in this wonderful fact?

Christ did such a perfect work for you and for me that we come into His presence with no condemnation. No one is going to be able to produce any evidence in the presence of God that you and I were ever sinners. No wonder we sing that song, "Hallelujah! What a Saviour!"

What a wonderful thing to be saved, to know you are saved and that you can come into the presence of God at any time and have fellowship with Him.

Now, why don't you do that today?

Read Romans chapter 8, come into the presence of the Lord and discuss the matter with Him. Discuss the chapter with Him. Pour out your heart to Him. He just loves to have you come within the veil into His presence and to have you talk to Him face to face. This is why He made you the way you are. He gave you the power to communicate with Him. Why don't you do it? Enjoy the Lord. Don't endure some "religion." Enjoy the Lord Himself. Enjoy your salvation in Christ Jesus. The Lord wonderfully, richly, marvelously bless you as you do this.

And I tell you again, my friend, it is a wonderful thing to realize that we have been delivered. The one law—the law of the Spirit of life—has delivered us from the other law—the law of sin and death. The law of the Spirit of life in Christ Jesus has emancipated us from the law of sin (which you find in chapter 6) and the law of death (which you find in chapter 7 where he says the Mosaic law makes sin exceedingly sinful). The law is the strength of sin as you have in I Corinthians 15:56. The law is a ministration of death as you have in II Corinthians 3:7.

But we are free now to serve God. We are free now to live for Him, free now to live a new life for Him which we did not have under the law. The law demanded. The law could not do in that it was weak through the flesh. Paul said, "I had not known sin until the law said, 'thou shalt not covet,' and the law which I thought was going to give me life, behold it brought death." All the law can do is to slay, to kill, to condemn, to curse. It can't do anything else.

You see, the law of the Spirit of life in Christ Jesus has set me free from the law of sin and the law of death. The law never supplied anyone with power to perform what it demanded. It did not produce holiness in a life. It demanded holiness. So how can one be emancipated?

"God sending His own Son in the likeness of sinful flesh, and for sin (because of sin), condemned sin in the flesh." What for? "That the righteousness of the law might be fulfilled in us"—

not by you or through you but "in you" who walk "not after the flesh but after the Spirit." What the law could not do, God's Son, Jesus Christ, did.

God sent His Son into this world where sin reigned, where death reigned. What for? In order to deliver you and me from the law of sin and death.

I want you to mark that.

Why did He come? Because man was totally hopeless, totally helpless, void of righteousness. And the law says you must die. He appeared once in the end of the age to put away sin. The sinless One was made sin for you and me.

He became a man that "through death He might destroy him that had the power of death, that is the devil, and deliver us who through fear of death were all our lifetime subject to bondage."

I like to quote II Corinthians 5:21 like the old lady who had been delivered out of a life of bondage to alcoholism. This dear woman didn't know much about schools; but, believe me, she knew the Lord. And I remember her testimony: "Jesus Christ, who knew no sin, was made sin for me who knew no righteousness that I, who knew no righteousness, might be made the righteousness of God in Him." This is what you have in Romans 8:3-4.

He made provision not only to put away our sin but to destroy the power of sin so you and I could go free—in order that (verse 4) the very righteous requirement of the law might be fulfilled in us who walk not after the flesh but after the Spirit. Our Lord released us from the bondage, penalty, and guilt of sin. He judged sin in its stronghold. He bought us and set us free. Sin has no more right to the Christian. It comes as a trespasser. And what is the result? The very righteous requirement of the law is fulfilled in us.

Friend, God did something the law could not do. He made possible a holy life for those who walk in the Spirit. What the law demanded and could not empower, the Spirit of God does in the believer. All that the law demanded is met in Christ for the believer. The believer in chapter 7 tried in his own power to *please God and could not do it.*

Now we come to chapter 8 and, in the power of the blessed Spirit of God who indwells us, each one of us can live the life that is pleasing to God.

Significant preaching of the meat of the Word produced significant results. From the founding of the school, such ministry produced—particularly among those students who stayed for the full three years—a sterling crop of young soldiers, equipped to do the work of the Lord around the world. Indeed, many became church and missionary leaders in their field of service.

Prominent among the file of letters Jack and Mary Mitchell saved through the years stands one written from a lonely outpost mission station near the Ethiopian border of the Anglo-Egyptian Sudan by Mrs. Claire Grieve, who with her husband Bob, a medical missionary, represent the mature fruit of Mitchell's ministry in his prime.

She graduated with Multnomah's first class in 1939. She had caught the vision of the foreign fields from her teacher and had left home and loved ones to serve a people who knew not God.

Italian bombers strafed her missionary compound shortly after this letter was written. Dr. and Mrs. Robert C. Grieve became Multnomah's first missionary martyrs.

Sudan Interior Mission
Special Bag to Kurmuk
c/o Postmaster, Khartum
Anglo-Egyptian Sudan, East Africa

Dear Mr. and Mrs. Mitchell:

Greetings in the Name of our Precious Lord! How He does grow exceedingly more precious each day as we are thrown upon

Him for our every need.

We are really ashamed for not having written you long ago. We think of you and our friends at the "Classes" so often. The songs we sang there together stand out as among the best we have ever sung and the spiritual refreshment each Sunday morning we'll never forget. How much we'd like to drop in and fellowship together with you, even for one day.

The place to which the Lord called us is all we desired—for it is a place where Christ is not known and where there is also great need for a medical work. As you know, we're working at the Doro Station, among the Nubians. There are many Arabs through this region at certain times of the year, for they are typical nomads, taking their flocks farther south to the water during the dry season and going northward during the rains.

We are only 43 miles from Mal and Enid Forsberg. They are stationed among the Uduk peoples at Chali el Fil, about 30 miles from Ethiopia. The Lord is opening both of these stations to a very fine work—and we do pray that the Word given out may soon bring forth much fruit. The people are really listening to the gospel with much interest—though they as yet seem to have no conviction of sin and therefore they realize no apparent need of a Saviour. God will bring about this change in their hearts, we know.

Bob is so very busy with the medical work, and more and more cases of a serious nature are coming to him from near and far. This is a cause for rejoicing, for these people have perhaps more superstitions than any of the neighboring tribes.

One little girl in our village has spinal meningitis. Do pray with us that there may be no epidemic and that Bob particularly may be protected from these terrible diseases he treats daily. He has already suffered a spell of amoebic dysentery in Egypt and bacillary dysentery here at Doro. This damp climate is also naturally hard on a person with sinus trouble—so he has suffered already from upper respiratory infection. I shall surely appreciate your remembering him.

Also, Malcolm (Forsberg) seems to be having plenty of illness. (Their little) Peter Leigh is getting along some better now. This zone in which we work is one of the most difficult climates in the world—but the Lord can and will put His arms of protection about us during this rainy season, I'm sure.

I've been spared any major illness myself, as yet, and am praising the Lord for it.

The way this old world is going, we wonder how long before our dear Lord shall come to straighten things out. Even this part of Africa may have a shaking up if Italy decides to fight. In the meantime, we just pray God will use us to the fullest extent here before any evacuation might be enforced. There is "talk," that is all thus far. We thank the Lord that "He holds the key to all unknowns." It would be far more difficult to have to plan our own steps.

Could you tell me what has happened to the Herbert Ebys? Are they in Christian work somewhere now? Also, we wonder how that beautiful little home of yours is progressing. Is the garden a source of "workout" as you had hoped it would be? I think your home is one of the most beautifully arranged ones I've seen for a long time. Wish you might drop in here and pay us a visit.

Our little home isn't particularly a thing of beauty, but we love it—our first. It is of red burned brick—burned here on the mission compound. Iron roof, cement floors, mud plastered walls. It is a grand feeling when the great tropical storms come to know that your house is a safe retreat from all the wind and terrific downpour.

Forsbergs set up their refrigerator yesterday, and two of the workers from this station, who went along to help set it up and get it started, shared in the delicious ice cream Enid made. Little Peter Leigh found it a bit cold—he hadn't the faintest memory of having tasted anything so cold—but he liked it, they said. We're so happy for them. They need it.

Mal and Enid hope to make an itinerary trek through all their Uduk tribe and drop in to see us in July. What a treat that will be. We are so cut off from all other white people from now on until the latter part of December, when the rains cease.

Should there be any bad sickness at Chali, Bob will have to wend his way there by mule or donkey or horse. There are none such as yet at this station. We have no means of transportation as yet.

Well, I've rambled on at great length, but have told little, I'm afraid. However, even this may give you a few things for which to ask prayer. We think often of Mrs. Kipp and Mrs. Hamilton and the Worshams, and ever so many of your folk there. Would you tell Mrs. Kipp I'll answer a letter if she'll write one first.

Remembering you and your flock often at the Throne of Grace—and thinking often of our good times together in Him—

We remain,
Lovingly yours,
Claire and Bob Grieve

In the spirit of our Lord's answer to the disciples of John the Baptist, God was using Jack Mitchell's Bible teaching ministry to open blind eyes, to heal the sick, to cleanse the lepers, to make the lame walk and the deaf hear. The dead were being raised to life and the poor of many nations were hearing the Good News.

Missionaries were dear to the hearts of both Mitchells. They sent them forth with joy. They prayed daily for them— Jack participated in the Portland area Overseas Missionary Fellowship prayer group through the years. They ministered to missionaries at furlough time and pressed upon the students at Multnomah that the fields of the world were indeed white unto harvest.

Although the Portland Union Bible Classes had been holding monthly missionary meetings since 1926, Jack organized a Women's Prayer and Missionary Union in 1933 to foster prayer for local and foreign missionaries. He scheduled its meetings to follow his weekly Wednesday afternoon class and also added some occasional monthly gatherings.

In 1934, the missionary budget was $915.00. By 1939, it had increased to $3,313. And through the years it grew.

In 1936, the council planned a meeting once a month and a conference once a year to emphasize missions. It was about this time that the first missionary, Roy MacNaught, went to El Salvador. Marian Carlson, who later was married to Eldon Whipple, was the next missionary to go.

In 1937, Mrs. Ella Collette was appointed missionary secretary for the church, an office she held for many years.

By 1941, the Sutherlands, Edith Nanz, Marjorie Giblin and Janet Hamilton had also left for foreign shores.

Year by year, the Bible Classes and then the Central Bible Church added missionaries to the list of those it supported. The bottom line was Jack's conviction that one did not go to the mission field because it was there. One went because he was a bond servant of Christ—as the experience of Maxine Sloan illustrates:

I was attending a Sunday evening service of the Portland Union Bible classes at the Behnke-Walker auditorium. Jack had preached the message, "Bondslave of Jesus Christ," about the person who was completely yielded to Christ.

And at the closing prayer—I was a college student at St. Helen's Hall—I yielded myself as a bondservant to the Lord Jesus Christ. I would now have no will of my own, no plans of my own. My whole life from then on would be committed to the Lord.

And, when my boyfriend Bill Sloan called me from Victoria where he was on staff at his home church, I told him of the message and of my decision. And he told me that some years before, Dr. Mitchell had preached a similar sermon in Victoria and he, too, had dedicated his life and yielded himself to become a bondservant of Jesus Christ.

So, when Dr. Mitchell—Uncle John—pronounced us husband and wife, we went with one heart and one mind together to serve the Lord.

The Sloans entered the ministry and Bill, before his death, served as interim pastor of Central Bible Church.

Jack loved to marry young people who had dedicated their lives to serve Christ. An old romantic at heart, he loved to be part of the happiness that went along with weddings.

He not only tied the knot for Bill and Coral Snyder (later, missionaries to Zaire), but he also drove the getaway car.

"We careened down the backroads of Beaverton and Aloha—almost ending up in a filbert orchard when he turned off the lights to fool the chasers," Coral remembers. He loved fun!

Claude and Barbara Leavitt (later, missionaries to the Trio Indians in Brazil) remember that, after their ceremony, he returned the honorarium for their first breakfast.

For many Multnomah graduates, a wedding was not a wedding without Dr. Mitchell officiating. As teacher and pastor, he had had a spiritual ministry in the hearts of many of them. It seemed only fitting, they felt, that he should have a part in the service that united them to their loved one.

Mary Mitchell took pleasure in ministering to some of the single young missionary women who returned on furlough after years of jungle life or life in other cultures where styles of dress seldom changed. Her interest lay in those who had no family to refurbish them. She would call them up when they came into the city and invite them to go shopping with her. She realized that, when they came back from the mission field, they had neither money nor clothes and yet had many speaking engagements that put them in front of people.

It was her habit to completely outfit the young woman and pay for everything so that she would be ready—at least sartorially—for a year's deputation. In the process she would let each one choose what she liked and what she felt comfortable with. She only insisted that her shopper not know the price. Often that gesture on her part marked the beginning of a deep personal relationship between the two.

One of the big events of this period was the purchase by the school of the campus on N.E. Glisan Street on which it now sits. Jack loved to retell that story:

Well, we were in the 703 building on N.E. Multnomer Street and we'd already rented a couple of houses close by Emily Neil's place and used both for dormitories. We all ate at Emily Neil's.

And then we built a building of about two stories. We made the foundation so that we could put three or four more stories upstairs to serve as dormitories and classrooms.

That building had a large classroom downstairs with cloak-rooms in front and restrooms in back. Upstairs, a large dining hall served also as chapel and as a classroom for larger classes. A kitchen adjoined it.

And then Peter Scruggs came to us and he said, "You know, the city is putting the blind school up for sale and the minimum bid must be $190,000. Let's bid on it."

Well, the board got together—there were only six or eight of us—and we prayed about it and talked about it. One said this and one said that.

We got back on our knees again for the Lord to direct us.

And I'll never forget it because when we got up off our knees, I said, "You know, I have a feeling that if the Lord wants us to have this property, He'll give it to us. He'll hold it for us."

Now the Methodist church wanted it to build a senior citi-zens retirement home. The Lutherans wanted it, but they found a place in Seattle they liked better. A group of doctors wanted it to build a hospital there, but the city wouldn't give them·the license to do that. So it was left between the Methodists and us as far as we knew.

So, the bids were to be in before Friday noon.

Peter called up Salem on Friday afternoon and said, "What about the property in Portland? The blind school. Did anybody bid on it?"

And they said, "No bids."

So the next morning, Dr. Willard called me up and said, "You know, how about offering them $190,000. That's the lowest bid you can make. And send a check for $5,000 as a firm bid. We can't lose anything. If they don't take our bid, then we get our money back."

So I called up the different men on the trustee board and we all agreed we should do that. We sent it special delivery on Saturday morning.

Now the sequel to that is amazing. Monday morning the Methodist group committee was meeting in the YMCA. And they had an architect there with plans for how they could change the buildings of the blind school and fit them for the kind of home they had in mind.

And while they were discussing the changes of the building—which they hadn't gotten yet, by the way—one of the older men said, "Gentlemen, we've got the cart before the horse. We haven't got the property yet. We've got to find out if the property is sold."

"Aw," they said, "don't worry about it. The only group that is interested in it is that little school called the Multnomah School of the Bible. They've got no money."

"Well, I'll feel better if you call them up."

So they called up Salem Monday morning.

And they were told, "Yes, it was sold this morning to the Multnomah School of the Bible."

And the amazing thing was that the State turned around and offered to lend us money for the transformation of the building at a very low percentage, by the way. And they held as collateral that two-story building we had down near Seventh and Multnomer.

Willard Aldrich says that to him the remarkable thing about that transaction was that "the State accepted the $5,000 down payment with a condition that we could be released from the purchase if we couldn't sell the property we already owned to the Lloyd Corporation. They accepted it as a bona fide offer even though we had a way out. And that added to the unusualness of this transaction."

The move gave the school a more than adequate campus in the heart of northeast Portland. Students found it easy to get public transportation to jobs and to downtown. It was close in, but it was private. As time passed other buildings were added. For the most part, the board waited until it had the money in hand before it went ahead with construction.

The board of Central Bible Church subsequently bought property in the next block and erected its new facility there.

Though he would deny it and say it was all of God's grace, the new campus and the new church building stand as monuments to Jack's administrative leadership and zeal. When the opportunity came, he was ready—always ready— and his people rallied round to support him.

Another notable aspect of the Mitchells' middle years— namely, travel—emerges time and again in diaries and in publications of the school. In 1959, Jack and Mary flew to Southeast Asia for ten weeks, visiting Multnomah and Central Bible missionaries and speaking at conferences. They went to Japan, Korea, Formosa, Hong Kong, Bangkok, Singapore, Saigon.

In 1960, Jack had gall bladder surgery in June and they stayed home.

In 1961, they went to Venezuela, California, Montana, and Colorado.

In 1962, they took the train to Colorado Springs, the train to Memphis, the plane to Los Angeles. Mary's diary says: "Each place—speaking engagements, people to see, days and nights filled full."

In August they took a train to a Navigator conference in Colorado Springs. From there they went to a conference at Winona Lake, Indiana, to speak "most every day." In

October, Jack went to Omaha, Nebraska, to speak in the Bible Institute. In November he ministered in Memphis and Dallas. Every year, he went to Dallas in February to lecture at the seminary.

In 1964, they went around the world, visiting relatives and their many missionary friends.

Mary wrote a letter from Singapore that Helen Carlson printed in the "Multnomah Alumni World" publication. An excerpt reads:

When we went down the steps from the plane at the Ethiopian airport (in Addis Ababa), we saw Doris Lacy waving and smiling. We could not keep the tears back for this was a special joy for us. We had really not expected to see her in Addis for our plan had been to go directly to Goba. However, plane schedules had been changed and we could not go until the following day. Not knowing just what would work out, she had come in to have the extra day with us in Addis.

Harry Atkins had also come from Wondo and Diana Elsdon was there. In the afternoon, the three of them took us for a tour of the city. We saw the beautiful new United Nations Building of Africa, the palace, the university and also visited the school for missionary children.

Our stay at the S.I.M. home was a great blessing. John spoke Sunday morning at the English service. Mr. and Mrs. Pete, Ackley of Yakima took their seats with a look of real surprise for they did not know we were there. They have had to leave the Sudan and are waiting for permission to remain in Ethiopia. Dr. and Mrs. Lindsey McClenny are also waiting at Aden.

Our plane for Goba left about noon. . . .

Obviously, the report took many pages as she narrated something about her visit with each missionary.

In 1966, the Mitchells went again to the Orient in June. In Thailand, Jack spoke through an interpreter to a Thai man who said he had never heard the name of Jesus. Jack often spoke later of the impact this had made on his heart.

In October of that year, they flew to Hawaii for ministry and rest.

In 1967, Jack turned in his resignation as pastor of Central Bible Church.

Wherever he went during those years, his ministry brought blessing. And the busy schedule did not end with his leaving the pastorate.

But a poem Mary wrote for her Christmas card one year reveals the character of life and heart that had characterized them both in the midst of unusually heavy schedules in ministering to the Lord's people:

> *"Another Christmas!*
> *And the joy of wishing*
> *For you, a blessed day,*
> *a bright New Year.*
> *With warmth of friendships,*
> *true and satisfying,*
> *The happiness of having*
> *loved ones near.*
>
> *The quietness of heart*
> *in simply trusting*
> *The One who always meets*
> *your every need,*
> *In knowing that*
> *whatever comes tomorrow,*
> *You will go safely*
> *Where His love may lead.*
>
> *M.M.*

Chapter Twenty-Two

Broadcaster

Letters from listeners came daily to the *Know Your Bible Hour* office after Jack Mitchell's death. A sampling of those that arrived include the following:

"I have found Dr. Mitchell the best Bible teacher I ever heard on TV or radio. I loved his warm voice. He is one of the few who always made Jesus the center and not himself. His love for his listeners was real. He even wrote a little letter to me himself—not his secretary. He was the only one who ever did that. I got to loving Dr. Mitchell the first week I heard him. He taught me so much about Jesus, and I knew he was telling the truth. . . ."

* * *

I often listened to Know Your Bible Hour over station KGNW. Dr. Mitchell radiated Christ, his love for his Lord and Saviour and his love for people to know the Word and to know and love the Saviour, too. . . .

* * *

"I do miss hearing Dr. Mitchell's voice on Know Your Bible. Even his voice radiated his love for our Saviour, and I feel my life was enriched through his ministry. . . ."

* * *

It is difficult to explain the sense of loss I experienced when

Dr. Mitchell no longer joined me in my kitchen at 9 a.m. over KBBO for a time of refreshment and challenge. Jesus Christ was always exalted as Dr. Mitchell reverently led us into a deeper appreciation and a greater understanding of our Wonderful Lord and Saviour. . . .

A principle of Jack Mitchell's life was "God rewards faithfulness, not greatness."

Daily, faithfully for many years, the voice of Multnomah School of the Bible came across the airways of the West via the *Know Your Bible Hour* radio broadcast. Since the early 1930s, Jack had had a radio program as part of the ministry of the Portland Bible Classes and then of Central Bible Church. Morning and evening services were broadcast.

When the *Know Your Bible Hour* went on daily with Con Robinson as the announcer and Frank Eaton as soloist, Dr. Mitchell would have marathon recording sessions in which he would tape five or more broadcast messages at a time.

The response was instantaneous, and letters like the following continued to pour in over the years:

The Holy Spirit has used your broadcast to encourage me and to strengthen my faith in times of deep need. More than once the Spirit has awakened me in the early morning to listen to your program and has dealt with my heart from the words which were spoken. For this I thank the Lord! I want to encourage you to keep declaring the Words of Life, because the Lord has, He is, and He will continue to touch hearts through your radio ministry. He always honors His Word!

* * *

I listen to you almost daily over KPDQ-FM and delight in two things in particular: 1) Your unabashed

*love and devotion to our Lord. 2) Your teaching on
the grace of God, especially as you contrast and compare grace with law. . . . Your program is such a blessing to me each day.*

* * *

*My thoughts of you are all prayers turned heavenward.
Never could I express how many times your prayers
and notes of encouragement kept me, as a mother,
going.*

Unlike many radio commentators, Dr. Mitchell took the
time to pray himself for those who wrote him with requests.
He also responded to every letter and signed each letter himself, often adding a personal note.

His secretary, Marian O'Connor, who served him for 12
1/2 years, says, "He was always punctual. He always took his
work seriously. He especially had a real interest in communi-
cating with the radio listeners who would write to him. He
would spend many hours each week acknowledging the gifts
that people had sent into the broadcast.

"He would write a new letter each month that went
specifically to the donors that month, and he would sign each
letter personally. If there were prayer requests or questions
that people had, he would try to acknowledge them at the
bottom of his letter. Every day I would give him more letters
to sign, and he would take time to pray for those requests. I
know he would gather the requests at the end of the week and
bring them home to Mary Mitchell, and they would pray
through those requests together."

He also took the time to see people. He would see students who had questions. He would see radio listeners who
would call for an appointment for counseling. People would
come in off the street and walk into the office and ask if they
could talk to him. And as long as his schedule would allow that,
he would welcome them into the office and pray with them

about whatever problem or situation they had on their mind.

"He always had time for people," Marian says. "It seems that he knew that people were important, and he would make time for them.

"I could never hear what he was saying in his office to people. When someone would go into his office, he would generally close the door; but I could sense when people left that it had been a good meeting, a helpful meeting—certainly a time when they had prayed together."

Jack and Con Robinson spent many hours together, sharing burdens with each other and bringing them before the Lord and praying. Marian says she would see Con leaving the office, and she could sense that a burden he'd been able to share with Dr. Mitchell had been lifted.

Not all of the letters they received were positive and encouraging. Sometimes, people would take their teacher to task, letting him know what they thought and spelling out in what area they thought he was wrong.

"I know his feeling was you cannot force someone to believe what you believe," Marian says. "You know it has to come from the heart. You cannot ever force your faith or opinion on someone else. He handled those letters in different ways. Sometimes he would go into depth and show why he believed what he believed. At other times he would just thank the person for sending the letter and basically say, 'The Lord bless you in your walk with God.' He didn't want to get into an argument that would be futile; but he did want to let the person know that even though there might be some disagreement, 'we can still both walk with God and we can still have fellowship.'"

He was always concerned when he got behind in his correspondence. He wanted to acknowledge every letter that came through the office, and he did the best he could with that.

"I think that was such a unique aspect of his ministry,"

Marian says. "People remember him as a great teacher, as a Bible scholar, as a speaker. What I saw was someone who was concerned about individuals who wrote to him. He wanted to let them know that he received their letter. It wasn't always possible, but he did his best.

"Sometimes I just had to laugh because he was so meticulous about keeping up with his correspondence that I would start taking a letter from him only to find we were thanking people for *their* thank you note. And that's just the way he was. He was so appreciative of their taking time to write him that he wanted to reciprocate."

Most of the time he dictated into a machine he had in his office. Generally, each afternoon after teaching, he would go through his letters and dictate several at a time. But when he began to tire near the end, he would ask Marian to come into the office and take dictation because he didn't have the strength to use the machine.

Marian says: "His last day in the office was spent signing letters to radio listeners. And I know he wasn't feeling well that day, but he came in anyway; and I had a stack of letters on his desk as usual. He signed those letters and it took him quite a while.

"I was wondering how he was doing because it was so quiet in there. I was a little concerned because I knew he hadn't been feeling well. But eventually he came out with the stack of letters all signed. He also had a handwritten letter to some friends he had become acquainted with because of the radio broadcast. They had become close friends so that, in that particular case, he had decided to handwrite a letter to them. But that was his commitment.

"I think many listeners felt they knew him personally because of those letters, those little notes," Marian says. "Every month for some of them there would be a little note that he would write, saying, 'I'm praying for your family.'"

At the heart of the Mitchell radio ministry stood its creed: "We are in Christ Jesus. We have a new life experience in the power of the Spirit. We have been brought into forgiveness of sins and into a wonderful joy through what our Lord Jesus did on the cross. We are no longer under condemnation. We have union and communion with Him, and nothing can separate us from the love of God."

His yearning for sinners to come to the Saviour colored the conclusion of many broadcasts. His yearning for saints to walk in the good of all they have in Christ struck home in many hearts. Listeners wrote such responses as those that follow:

> *What a gentle shepherd Dr. John Mitchell is. Your program is a refreshing for me every weekday morning. Daily, it improves my focus on the Author and Finisher of my faith. What a blessing!*
>
> ** * **
>
> *I personally am greatly blessed by the teaching of Dr. Mitchell. Having been a Christian for about 5-1/2 years now, it is very difficult to find a source of teaching that is sound, consistent and Christ-centered. I spent many years in drug and alcohol addiction before the Lord graciously saved me.*
>
> *Having never attended church before or read the Bible, I fell into all the current false teaching that is going around today.*
>
> *Dr. Mitchell, if you ever wonder if God is using you mightily, rest assured that there is one new believer right here that will be eternally grateful for your love for Jesus and your faithfulness to His Word.*
>
> *It is because of believers like you that believers like me are no longer tossed to and fro by every wind of doctrine. May the Lord Himself express my gratitude—I don't know if I have the words.*

* * *

The number of times I am able to listen to your pro-
gram is no measure of how much I value it. I know of
no one who can make the love of our Saviour as real
and precious as Dr. Mitchell can. I love to hear him
speak. . . . Once you've heard him, you can never for-
get that Jesus loves you.

The letters from listeners brought him great joy, Marian
says.

"How he loved to pray over them and answer them.

"When I think of Dr. Mitchell, I think of a man of
prayer. That seemed prevalent in his letters to people. He
would always bring them back to prayer and to the daily walk
with God. He loved to encourage those who wrote him to
seek the Lord Himself for the answer to their problems. He
loved to call them on to live a godly life 'in daily fellowship
with the Lord Jesus.'

"He would tell them: 'No matter what your problem, no
matter what your situation, no matter what someone else is
doing, be sure you are walking daily with the Lord.' "

Perhaps Dr. Mitchell's principle that "God rewards faithfulness, not greatness" might in his case be modified.

Sometimes, God rewards faithfulness *with* greatness.

Chapter Twenty-Three

Humorist

Uncle John had a wonderful sense of humor, but his stories weren't what one would call "hilarious." Most of his humor was wry. It was personal experiences he'd gone through that he'd chuckle over. His wasn't a raucous humor. He had a good sense of humor.

He would never downgrade another person by getting people to laugh at him or his failures. It was always some experience he'd had that he'd found amusing or one where the joke had been on him. He was always cute.

He had some ridiculous stories he loved to tell and, of course, we all laughed with him.

—Norm Cook

If Jack Mitchell had a group of people he liked to tease and bring down from their high horse, it was members of the clergy. He knew the temptations and weaknesses of his brethren, and he never let them get away without a nudge in the ribs.

Norm Cook tells about a leading Bible teacher and evangelist living in Hong Kong, who raised himself up as a self-appointed bishop over his fellow pastors. When Norm set up pastors' conferences on the island of Taiwan, this gentlemen would insist that he should eat in his room, away from the other men. Then he would come onto the platform and do his speaking.

The year Dr. Mitchell spoke at that conference, he recognized the problem and insisted that the brother come down and eat at the round table with six or eight of the other men. They would all dip in the same bowl and eat the same food.

The elder insisted that he should stay in his room.

Dr. Mitchell insisted that he should come and be sociable.

"Uncle John won that one and he laughed for a long time over how he had put one over on his Chinese brother."

Dr. Mitchell developed his own dialect in Chinese and impressed many people with his fluency. Norm tells how he even used it on the Chinese themselves.

He loved the Chinese people and it frustrated him that he couldn't speak the language. So he developed a sort of Chinese doubletalk. He had all the phrases and tones and things like that, but it didn't make any sense. He had learned a few words each of Mandarin and Cantonese that he could pronounce, and he'd throw them all together. It sounded very good, very authentic.

He really had the pastors mystified when he started joking with them and going off into his Chinese act. They would come to me so seriously and say, "We know he's speaking Chinese, but we don't know what dialect."

He called it Haka.

It was so funny!

He reverted to it many times in later years when he was embarrassed and didn't know what to say or when conversation lagged and needed a little spicing up.

It always brought laughs.

One of Dr. Mitchell's very favorite stories was over the dilemma he found himself in at a banquet the Chinese pastors put on for him. This is the way he would tell it:

During the meal, someone brought a whole fish and put it on the table in a grand fashion. By custom, the head of the fish was to go to the honored guest.

I was the honored guest.

So one of the Chinese men, David Liao, rose and with great ceremony brought me the head of the fish and put it on my plate.

He announced, "In Chinese, we honor the elder and so you must receive the head of the fish."

He had put the token of esteem on the plate of a man who, though he had no taste at all for the heads of raw fish, in no way wished to offend his brethren.

You can believe I said a quick prayer.

Then I rose with great solemnity to my feet and lifted the plate of fishhead into the air.

"In the Scriptures, the Apostle has given us an admonition—that in honor we are to prefer one another," I said.

And with that I put the fish with much ceremony on David Liao's plate!

Norm Cook took Jack bowling once.

We were bowling away and then he missed. The ball went into the gutter and he said, "You just sit down. Sit down."

And he kept throwing three or four or five balls until he started getting the balls in the middle of the alley.

And then he said, "Now you go ahead and bowl."

He had made a fun thing out of that and we laughed together.

Not everybody recognized Dr. Mitchell's humor for what it really was. Spencer Durr recalls:

We had him as a speaker in family camp when we were in the ministry in Montana. We were crowded out with people and had to serve food in lines rather than family style as we usually did.

When Dr. Mitchell got up to the servers and saw the slab of beef that was put on his plate, he said, "What are you giving me all that fat for? I can't eat fat!"

Of course, I heard the ring of laughter in his voice; but evidently nobody else did.

I never could get the cooks to even go to chapel after that.

Perhaps the story he is most noted for, the one he told over and over again to laughing audiences of students and adults, was his famous "candle story." It concerned a family that had difficulty extinguishing a candle because each member talked out of a different side of his mouth.

The daughter talked out of the left side of her mouth. The son-in-law talked out of the right side of his mouth. The mother talked across a retracted chin and the father—sans an upper plate—talked with a protruding chin. Dr. Mitchell loved to tell the story, holding a candle and changing his mouth appropriately for each character.

He told this version to the Grad class of 1983:

There was a dear man and woman who ran a little grocery store. Their daughter used to live with them, and she used to wait on the trade.

But she felt that she couldn't go with any young man because (mouth left) she talked this way.

(Mouth normal) And one day a young man came in and he said, (mouth to the right) "I want a package of cigarettes."

(Mouth left) "Who are you making fun of?"

(Mouth right) "I'm not making fun of you."

(Mouth left) "Yes, you are."

(Mouth right) "No, I'm not."

(Mouth left) "Yes, you are."

(Mouth left, high falsetto) "Oh, Ma!"

(Chin in under upper teeth) "What's the matter now?"

(Mouth left) "Well, I've got this man that's making fun of me."

(Mouth right) "I tell you I'm not making fun of you."

(Mouth left) "Yes, you are."

(Mouth right) "No, I'm not."

(Chin in) "*Well, now, daughter, maybe the boy can't help it.*"

(Mouth normal) You see, she couldn't get a fellow

(Mouth left) because she talked this way.

(Mouth normal) And he couldn't get a girl (mouth right) because he talked this way.

(Mouth normal) So they finally got it all together and went the way of all flesh and got married.

And, because of the fact that they were like that, they were living with—you see, the parents were kind of old—and so the young couple came in and stayed upstairs, too—in the apartment upstairs.

And one night while they were getting ready for bed, the lights went out.

(Mouth left) And she said, "Honey?"

(Mouth right) And he said, "Yes, dear."

(Mouth left) "Hadn't you better light the candle?"

(Mouth right) "Give it to me."

(Mouth normal) So he took the matches and took the candle and lit the candle as you see. *(Mitchell lit a candle.)* And they talked together about different things of the day, and it was time now to go to bed.

(Mouth right) And he said, "Honey?"

(Mouth left) "Yes, dear."

(Mouth right) "I think you better blow the candle out."

(Mouth normal) So she took the candle. *(Dr. Mitchell blew twice out of the left side of his mouth, paused, and blew again.)* Nothing happened.

(Mouth right) "Give it to me."

(Mouth normal) He took the candle. *(Dr. Mitchell blew twice out of the right side of his mouth, paused, and blew again.)*

(Mouth right) "I think you better call your mother in."

(Mouth left, falsetto) "Mother!"

(Chin in) "What's the matter now?"

(Mouth left) "I can't blow the candle out."

(Mouth right) "Neither can I."

(Chin in) "Let me try."

(Mouth normal) So she took the candle. (Dr. Mitchell sucked in his lower lip and blew down twice, paused, and blew again.)

(Chin in) "I think you better call your father in."

(Mouth left, falsetto) "Father!"

(Jaw protruding) "WHAT'S THE MATTER NOW?!"

(Chin in) "Well, daughter can't blow the candle out."

(Mouth right) "Neither can I," the boy said.

(Chin in) "Neither can I," the mother said.

(Jaw protruding) "Well, give it to me."

(Mouth normal) And the old man took the candle.

(Dr. Mitchell thrust out his lower lip and blew up twice, paused and blew again.)

(Jaw protruding) "Daughter!"

(Mouth left) "Yes, Dad."

(Jaw protruding) "Stand at the window and look out there for help."

(Mouth normal) So she went to the window. And believe it or not, there was a graduate of the Multnomer School of the Bible going down the street.

(Mouth left) "Oh, boy! Oh, boy! Come up here."

(Mouth normal) The boy came up.

(Mouth left) "You see that candle?"

(Mouth normal) "Yes, ma'am."

(Mouth left) "Well, I can't blow it out."

(Mouth right) "And I can't blow it out."

(Chin in) "And I can't blow it out."

(Jaw protruding) "And I can't blow it out."

(Mouth left) "Boy, you blow it out."

(Mouth normal) So the boy picked the candle up. He was a graduate of Multnomer. He wet his fingers, and he put it out.

People clamored for that story everywhere he went. It

helped break the ice for him when he spoke at conferences and camps. It helped show the world that he was, after all, human and did love fun.

Dr. Willard Aldrich believes that the all-time success of the candle story was at the Wecks's home.

It was a trustee meeting, with a few faculty thrown in, in the early days of the school when Mr. Wecks Sr. lived in town.

Mr. George Kehoe was alive then and he and Jim Braga were at the party. And both of them had a great sense of humor. When they got tickled—well, they both got to rolling with laughter over the candle story as Dr. Mitchell was telling it. Dr. Mitchell couldn't go on—he got to laughing so hard, laughing at them. We all were laughing.

It was wonderful.

Chapter Twenty-Four

Man of Prayer

Dr. Mitchell's last public prayer was given when he opened his Grad class with this prayer on March 8, 1990:

Father, how faithful You've been through these many, many years. There's one thing we can be sure about, and that is that You will always be faithful. You will always love us, and Your mercies are new every day. Thank You again.

We glorify You.

We praise You.

We worship You this morning.

For You are the One who is worthy of all our worship and praise and thanksgiving.

We pray Your blessing upon each fellow and girl in the class today, and upon the whole school. Lord, may Your blessing be upon this school and its ministries as the testimony goes out to different parts of the world—that it would be in the power and blessing and joy of the Spirit of God.

I pray Your blessing now upon the class as we wait before You. May it not be just another class, not just another class to attend and hear something about Your Word. But may it be a time of really rejoicing in Your presence.

Have our minds and our hearts open to the One who's

altogether lovely, that we may indeed be in love with Him.
Grant this we pray, in Jesus' blessed name. Amen.

The window into a man's character—and soul—opens widest when he prays. If he is familiar with the Person of God, with the Word of God, with Christian living in frailty and strength, then the depth and breadth of that familiarity will show best when he prays.

Jack Mitchell brought into each prayer nearly a lifetime of fellowshiping with God and of pouring over His Word.

Drop in on him in his office and he would pray with you before he let you go. His prayer would be like this:

Our Father, as we bow before You this morning again, we thank You for our fellowship together. We thank You for the wonderful, wonderful fact that we are Your children, the objects of Your love, affection and devotion.

We can't get away from it, Lord, the wonder of it all. Why should we be so favored to become Your channels of blessing to people, to communicate the precious Word to men and women everywhere. Thank You for the grace that You manifested, Your patience and longsuffering with us.

We just want to glorify You these days.

And we think of these precious young people, many of whose lives have been changed and transformed while they've been here at the school. We pray, as they go out, You'll get them to do the job You want done, that they might be channels of blessing wherever they go.

Grant at least to some of them the opportunity, the joy of giving the Gospel where they haven't heard it for years, to see lives transformed. We just plead with Thee for this.

Take out of our hearts, out of my heart and the hearts of the faculty and staff—all of our hearts—any coldness and indifference for men and women who are out of Christ.

We remind ourselves that You were accused of being the friend of publicans and sinners. Lord, may we never lose that passion to see men and women saved and believers built up in Christ so that they in turn may become channels to their friends, to their neighbors.

Thank You again for another year of blessing. And, Father, we pray that You will undertake for us especially in the material needs of the school these days. We pray that You'll undertake and put it upon the hearts of Your people to give.

Then he would pray for you. And then he would continue.

Thank You for this fellowship together. Lord, how wonderful to know that we are one in Christ, and we pray that we shall ever be in that place where You'll find us usable.

Thank You again for these few moments together in Jesus' blessed Name. Amen.

And you would go out of his office, walking on air.

* * *

He preached a series on Romans 8 several years ago and concluded each sermon in prayer. Those prayers, recorded at the time, reveal the man and show the depth of his knowledge of God.

Through the years, he had chosen the better part. Like Mary of Bethany, he had sat at the feet of the Lord Jesus, the Master Intercessor, and he had learned to pray.

Excerpts from his prayer following his sermon on Romans 8:1-3:

Our Father, as we bow before Thee this morning, we thank Thee for the marvelous provision made whereby we can not only rejoice in a Saviour, who has pardoned us and forgiven us, but a Saviour who lives. How we rejoice that the law of the spirit of life in Christ Jesus hath set us free, once for all forever, from the law of sin and the law of death.

We are new creatures in Christ. We belong to Him. We are accepted in the Beloved One, indwelt by His Spirit that we may go forth in this world to show something of the character, something of the beauty, something of the sweetness and love and grace of our Saviour to men and women.

Exerpts from his prayer following his sermon on Romans 8:12-17:

Our precious Father, as we bow before Thee this morning, somehow words seem to fail us in presenting this amazing, amazing fact that there is a family being built up by the Spirit of God, made up of redeemed sinners, justified by Him, declared to be the sons of God, able to come into Thy presence with that peace and yet with that wonderful confidence and say "Abba, Father."

Oh, Lord, in some way make these things real to us by the Spirit.

Make us go forth this day with a conscious realization we are the sons of One who is God. And not only may we revel in that marvelous grace and relationship and union but also recognize the privilege, the high privilege and honor of being Thy representatives with the responsibility of bringing to others the wonderful story of redeeming grace.

Oh, to realize that we are no longer under the control of sin or the flesh and are delivered from the powers of hell and emancipated and redeemed and reconciled and fitted for eternal glory.

Father, this morning make Thyself real to our hearts that our lives may show forth Thy praise and Thy glory.

Excerpts from his prayer following a sermon on Romans 8:18-25:

Our Father, as we bow before Thee this morning, we find words are inadequate to express what is in our hearts—the glory, the majesty, the wonder of it all—that we redeemed sinners, children of God, have been left in the world to represent Thee.

This same One who has declared that we shall be made just like Him. Oh, Lord, we plead with Thee this morning, for the Spirit of God to take His rightful place in our hearts, in our lives, in our minds, in all that we are.

Lord, teach us to live in view of the glory, to remember that the hope of this body is immortality, that we shall be glorified together with Him.

Excerpts from his prayer following his sermon on Romans 8:26-27:

Father, we just thank Thee again this morning for the Spirit of God who indwells us, who has come to lead us and to guide us into all truth. And we would confess, dear Lord, humbly confess that these minds, these finite minds of ours can't begin to delve into the wonder and glory of Thy purpose. To think that You've picked us up and redeemed us and justified us and brought us into Your family, united us with Your Son, given us a wonderful hope and then the Spirit of God to help our infirmities. And You guarantee that that hope will be realized, that that hope will be consumated.

How we thank Thee because You will never be satisfied until every, every believer in Christ—the weak as well as the strong—shall stand in Thy presence, conformed to the image of Jesus Christ.

If it please Thee, may some of us know something of this fellowship of intercession, when the purpose and call of God will get a hold of our hearts and we will cooperate with the Spirit of God that others might come to know Thee whom to know is life eternal.

Excerpts from his prayer following his sermon on Romans 8:28:

Dear Lord, we may fail Thee, but You will never fail us. Oh, make us to appreciate it. Make us to live for Thee. May the Spirit of God, who helpeth our infirmities, lay hold of us more than ever before. May we go forth as living testimonies of the grace of God; and, as we separate this morning, may Thy wonderful love and may Thine infinite mercy and that wonderful grace that redeems be the portion of each one of us.

Until we see Him face to face. Amen.

As Dr. Mitchell concluded one of his final sermons at Central Bible Church on August 13, 1989, he led up to his closing prayer with words heralding his own expectation of joy and glory; and, as always, he expressed his deep yearning that those who have not yet trusted Him will "come to know and love the Saviour."

What I'm trying to get to your heart this morning is that we have a Saviour who cares for you and He cares for me. And He's made provision that not only shall we have a wonderful place in Glory, but I believe we're going to have the joy of being with Him in His kingdom and have dominion over the works of His hands. I believe the Eighth Psalm is yet to be fulfilled. I believe the promise to Adam and Eve is still yet to be fulfilled. He's going to do it just as He purposed—that man shall have dominion.

And we say to ourselves, "Oh, boy! I'd like to go to Glory."

I know that's very nice, but I'm still down here. That's the problem. I'm not in glory yet. I'm down here with my frailty and my failures and my weaknesses; but the throne of grace is always open and on that throne is a Man, the Man Christ Jesus.

I come back again. I can't get over the fact that there's a Man at God's right hand who cares for me, who cares for you.

I think I've said enough.

I couldn't help but think this morning when I was meditating upon this which we sang last Sunday:

Holy, Holy is what the angels sing
And I am going to help them make
The courts of heaven ring
But when I sing redemption's story,
They will fold their wings,
For angels never knew the joy
That our salvation brings.
Hallelujah! What a Saviour.
Don't you love Him?
(Faint response)
That's pretty weak. Do you love Him?
(Loud response)

All right, then, walk before Him, obey Him, enjoy Him, love Him, worship Him, praise Him.

Father, it's hard to find words to express the marvel of this relationship that Your purpose for the earth is yet to be fulfilled and that You've redeemed a people to have that fellowship, to fulfill that purpose.

Thank You for a Saviour who understands, touched with the feeling of our infirmities and praying for us, representing us, our Anchor, our Hope, our Forerunner, our Refuge, our Advocate. All that I need to stand before You is in my precious Saviour.

Father, may we—as a people and as individual members of the Body of Christ—walk in the intimacy of Your fellowship, in obedience to Your Word; and, while we are still here, may each one of us have a testimony that will attract others to the Saviour—that they might know You whom to know is life eternal.

And, Father, should there be any who have never come into this relationship with the Saviour, we pray that even today they will come to know and love the Saviour and become a member of the family of God with an inheritance that is incorruptible and undefiled—that never fades away, reserved in heaven for us who are kept by the power of God through faith unto a salvation yet to be revealed.

And may we as Your people fall in love with You and become usable in the Hands of the Spirit of God in reaching our generation while it is still called today—for the night cometh when no man can work.

Bless these dear people, O Lord Jesus. Bless everyone of these men and women. Bless these precious young people. Make us to be channels of blessing to our generation—we pray in Jesus' blessed Name.

Amen.

Chapter Twenty-five

Co-Worker

I never had the feeling that he was living a life that contradicted what he taught and what he believed in. And I say that because of the way he treated people and the way he treated me.

I enjoyed the way he signed his letters when he would be away for most of the summer. He would always keep in touch, making sure that I had the materials to keep the ministry going as far as letters from him were concerned.

His letters were always friendly and warm, sending greetings to my husband and me, to Con Robinson and his wife. And then he would sign his letters to me: "Your co-worker in Christ."

That always spoke to me that that was how he saw the radio ministry. We were co-workers together. We were a team. We were not one over the other; but we were equally important, doing that part of the ministry that each person could handle.

For him, it was being the radio Bible teacher, corresponding with people. And for me it was preparing the letters for him to sign and helping him in any other way.

He saw it as being co-workers together.

—Marian O'Connor
Secretary

There was no disputing it. Multnomah was Mitchell country. He, as founder and chairman of the Board, could go where he liked, when he liked, with whom he liked, and virtually do what he liked. Wherever he went it was "Church of the Open Door" because glory filled his soul and working people all around campus loved to have him come into their offices and share it with them. He didn't do it to win any popularity contest. He really loved people and wanted to communicate God's love to them. Co-workers always greeted him with welcome smiles, and he always responded with humor and encouragement.

He knew almost everybody. Some of them like Helen Carlson, Vivian Kepler, and Hazel Oliver had been with him since 1936 when the school first began.

Faculty and staff retention at Multnomah was high. The continuity and stability that that afforded gave character to the school. Graduates could return years later and find the same teachers and secretaries and librarians and cooks that had been there when they were students. A family spirit blended people together. Faculty had a voice in managing school affairs. Mutual high esteem and common spiritual interests made happy co-workers of all the employees—faculty, staff and administration.

And, at the heart of it all, was John G. Mitchell.

His co-workers say it best:

Multnomah School of the Bible owes its existence to Dr. Mitchell. He was able to gather a team together that stayed with him and felt very, very happy in working with him. . . . He was not the kind of a person who was dominating and insisting that his way be done at school. His way seemed to be more that he found the kinds of people in whom he had confidence and let them run with it. And it was very pleasing to work with him because of this.

He could have been a headliner in the Christian world if he wanted to be; (but he chose) to stay where God had put him, to be faithful and to do a good job. It means that we have a Bible school now that is second to none.

It is hard to find an enemy of Dr. Jack. He was a man with no guile. He was a man who wanted the other person to succeed and who prayed that that person would succeed. He had a good word for everybody. He had a fantastic mind. It was so retentive that the Lord was exploited in his ministry.

He was a challenge to me.

—*Ed Goodrick*
MSB Professor of Greek

I came on the faculty in 1955, and it was a thrill to get to join the work that Dr. Mitchell had founded. I felt it a tremendous privilege. . . . He cared about the people who worked here. He stopped by to talk from time to time. He had a busy schedule and being an older man he didn't have the strength of youth in his later days. But he took time out to talk to those of us who worked here.

One of the girls in my office got married and all during her romance he would stop and say, "Well, how is my Miriam today?" And when she was married, he was almost as thrilled as she. He cared about the personal lives of us who are here.

—*Joyce L. Kehoe, Registrar*
Director of Admissions

My fellowship with the school was made very sweet because of Dr. Mitchell's presence. We as a school had difficulties down through the years, but there was no difficulty that wasn't made sweet and pleasant by Dr. Mitchell. He really served as a sweetener in the midst of all kinds of trials and difficulties, and I really thank the Lord for the opportunity of working under and with Dr. Mitchell and his wife.

—*Roger D. Congdon*
Professor of Bible

I was his first secretary. It was the first time he had let anyone else help him in any way with his personal mail. As I typed his letters for him, I felt I was sitting at the feet of a master teacher.

I thought of him as kind of a second father. He was always considerate, always very thoughtful. The last day I worked for him—I was leaving to get married—he wept out of concern and love. He told Chuck he better be good to me or he would beat him with a shillelagh.

—Barbara Lidbeck Darland
Multnomah Professor

The secret of his power was that he lived in the Word and the Word of God lived in him. When he spoke, it was the Holy Spirit speaking through him and that word became living. I remember him saying over and over how much time he spent in the Word of God himself.

His life showed how the grace of God can reach a man. . . . and how through his study of the Word, his love for the Lord and his desire to serve the Lord, the Lord blessed his ministry.

—James Braga
Professor of Bible

He did not consider himself a great man, and I suppose he wasn't by worldly standards. His greatness lay in his walk with the Lord and the blessing God gave to his ministry.

He always seemed to want to illustrate the fact that he was just clay like other men. And, in telling about the "greats" of bygone days with whom he had enjoyed acquaintance and fellowship, he would say, after telling about their wonderful ministry, "But they were just men."

—Charlotte Lawrence
Faculty wife

Bill Wecks, a close associate of Dr. Mitchell's, spoke of him at the memorial service:

It is very difficult in a very brief time to speak of all that Dr. Mitchell meant to us, but there's a part of a verse that fits him very well. You remember II Corinthians 5:14 where the Apostle Paul says the love of Christ constrains us. Now that word "constrain" does not mean "restrain." It means—in one of the translations—"compels."

I like the word. It "motivates" us. To me, this speaks of Dr. Mitchell. The love of Christ certainly motivated the great Apostle Paul, and I'm sure that it motivated Dr. Mitchell, too. He always gave evidence in all the times I met with him that he knew what the love of Christ was. And he loved Christ for His love for him.

I remember the rainy day when my father and he and I walked in the woods out there in Trout Creek. They were going to decide where that first building should be for the camp. The woods were wet and he was wet and my dad was wet, but they decided. And it was all for just one reason, and that is that they would reach boys and girls with the Saviour.

He had a tremendous love for the Saviour.

In fact, just recently, Dr. Joe Aldrich and Johnny Van Diest and I planned to get together to talk about the ministry of Trout Creek Camp. Dr. Joe brought Dr. Mitchell along for that luncheon. His hearing I'm sure was bad, and I don't think he heard too much of what we were talking about.

But, finally, Johnny asked, "Dr. Mitchell, do you have any thoughts on the camp?"

And right away he acted like he was a 20-year-old and very, very enthused about the idea.

"Why don't you start some Bible classes all over Portland. Teach the children about the Word of God, and then send them out to camp," he said. "And, when you get them out to camp, then you can show them what the love of Christ is."

This was very, very typical of him. But his burden was not by any means limited to children. His heart went out to people of any age.

Not too long ago, he and I took a number of funerals together. He would speak at the main service, and I would take the graveside because he was getting a little bit shaky as he was walking. But he himself took one particular graveside service because it was for a lady who had accepted the Lord in the Sunnyside Congregational Church in 1929 under his ministry.

That day, he almost lost his balance.

He said, "Bill, come here and you hold me up." And I held him up as he continued the message. It didn't bother him one bit. He really gave it to them. It was tremendous.

And then I went to his house one time because we were going to have a funeral service together and I wanted to be sure everything was in order. After we had talked about it a little bit, he said, "You know, I've been thinking of something here lately."

And for about 10 minutes, he expounded some truth that was really tremendous. I wish I had had a tape recorder and could give it to you. It was just a thrilling truth. And he expounded that as if he had an audience of a thousand, but he had just one in the audience and that was me.

He was so excited about some of these truths. The thing that struck me as he got up into his 90s was he never stopped learning new truths. It just thrilled him when he saw something that he had never seen before in Scripture. And it thrilled him to see someone come to the Lord and then to see that person grow in the knowledge of the Lord.

The other night, after Dr. Mitchell had passed away in the morning, my wife and I began to name some people we thought were in glory now that he knew. Many of them are there because he led them there.

You know, that's a tremendous thing and it certainly should be a motivation to all of us as we think of this because when he went to Heaven, I'll guarantee there were many—probably thousands—there that had been under his ministry. And what a joy that would be for him!

You know, some day we're going to be there, too. And we need to think of these things.

Certainly, the Homegoing of Dr. Mitchell should inspire us to be more faithful and devoted to the Lord than ever before.

The director of Multnomah's library saw another side of John G. Mitchell:

Shortly after I came to Multnomah, Dr. Mitchell came to my office and said, "What are you reading?"

I held up "Christianity Today."

He replied, "I don't mean that. I don't mean your Bible either."

I was puzzled.

But he continued, "Jim, you're like me. You no longer can golf, jog or go on long walks. You need to do recreational reading. Now what are you reading to relax your mind?"

He proceeded to tell me that he owned the complete Zane Gray collection. He said, "Have you read any Zane Gray books?"

I replied, "Yes, many years ago."

"Well," he said, "you should get The Riders of the Purple Sage.*"*

I couldn't believe what I was hearing. The holy, godly Dr. Mitchell was saying it was okay to read Westerns. I had been led to believe it was somewhat less than spiritual to waste time on such material. But since it didn't hinder Dr. Mitchell, I figured it would be worth a try. Besides, I thought he would probably be asking me if I got the book and was reading it. (And he did a few days later.)

I did enjoy the book and some other Zane Gray books as well as all of the paperbacks of Louis L'Amour.

—James Scott
Librarian

Dorothy Randal, widow of former MSB librarian Lewis Randal, wrote Mary Mitchell a note after the funeral:

His love and dedication to the Lord and his loving ministry through the years influenced many. Because he was God's instrument, others have gone all over the world, teaching God's Word learned at Multnomah.

God's love was manifested through his life as well as through his teaching and both were a blessing to me.

When I was helping Lewis in the old library and Dr. Mitchell would occasionally come in, his love and sense of humor lightened the day for all of us.

Helen Carlson attended Multnomah as a member of the first class. After her graduation in 1939, she stayed on as a teacher of missions and as alumni secretary. She said of him:

He grew and matured down through the years. He always impressed me as a tremendous teacher but also as one who had a real love for the Lord and a compassionate love for the Word. . . . He was a man who lived what he talked and he made the Scriptures live for us. He certainly had a pastor's heart, a shepherd's heart. He had a constant desire to reach others with no sense of competition in the Lord's work. That isn't true of many of our "great" men. He supported anything that was really of the Lord and was very pleased when other people were successful.

Dr. Mitchell, at a Multnomah School of the Bible faculty retreat, was asked what advice he would give to his co-workers there at the school. These are his words:

The one thing that is on my heart is that not only shall we teach the Word of God academically, but I'd like the Truth to get a hold of every one of our kids. I can only impart what's living in me.

I think God raised up Multnomah School of the Bible to do a specific job—to saturate young people with the Word of God and to help them have a personal, real relationship with the Saviour.

I think we need to stress more and more that life can only come through relationship. Unless I'm related to a Person, I can't have life. If I have that life, I will manifest it in what I say, in what I do, in and by my very actions. And I believe that we've got a tremendous responsibility to do this.

I've often thought—each year we wonder how many students will God give us—and I always think to myself, "Well, Mitchell, how many can God trust you with."

We're taking young lives who are going to leave us in three, four years, one year as the case may be. They're scattered all over the world. What are they going to present to our present generation? They can only present what lives in them.

And I think we as a faculty have a tremendous responsibility to so walk before God in the intimacy of His fellowship that unconsciously we will display something of the sweetness and the beauty and the love of our Saviour.

I think in our pastorates today we need men in the pulpit who won't use a club on God's people but will manifest that tenderness and compassion of our Saviour which He had for men and women. Always remember, never one soul ever came to Christ with a need but that Christ met that need.

Whatever aspect of the ministry we may have at Multnomah, I think all of us ought to be sold on the one thing that "If it's Bible you want, you want Multnomah." But we must saturate our own hearts and minds and lives with the Word of God so that it will be imparted by the Spirit of God as a living thing in the lives of these precious fellows and girls.

That's what keeps me going when I see these kids. I yearn for them that in some way every one will be gifted—not to try to imitate somebody else. You can't imitate spiritual gifts.

But I really believe that verse in I Cor. 12:27—you know it? (Pause)

Oh, you don't read your Bibles! (Laughter)

"We are members one of another and members in particular." Every student and every believer is very particular to God and has a special place to function in the Body of Christ. It's not for me to tell a student where he shall go or what he shall do. He

must be in touch with the Saviour and go where God wants him.

It would be nice if some of them were to have a big church, a big organization. But God is not interested in that. He's interested in them as usable men and women. And I believe that, as we walk before God, He will use them. I think at the judgment seat of Christ we're going to see some surprises. Some little folk we never knew, way off in some old stick, will be rewarded more than some of these fellows that have got big churches and big organizations.

God rewards faithfulness to Him personally. And I repeat it, we are very particular to God. You are. I am. Nobody can take my place. Nobody can take your place. But I am responsible to the Saviour that I'll be a vessel usable in His hands for reaching men and women for Christ and for encouraging God's people— most of whom are babes, not having been taught the Scriptures.

I wish you could read the notes I get from my radio audience. It would break your heart sometimes. They're starved. They don't know where to turn. We need to be men and women today, especially in the school, who will stand for the Word of God and for the glories of our Saviour. We need to be men and women usable in His hands for bringing these fellows and girls into a real relationship and fellowship with the Saviour.

That's the burden of my heart.

If I wanted to be remembered—which I don't—but if I was, I would say that I was a man that gave myself to the Word of God, to the exaltation of the Person of our Saviour.

That's the only ambition I've got, the only ambition I've had.

Chapter Twenty-Six

Teacher

John G. Mitchell in class:

Let's begin at verse 20.

You all got it?

Let me see your Bibles. Come on. Lift them up.

Got to be opened up. Are they all open?

Some of you didn't bring your Bibles.

Hunh?

Who didn't bring their Bible? Put your hands up.

All right. Put your Bibles up. Let me see.

Come on. Haul them out from under the seat there. You're sitting on them.

Put them up!

Some of you haven't got your Bible up yet. Come on.

Come on, fella, put your Bible up. That's it.

Colossians chapter one. Anybody—

Wait a bit! Keep them up. Let me see who else is holding out on me.

Hey, you fella, fair-haired boy. Where's yours? Is yours up? (Laughter)

Don't you try and cover him up now!

I n those day there were giants in the earth.

Chief among them, particularly among those who rode the rostrum in classrooms worldwide, stood John G. Mitchell, master-teacher.

No better description of his teaching and no better tribute can come to such a man than can come from students who sat before him through the years:

My life was incredibly impacted by Dr. Mitchell's life and ministry. His love for the Lord, the Word, the students, and life were so obvious and so contagious. My life will never be the same after knowing such a great and godly man.

—Bill Thomas, '88

I remember Dr. Mitchell's Spiritual Life classes. I just gobbled it up, you know. I would just sit there. I was really challenged. I wanted to memorize Scripture and be able to quote verses like he did and support what I believed. And I was really challenged, like never in my life, to really dig into the Scriptures and really study and really know what the Scriptures taught and what I believe.

My first two years of Multnomah were a mountaintop experience of digging into the Word.

—Karen Diggins Wheaton, '70

Dr. Mitchell spoke at Word of Life college in New York. Jack Wyrtzen, its founder and director, retained vivid memories of that occasion:

I can still hear him turning to our 350 students here at Word of Life Bible Institute and teaching us his songs with his beautiful brogue, and how we still rejoice when we can hear his voice: "Cheer up ye saints of God, there's nothing to worry aboot. Nothing to make you feel afraid, nothing to make you doot."

I remember one of our young people—one of our students—

asking, "Dr. Mitchell, what method do you use to memorize Scripture."

"Ah," he said, "I've never tried to memorize Scripture. I just pray over them and read them over and over and over again until they become part of me and then I know the Scriptures."

Evangelist Luis Palau took Multnomah's grad course before embarking on his world-wide ministry. He has many memories of Dr. John G. Mitchell:

I thank God for the youthful, contagious enthusiasm that he always showed us in and outside the classroom.

I was impressed with the amazing memory he had, particularly for Holy Scripture. I'll never forget in class when he would say, "Oh, yes, it's in the book of Joel. It's on the right-hand page, at the top of the page, about the fourth line down on the right-hand side." I always was impressed by this, and I know that it stirred me to love Scripture and to memorize the Word of God.

He always remembered so vividly the details of his visit with us in Mexico City. We were missionaries there and he was so kind to our children and all of us, and he never forgot it.

The thing I thank God most for is his Bible studies. I have used his notes on Romans to preach across the Spanish-speaking world on radio and television. They were invaluable to me in preparing those messages.

But I'll never forget coming to class and suddenly, instead of opening up the Bible study with a passage of Scripture, he would start singing, "There is a Fountain Filled with Blood Drawn From Immanuel's Veins." Every time I sing that song, whether I am in Latin America or Europe or anywhere in the world, I think of Dr. Mitchell and his love for Jesus Christ and the blood of Christ that cleanses us from all sin.

Do I have anything to say about Dr. Mitchell that is negative? I certainly do. I will never forget it. He was the only one who ever gave me a "C" at Multnomah School of the Bible. And it was in his class on Hebrews. Now, how did it happen? It was my fault, was it?

All right, it's true. I was courting Pat, who later became my wife. But after a perspective of half a lifetime, I am glad he gave me a "C" in Hebrews. He got his "C," and I got my wife; and in the perspective of history, I'm glad to have my wife.

Just one last thing. When Dr. Mitchell realized that I would become an evangelist, one day he said to me in public—although he said it to the whole class, but he addressed me, "There are three things you better watch, Luis—and all of you who want to be evangelists. First, evangelists run the risk of pride. Secondly, watch out for the love of money. And thirdly, watch out for sexual temptation."

How I thank Dr. Mitchell for all the teaching, the advice, the humor, the joy, the memory, and the singing.

Lorne Sanny, who worked at the right hand of Dawson Trotman until he himself took over direction of The Navigators, had vivid recollections of Dr. Mitchell's Bible classes for the many young men and women in his organization:

Dr. Jack spoke from a well that never ran dry.

As a young man with the Navigators, I remember sitting and listening to him expound the Word to a group of sailors. After an hour and a half, Dr. Jack would stop and say, "Have you had enough or do you want more?"

Members of the audience would yell, "More! More!"

Dr. Jack would smile and say, "Well, okay."

He loved it, and so did we.

Early on, I learned never to sit in the front row when he was speaking. You were very likely to be embarrassed by a question you couldn't answer and then hear the admonition, "Why don't you read your Bible!"

He said one of his purposes was to give us a hunger for the Word. And he did that like no other.

Dr. Jack was a remarkable human being, deeply dedicated

*to Jesus Christ and the Word of God. He set a standard for us
that was scriptural and still only rarely equaled.*

*I know he left his mark on me and on many, many
Navigators—a mark that can never be erased.*

Charles R. Swindoll has vivid memories of Jack
Mitchell:

"My first face-to-face connection with Dr. Mitchell
came when I was a student at Dallas Theological Seminary in
the fall of 1959. He was a visiting Bible lecturer. In fact, he
returned for other series of lectures more than once before I
graduated four years later.

"I was so taken by his 'scriptural saturation' (I don't
know of a better way to put it) that I told my wife Cynthia
that she must attend the evening meetings in which he spoke
to the general public. She and I never missed from then on.
We shall forever remember his frequent exhortation to 'read
ya Bible!'

"We had never heard such a Bible teacher as Dr.
Mitchell . . . and we had heard many in our lives. His delivery
was altogether unique—who will ever forget that Scottish
accent?—his grasp of the written Word was incredibly com-
prehensive, his ability to trace various themes through the
Bible was mind-boggling, and his devoted love for the Saviour
was contagious.

"I shall never forget how he often began his lectures with
a gracious but firm reproof, concerned that we at the seminary
might be getting an intellectual understanding of God's Word
but failing to have our hearts touched by the truth we were
studying. His concern for our spiritual welfare melted me.

"In the years that followed it was my privilege to hear
Dr. Mitchell on numerous occasions—in churches, at conference centers, at schools and other seminary settings. Each
time I loved the Lord more after he spoke than I did before.

Being in his presence was nothing short of being near one of the most Christlike men I'd ever known.

"I recall one particular occasion when Cynthia was unsettled on a rather complicated subject. She and I had been taught a certain interpretation by one well-known Bible teacher and then a different interpretation by another respected scholar. Our confusion only intensified as we went to the Scriptures on our own and came to yet another conclusion.

"At that time, Dr. Mitchell happened to be speaking nearby, which gave us the opportunity to attend the meeting and talk with him alone afterwards. With keen perception and in a quiet, gracious manner, he patiently listened to our dilemma and then explained the issue as he understood it (quoting numerous passages of Scripture in the process). Ultimately, he helped us both come to terms with an interpretation that squared with Scripture and made sense. We must have been with him for thirty or more minutes, yet he never seemed hurried or irritated. What a man!

"In later years, it became my privilege to speak alongside Dr. Mitchell at various gatherings, and at his invitation stand before his students at Multnomah School of the Bible and teach God's Word . . . an honor I never took for granted. There he sat listening to me (of all people) and apparently enjoying the reversal of roles. He never failed to speak encouragingly as he affirmed God's hand on Cynthia's and my lives . . . as he took delight in our growth . . . as he found pleasure in the ways we were being used.

"His quick wit often lifted my spirit. His passion for truth drove me deeper into my study. But it was his humility that impacted me the most in our final years of friendship. Never arrogant, never demanding, never jealous of another's success, and never selfish for the limelight, the man modeled genuine greatness, authentic servanthood.

"I have not walked in the shadow of many giants in my

lifetime but John G. Mitchell was certainly one. My life is richer and my love for Christ is deeper because of his towering presence and godly influence.

"To this day, when my spirit is heavy or my mind gets overwhelmed or my heart begins to grow cold and indifferent, the memory of that faithful, dedicated servant of the Most High draws me back to the path of absolute obedience and the life of simple faith.

"I say with great gratitude, he, being dead, still speaks."

Others testify how Dr. Mitchell, master-teacher, marked their lives:

There have been four key people who have influenced my life for Christ. Dr. Mitchell is the only one of the four, however, whose life was without question as to his integrity and moral character.

What Dr. Mitchell was actually stands out more to me than what he said. And because of what he was, it made me want to heed what he said and taught.

I remember he would begin a class with "Are you saved?"
The response would be a low murmur.
Again, "Are you saved?"
This time, the murmur was a little louder.
Once more, with emphasis, "Are you saved?"
Finally, a strong affirmative response from the class.
Now he was ready to begin teaching.

—Chuck Forster, '51

Even though by the winter of 1977 his eight-plus decades were catching up on him, Dr. Mitchell hardly missed a class and never a good joke.

As our grad class sat one day in the large lecture hall, waiting for his tardy arrival for our Spiritual Life class, we decided to do something he'd never forget for his upcoming birthday.

Providentially, there were as many grads as Dr. Mitchell had years. So on birthday day, we hurried to class, passed out candles and matches and stationed a spy to warn us of his coming.

As he came to the door, he was momentarily confused by the lights being turned out. Then the glow of 85 candles and a cheerful rendition of "Happy Birthday, Dr. Mitchell" set his face into a smile.

He made his way to the stage, sat down and just grinned— for several memorable moments at a loss for words.

—Jeanne Doering Zornes, '77

Many times, I've been discouraged in my relationship with God, believing that He'd never use me as He used D. L. Moody or C. S. Lewis or even Dr. John G. Mitchell.

God lovingly corrected my perspective through a conversation I had with Dr. Mitchell. He quickly reminded me that though God has seen fit to use him in great ways, he is still just a redeemed sinner saved by grace.

"Tracy, God never rewards greatness, but He always rewards faithfulness," he said.

"Every believer has a special place before God. I can't take your place, and you can't take mine," he said. "All God wants is you. Nobody can take your place because God has placed you in the body, right where you are, for the exaltation of Christ."

—Tracy Smith, '90

When David and I were juniors, we started going together and sitting together in classes. In Dr. Mitchell's classes we'd been sitting on the opposite sides of the room until then.

We didn't think anyone had noticed.

But one day, Dr. Mitchell stopped in mid-sentence and said, "Debby, what are you doing sitting there?"

We turned beet red.

—Debby Yost Heidel, '73

Dr. Mitchell—
   Dr. Mitchell is our friend,
   And we like him well,
   He will go to any end
   The Gospel for to tell.
   He teaches in "Multnomer"
   The subjects that we need.
   His favorite book is "Joner,"
   To this we are agreed.
   We like his way of teaching.
   He really knows the Word.
   He's very good at preaching.
   His all is for the Lord.
               —Author unknown

Gordon Donaldson, '51, took the initiative and struck a vein of gold he mined most of his senior year:

It occurred to me that it was a shame to be so close to this man and not get next to him in such a way that some intimate knowledge of how he operated and what he thought could be gleaned on a personal basis. So I went to him one time at Central Bible Church (then downtown, of course) and told him, "Dr. Mitchell, I'd like to get some personal time with you. Would that be possible?"

"Yes," he said. "Let me know when you want to come to my office, and we'll take an hour together."

"Well, actually," I ventured, "what I really want is to meet with you personally every week."

He was a bit taken aback. I don't know whether a student had ever asked such a thing of him.

"All right, give me your schedule," he said.

The thought that came across was that he would fit my schedule, as though I were the busy one! I rather laughed off his answer, feeling it was not my place to dictate the time.

Two or three weeks later as I was leaving church again on a Sunday morning, I said, "Dr. Mitchell, when are we going to get together?"

In his animated "big bear" manner, he remonstrated, "Well, I told you to give me your schedule and you didn't do it!"

So I scrambled quickly, checked my schedule and told him Tuesday early afternoons.

So for more than a whole semester I met him at his car at 2 on Tuesdays, following his 1 o'clock class. It was an arrangement in which we talked as he drove to make visits on church people. While he was in visiting, I sat in the car doing homework. When he came out, he would describe the situation and where the person or persons were spiritually as fully as he could (without betraying confidences).

And then he would ask me, "Now how do you think you would have handled that? What would you say to these people? What Scripture would you have used?"

After listening to my ideas, he would then describe what he had done, how he approached the situation, why he had taken a particular tack, and what the response was. These were invaluable times of insight into his heart as well as learning his use of the Scriptures in ministry to people.

Sometimes we would spend the driving time talking about things theological or problems I was having with something from his classes or the classes of other teachers.

On at least two occasions that I remember, he came out to his car at MSB and said simply, "I'm not going calling today. I'm just going back to the church," as if to say "There's no point for you to go with me today."

To which I answered, "That's OK. I'll just ride with you and take a bus back to the school."

On the two occasions I mention, we got to the church and I started to open my door when I realized that he hadn't budged. We were in the middle of some discussion and he was in his ele-

ment, talking about the Lord and the Word.

I quietly closed my door—and we sat there for over an hour together while he continued to pour out of his vast store of Biblical knowledge and, more importantly, his heart for God.

In later years, I heard that he did this on a personal level with other students, perhaps even on a regular basis.

I have looked through my old MSB notes from his classes (believe it or not they are still around after 40 years!) and I have some of his memorable quotes:

"If your heart is right, your feet will track right."

"The study of the Word without the Spirit leads to rationalism. Speaking about the Spirit without the Word leads to fanaticism."

"When you imitate anybody, you always imitate his weaknesses—for you cannot imitate his strengths. Strength is inimitable."

"Unbelief looks at what we have. Faith looks at Who we have."

"True discipleship leads to freedom."

"Wanted: Wicks to burn out; oil supplied."

"Neither age nor experience is a guarantee against failure."

Regarding women's cosmetics: "A little red paint never hurt a barn."

Many others were marked by Dr. Mitchell's life and teaching:

One of the earliest things he did for me was lead me to a real knowledge of salvation in my early MSB days. When I told him I wanted to talk with him, he offered to meet me anywhere and any time at my convenience. It really impressed me as a new student. Of course, I was also on the receiving end of many of his teasings.

—Mary Collette, '45

I know that I'm saying what thousands of others have said when I say that there would not be enough time or space this side of eternity to measure the great impact of his ministry on my life. His greatest help to me was in helping me to fall more in love with the Saviour and to appreciate His grace.

　　　　　　　　　　　　　　　　　　—David Croy, '60

He made learning fun. I remember most the twinkle in his eye—the twinkle of the Lord.

　　　　　　　　　　　　　　　—Donna Jarrell Sexton, '84

We remember him for the good solid and practical teaching while we were students at Multnomah. A cherished part of our notes was the big "D" for digression as he enlarged on the present study to share a rich spiritual truth.

　　　　　　　　　　　　　　　　—Inez Kellogg Wilson, '45

In September 1941 I first met him. I had hitchhiked out to Portland from Nebraska to attend MSB. I didn't know the requirement of being accepted as a student before I came. I just arrived! And since I had come so far, he and others graciously allowed me to stay.

My first recollection of his ministry was four hours of Romans each week. It still is an amazement to me to think of how a group of young people could be so captivated by the study of Romans. Soon I was caught up in the same spirit. Ever since, Romans and Dr. Mitchell are synonymous to me!

　　　　　　　　　　　　　　　　　　—Don Rubesh, '47

He was a man of the Word, exalting the Saviour of the Word. The fresh, new focus on the importance of the resurrection was one of the first things that thrilled me when I came in 1946. Somehow it was taught and believed, but not of vital importance in my circle in the East.

I had so many classes with Dr. Mitchell, but one I have valued above all others through the years—Spiritual Life (and not because it was an exam-free class either!)—and one lecture in particular: "The Effect of My Sin upon the Holy Angels, Satan, the Word, Believers, the Church, Me and my Lord."

He was a man who was a man—one who appeared to be gruff with a tongue which never did quite conquer "Jonah"—but a man with a tremendous humor (who could forget the candle story?) and the seemingly inexhaustible heart of love for each student. The man was maybe "feared" a bit, but certainly he was held in awe by his students and greatly, greatly loved.

—Emily Edmunds Dunbar, '48

I remember the delightful "favor" Dr. Mitchell and Dr. Aldrich did for me my freshman year at MSB. Every lunch hour they, in kindness and love, saved me their raisin nut bread and any other that was extra. They were my special friends—until the semester ended. I had gained 15 lbs. We had to find better ways to show our friendship to each other.

Dr. Mitchell's wonderful teachings to my heart have been passed on through my life and weekly teaching of several hundred women in Bible study. I thank God for him—and his dear wife Mary.

—Naomi Taylor Wright, '51

The favorite Books he taught so faithfully were Romans and Hebrews, and his emphasis on expository teaching has remained solidly with me. When asked by a pulpit committee in a church what my strongest area of stress was in proclaiming the Word, I always reply, "When I attended Multnomah School of the Bible years ago, Dr. John Mitchell always said, 'We're not so much interested in how you preach as how you teach, for the effective preacher must be a faithful teacher,' and expository preaching and teaching, as outlined by Dr. Mitchell, has remained with me to this day."

The expression on Dr. Mitchell's face that remains most with me is the one when he would look off toward the back of the *classroom and, with a wry smile and little squint to his eyes, he would come up with some bit of dry humor that would keep the class freshened and alert.*

           —*Edward H. Duerksen, '50*

    My appetite for the Word was enlarged and at the same time satisfied through his clear exposition of the Scriptures. But more than that, God gave me an intense desire to minister His Word myself as a result of his example. The exaltation of the Person and work of the Saviour through him have left an indelible impression on our lives and ministry.

    We anticipate that trumpet sound that shall soon usher us into His eternal presence. Then we shall be able to express more adequately our praise to Him for faithful men who taught others also.

           —*Dave Hazen, '49*

    How very delightful it is to remember the treasured year under his ministry. When I least expect it, a song like "Free From the Law" will bring back a flood of memories of time in class mulling over great truths and reaffirming the values we hold so dear. What good training!

    The privilege of being in Viet Nam while he was there for Doris Walker's wedding and watching him counsel the missionaries was another highlight for me. Coming at a crisis time in my life, I realized how many serious illnesses he had surmounted without breaking a lifetime of continuous service. What a good builder of hope he was!

    My appreciation of his teaching continues to grow. What a vision he had! The emphasis on God's omnipotence and the value of reading and re-reading the Word are two notes that continue to ring in my life.

           —*Jeanette Kistler Krause, '53*

I am still moved by his grasp of the Scriptures and his ability to relate scattered passages to any given subject.
—*Andrew Paschall, '50*

Dr. Mitchell was such a wonderful teacher. He not only gave us an understanding of the Word of God, but he made each class period such an interesting time. When he gave assignments, he expected us to do them.

I remember so well his asking, "How many of you finished your reading assignments?"

There would always be several who did not, and Dr. Mitchell would say, "Shame on you, spoiling the record of the whole class." Of course they were ashamed, but some of those assignments were to read the several chapters five times and even more.

Dr. Mitchell was a forceful teacher—exacting, yes, but no more than was just and right. He made those passages of Scripture stand out!

One day, he posed a question on Matthew 27:51-53. "Where did the saints go who arose at the time of our Lord's crucifixion?" Then he dismissed the class. Well, the whole room buzzed with conversation. The students gathered in groups and then passed from group to group, trying to find the answer to that question.

I repeat. Dr. Mitchell was a wonderful teacher.
—*Julia N. Spencer, '50*

What did Dr. Mitchell mean to me? Twinkling eyes, a smile on his face, an open Bible in his hand; quoting passages of Scripture, declaring he could never memorize verse by verse but only with continuous context; quoting outlines and the relationships of the books of the Bible to each other; Spiritual Life class . . . . no grades, no credit, but we wouldn't miss a moment of his wit or spiritual wisdom.

Biblical exposition well lubricated by recent practical experience from his own life. His unique love for grad students and ability to accept our arrogant attitudes and challenge us to love the Saviour. His love and gratitude for "Mary Mitchell, my wife." For teaching me to pray, "I love you, Lord Jesus." His high standards and passion for a Bible school spiritually devout, unshackled by scholastic striving.

A man of the Word who loved and revealed the love of Jesus to others.

—Lu Stevens, '51

A request...that we might have a double portion of the spirit of Dr. Mitchell...that we might be a blessing to others as he has been to us.

—Karl and Delores Baker, '56

Graduation time was fast approaching. . . .

The seniors were anticipating what was ahead. . . .

Dr. Mitchell's concerned and personal interest in his students was manifested to another graduating senior and me when he took time to give us some valuable advice. The Lord has brought this counsel to mind many times in the following years. It was:

"If you are certain you are where the Lord wants you, don't run when 'things get tough.'"

The Lord has used this bit of wisdom to keep *me and He has proven His faithfulness over and over again.*

—Verna Conkle Strong, '56

Our most pertinent recollection of Dr. Mitchell:

"Do you want to know the secret of understanding the Word of God? Here it is: Read it, then read it again, then read it again, then read it again, then read it again, then read it again. . . ."

—Graham and Dorothy Brotherton, '62, '61

Not only do I remember his clear teaching, but I shall never forget his unique sense of humor, that humor which turned a potentially dry Biblical study into a most pleasant, meaningful learning experience.

Like the time we were deeply involved with a problem passage in Hebrews. One student was especially reluctant to accept his interpretation. After repeated explanations of the passage, to no avail, I recall how Dr. Mitchell threatened to "whip" the next one who disagreed with him.

Sure enough, his next statement was challenged by the same student. Being true to his promise, he called him out into the hall.

I shall never forget the roars of laughter as the class listened to the sounds of the mock fight in the hallway. Needless to say, Dr. Mitchell broke the tension of that session and won, not only the point under discussion, but also the hearts of his students.

—*Virgil O. Vater, '60*

Not only did he keep me awake after a hard night's work, but the class was sheer delight.

Even though we played many tricks on him, he kept on teaching with a smile. His podium would wobble with a pebble underneath it. Or it was turned upside down. Our questions were many times irrelevant and stupid. The assigned reading had a 100 percent only three times. But he taught faithfully anyway, and we learned. Boy, did we learn!

In my eyes, he stood far above me. I think of him as mighty in wisdom, grace, knowledge, and understanding. Therefore, I deeply appreciated his humbleness in meeting me at my level. I enjoyed every wrestling match, mentally and physically.

—*Dirk Knies, '71*

My first recollection of Multnomah School of the Bible dated back to a Sunday School picnic at Peninsula Park about 1936. I can remember his telling me of this wonderful school that *was coming into existence that was to train young men and women in the Word of God.*

Little did I realize at that time that I would have the privilege of going to Multnomah ten years later and becoming associated with Dr. Mitchell in this work some time thereafter.

The most satisfying thing of working with him in this ministry was the assurance that God's Word was first and foremost in our curriculum and that His Person and work were magnified above academic excellence.

—Newton P. Scruggs, '50

Because he was a man who knew how to work with his hands, I felt I could identify with him; and this made his ability to handle the Word much more meaningful to me. I appreciated his ability to make the teaching of the Scriptures practical for everyday life.

Then, of most importance, he lived it before us in day by day contact that proved its quality. He had an unfailing, loving courtesy even under the pressure of a busy schedule. He urged us to immerse ourselves in the Book. He held before us the Person of Christ and encouraged us to know Him better.

—Bob Griffin, '50

I came to Multnomah in 1964 as a carnal Christian. Needless to say, I was selfish, frustrated, and miserable. I desperately needed a "doctor," a professional in the Word of God to diagnose my disease and tell me how I could get well. In my freshman Spiritual Life class, I found a man whose knowledge of the Word and clear explanation of it made me examine my heart.

It was during that class that I gave my life to God.

—Virginia Stanton Work, '69

One class in particular was a tremendous blessing at the time and has remained with me since. He was teaching Romans to the senior class of '56 in the spring semester. This particular day he had finished chapter 8 and then he took us over to chapter 12, verses 1 and 2. As he linked these two passages together for us, it was so quiet one could have heard a pin drop. The lunch bells rang. Still we sat—under the powerful influence of that Spirit-filled teaching. When he finally dismissed us, about ten minutes late for lunch, I for one was loath to leave even then.

—Helen Baker Miller, '56

Mitchell: For class tomorrow, read the book of Galatians six times. That's an order.

Student: (In shocked voice) How many times?

Mitchell: Read the book of Galatians 12 times.

Student: (In high-pitched voice) I thought you said six times.

Mitchell: Then read the book 20 times.

Class: (Laughter)

Mitchell: (Seriously) The man or woman whom God will use is the man or woman that knows the Book. Read the Book, then read it again; and, when you're done, read it some more. Never stop reading the Book. Know the Book, live the Book, and preach the Book.

The above may not be word-for-word accuracy, but I remember the occasion well. The challenge is ever before me, and I have accepted it as from the Lord for my own ministry.

—Gary Davis, '68

I look back on my memories of Dr. Mitchell and thank the Lord for his instruction and inspiration. There wasn't a class he taught that wasn't profitable.

I remember him joking around, feeling good and asking anyone if they wanted to box a couple of rounds.

One evening I had my chance to do so; and, before it was over, Dr. Mitchell had the last laugh.

That evening when the Board of Trustees was having a meeting after dinner, we were all waiting in the lobby to go in to eat. Earl McClannahan and I were playing around, punching at each other and otherwise enjoying ourselves.

Earl was wearing a gray sports jacket; and, after taking a punch at me, he made a wide circle behind me. Out of the corner of my left eye, I saw a gray jacket and immediately punched it in the stomach.

The wearer of the new jacket was Dr. Mitchell; and, when I looked around and saw who it was, I didn't know whether to run, fight, or laugh.

Dr. Mitchell realized this and decided to have some fun with me. He asked if there was anyone willing to hold his hat while he settled the matter with me. Everyone seemed as dumbfounded as I was for a minute.

Dr. Mitchell had his laugh and walked away contented.
                                        —Richard Hyde, '65

One thing was a big help to me. I had always thought that a person that spoke in public meetings like Dr. Mitchell had would not be afraid to get up before audiences. He was asked this one question by one of the students one day.

His answer was this. "I am afraid every time before I get up to speak before an audience."

This teaches all of us our utter dependence upon God and the leading of the Holy Spirit.

Then, too, as much as Dr. Mitchell has studied God's Word, this was a striking challenge. He said, "Always before a speaking engagement, I read the chapters of the book I am to speak on over and over again to saturate myself with the Word of God."
                            —Doris Countryman Davidson, '50

I met him back in 1949 in summer school. I wasn't saved. An alumnus of Multnomah who was pastor of a church urged me to go to summer school. I didn't have a job. I didn't know what I was going to do. I thought I might as well go there as everything had been paid by the GI Bill and they would pay my subsistence. So I went.

It was a six-week school. Dr. Mitchell was teaching "Spiritual Life." And when we were halfway through, I realized that I believed everything he was talking about. And I was saved. So I really have a great bond with Dr. Mitchell in that sense. Nobody dealt with me. I think it was just the way he taught "Spiritual Life" that reached me.

I felt like a sponge that summer. I was just soaking everything in. And when it was over, I thought, Well, I just might as well keep on going, *and I returned for school in the fall.*

—*Warren Yost, '53*

I remember when I was a senior, Dr. Mitchell was our class advisor. He told us a story.

His wife was such a help to him, he said, standing behind him, sometimes pushing him.

And he said that one Saturday—it was his custom to spend a lot of time studying—but this Saturday he just didn't feel like it. He thought he would go out and do something—or else take a drive, I guess.

She intercepted him at the door and she said, "You get back in there and study."

He told that on himself.

—*Eleanor Bower Yost, '53*

When I came to school in the fall of 1950 and sat in Dr. Mitchell's Spiritual Life class, although I had grown up in a believing home, I had never with understanding heard such teaching before. It opened up my spiritual life to me as never before. I thought he was an old man, even though he was in his mid-fifties. I could not get enough of his teaching.

I guess the greatest regret that I have is that I did not have more time with such a man of God. I saw him in many situations over 40 years and never was I disappointed in how he related to his Saviour or to the situation we were in. I am sure I caused him disappointment, but he never disappointed me. He was a wonderful man of God and of His Word. The only time I ever remember seeing him a little irritated at me was when I called him "Methuselah" and said I thought that perhaps the Lord would return the year he died.

                                      —*Rod Pence, '53*

A grad student during Dr. Mitchell's final illness wrote him the following letter:

Dear Dr. Mitchell:

I know a certain part of you must look forward to being with the Lord. I know the Lord is looking forward to being with you.

A lot of us in the grad class have been selfishly praying that the Lord would restore you so you can finish this year with us.

The grad class is not the same without you. We have so many excellent teachers and so many excellent classes, but there is only one class that has really transformed my understanding of the Saviour and that is yours. It is hard to express the impact you have had on my life in the short time I've sat in your class. I think a surprising number of my fellow students would feel exactly the same way.

In my other classes, I learn a lot about the Bible and God. In your class I get a glimpse of Him.

I do a great deal of work in my other classes. I do a great deal of growing in your class.

You often apologize to us for not sticking to the schedule, but we don't care about the schedule as much as we care about the insight and impressions of a man who has walked with Jesus for a long time.

Maybe you know how much we need that today.

Unfortunately, it is not everywhere to be found.

You should know that a lot of us are praying to the Lord on your behalf. We confess and repent for the selfish prayer. But we love you and need you. We know God will provide for us in your absence. We know that God's plan will always prevail. We are praying that His plan would be to return you to us refreshed, relaxed, invigorated and filled with a new vitality and strength that we all know can come only from God.

I think I speak for the whole class when I say we love you and will not be the same as a result of this class.

We anxiously await your full recovery.

Your brother in Christ,

Steve Rozsa, '90

Duane Hallof, a student from Multnomah who had endeared himself to Dr. Mitchell in his final years, spoke at the memorial service as a representative of current students. He quoted from *The Living Bible*, a fitting gesture since Kenneth Taylor, the paraphrast, had as a young man been a member of Dr. Mitchell's congregation.

It is my privilege to represent students of the past and of the present and to tell of my relationship with Uncle John.

I think students of the past would recognize and remember Dr. John for his faithfulness to Christ, for his perseverance to go forward, to stand in the gap and to do what it took to get the Word out through the establishing of Multnomah, through the shepherding of Central Bible, through his faithfulness to his radio ministry and to many of you who have received letters from him—handwritten because he wanted to extend that care.

I think, in remembering Dr. Mitchell, the classes of the past would remember him from Colossians 1:28-29. I'll quote from The Living Bible:

"Everywhere we go, we talk about Christ to all who will lis-

ten, warning them and teaching them as well as we know how. We want to be able to present each one to God, perfect because of what Christ has done for each of them. This is my work, and I can do it only because Christ's mighty energy is at work within me."

As a representative of the students at present, I think of Uncle John from I Thessalonians 2. And, again, I quote—"We speak as messengers from God, trusted by Him to tell the truth; . . . we were as gentle among you as a mother feeding and caring for her own children."

I think of going into his office many times and seeing him sitting there, laboring over letters, sometimes an inch thick from people who had written to him. He was writing back and giving each one a special word.

I think of my own visits to his office when again he was busy. And he would put his things down and come around the other side. . . (tears). . . the other side of his desk.

The verse continues: "We loved you dearly, so dearly that we gave you not only God's message but our own lives too. We talked to you as a father to his own children. Don't you remember? Pleading with you, encouraging you and even demanding that your daily lives should not embarrass God but bring joy unto Him who invited you into His kingdom to share His glory.

"And we will never stop thanking God for this that, when we preached to you, you didn't think of the words we spoke as being just our own, but you accepted what we had said as the very Word of God, which of course it was, and it changed your lives when you believed it."

I think of my freshman year, looking forward to being here at Multnomah and sitting right there watching Uncle John go through Spiritual Life class. My roommate and I just sat there, almost like the men on the road to Emmaus, our hearts burning within us, realizing how much was in his head and how much he embodied that in his life.

I think, too, as a representative of present students, we have a model in Uncle John of one who lived out "taste and see that the Lord is good"—through his 61 years of marriage to Aunt Mary and all the blessings that go with that; through good health of a man 97 years old who just continued to go, never gathering any moss; through his travels all around the world and his contacts with countless millions of people; through his daily provision of care by the God whom he served and spoke of so faithfully and the large family who cared for him. . . .

I think of Dr. Mitchell, too, as present students would, in light of the testimony of God's grace and blessing. I remember the morning that he passed away and Proverbs 4:18 comes to my mind, "The good man walks along in the ever-brightening light of God's favor; the dawn gives way to morning splendor." And how the life of Uncle John just continued to grow in more glory.

And, finally, Uncle John modeled one who never had lost his first love. I remember one of his favorite songs, and he'd often have us sing it in his class. It's "Jesus is the Sweetest Name I Know. And He's just the same. . .(tears). . .as His lovely Name and that's the reason why I love Him so."

As a representative of my relationship with Uncle John, he was a loving father to me; and he was a friend. I never realized how much I meant to him until his secretary, Marian, would come and get me out of class when he was having down days and let me know that it would be good to come by and see Uncle John today.

And how, just recently, someone told me that he had said that my name should have been changed to Mitchell.

He was a model husband to me; and, oftentimes, when my wife and I would go over to take care of Uncle John or Aunt Mary, he would ask Connie, "Is he being good to you? Make sure you kick him in the shins if he gets out of line."

He was a hero to me, one whom I could honor and respect.

He was a shepherd, who cared, and I learned much about pastoral care at his feet over these last three years. He embodied to me Jeremiah 3:15, "I will give you shepherds after my own heart who will feed you a knowledge and understanding." And all of that was wrapped in a love in the only way that Uncle John could do it.

In summary, I pay my respects to Dr. John Mitchell, whose life was marked by faithfulness to Christ, to integrity with His message, a model of a loving heavenly Father to all who have come in contact with him and a man caught up—in the wonder of the matchless Name—and the love of his Saviour.

Chapter Twenty-Seven

Family Man

Russ Lambert represented the Mitchell family when he spoke at the memorial service for John G. Mitchell:

Many of you knew Dr. Mitchell as "Dr. Mitchell," your pastor, your teacher, your friend. To us in his own family, he was "Uncle John."

We loved him dearly.

Last night, as a family, we got together and we thought what could we share with you today that would be meaningful about our Uncle John. And when we got going, we realized that you wouldn't have enough time today to hear all the stories we would love to share with you that have special meaning to us. And so I've tried to put it together in a little capsule to share with you.

The thing that all of us would say unanimously is that he was very consistent. We could count on him. We knew where he stood. He was faithful. He was a wise counselor and available to us. When any one of us would call him or go see him, he would take the time out of his busy schedule to let us sit down and talk and share. He always listened. And, oftentimes with a few pearls of counsel, he would help us get straight and then encourage us. He would pray about it and continue to pray about it.

He discipled us by his example. What you saw publicly as

far as his conduct is what you saw privately. He wasn't a two-person type of individual. He was consistent. He had a sense of humor, loved life, was always teasing and kidding us. And, sometimes he even gave us a little ribbing where we needed it if we weren't too happy.

He was tender. He would shed tears easily. That made an impression on all of us.

He was humble. That came through loud and clear time and time again. When things were going wrong, he'd say, "Now are we here to honor the Lord or are we here to honor ourselves? If we're here to honor the Lord, let's do that."

He was a role model. He never put others down, and he always was a gentleman. He always opened the door for Auntie Mary getting into the car. He always made sure that she was safe and sound before he got in. If she needed an umbrella, he went and got it. And that was a role model for us fellows in the family.

He loved people of all ages; and, if you were around him privately to hear some of his stories and to see some of his faces he would make for the kids, you'd say, "Is this really Dr. Mitchell?"

We have some vivid memories of Thanksgiving dinners and Christmas, family get-togethers, good times with his great-great nephews and nieces as well as those in my generation.

But the thing that impressed us the most was his love of the Word. We never went to his house on Saturday when he was pastor of the church because Saturday was devoted to studying God's Word so he would be prepared on Sunday morning. And that was an all-day affair. He never let that go because he wanted to be God's man when he stood in the pulpit before you.

He read the Word until he memorized it. I used to kid him. You know, he'd get up to preach and he'd never open his Bible. He'd just be quoting verses. He'd say, "Now look over in Isaiah." And then he'd have you in Revelation. And then he'd have you in John. And you'd think, "When is he going to open his Bible?" But he had it so ingrained in his mind from his reading and reading and reading that he didn't have to memorize purposely.

He would love to quiz us. I remember sitting around the table on more than one occasion and he'd say, "Okay, now where is this found? Where is that found?" More often than not, I didn't know.

We all remember the time he spent in the Word right up until the last week of his life. He was going through the Psalms and the Gospels. He would read and read and read and read. Nothing else seemed to matter at that time. He just wanted to get into the Word of God and spend time reading.

What a heritage we have.

What an example.

There's a passage in Psalms that was especially meaningful to him in Psalm chapter one, verses one and two. Many of you have memorized it, but I've paraphrased it for this occasion because this was one of Uncle John's favorite passages:

Blessed was Uncle John who walked not in the counsel of the ungodly nor stood in the path of sinners nor sat in the seat of the scornful. But Uncle John delighted in the Word of the Lord and in God's Word he meditated day and night.

Jack Mitchell loved to refer to home and family life in his sermons and classroom lectures. You knew he had an active domestic life and you knew "Mary Mitchell," as he always called her in the pulpit, was at the heart of it all. He was an artist at working these illustrations into the topic of the moment:

To think, that you and I can go morning, noon and night in perfect, blessed, intimate fellowship with God, where He will unveil before us the glories, the treasures of His counsel and of His heart.

Whatever your job may be—in the office, the shop, the store—you can do your job with your heart still in fellowship with God.

*Now that doesn't mean I don't do my work. It doesn't mean
I don't wash my dishes.*

*Now don't you go and ask Mrs. Mitchell if I wash the dish-
es. I don't. I used to do it twice a year—at Thanksgiving and
Christmas Day.*

*I always said that when the women work in the kitchen on
those two days, when they've got all the dishes, pots, and pans and
have used every pot in the house, a man should say to his wife,
"You go on in the living room and enjoy yourself and we men
will clean up the kitchen."*

*You'll never know how many pans you've got in the kitchen
until you try that, brother.*

But he would never tell family stories that might embarrass anyone. In fact, apart from "Mary Mitchell," he didn't
mention from the pulpit any members of his family by name.
He really didn't have to. Everyone knew his wife had been an
Eby and that Verna Eby, her sister-in-law, was at the piano
every service and that Verna's husband Herb was active on the
Board. Their four girls grew up at Central Bible Church and
worked their way through the Sunday School, the youth
groups, the college groups and on out into godly ministries.
Eby marriages attracted many guests. Eby farewells, when
Russ and Marianne Eby Lambert and Bill and Ruthie Eby
Berg went to the mission field, earned much notice. But Eby
family affairs went unreported. People respected the greater
Mitchell family and granted it privacy.

Dr. Mitchell's niece, Olga Mitchell McEwing, daughter
of John's brother Joshua, was nearly eight years old when she
came from England.

"I don't remember the first time I saw Uncle Jack," she
said. "Everything was so exciting and new when we came
from England. There was just too much going on. As far as I
know, the relationship between my father and uncle was very
close. My father's greatest love was music and he was musical

director for Radio Station KOMO for several years."

The Mitchells took Olga (the last surviving Mitchell) with them on a trip to Southern California in 1937 when she was in junior high school. On their return to Portland, they stopped in Northern California where Mary's brother Herb and his wife, the former Verna Rempel, were conducting evangelistic meetings. It was then that Jack planted the seed in Herb's mind that he needed more Bible training. The Ebys soon joined the Mitchells in Portland when he enrolled at Multnomah.

"The first time I saw Jack," Verna remembers, "right off the bat he crossed his eyes and acted like a spastic."

Sarah Mitchell, Jack's father's sister, came to Portland in the late 1940s and lived with the Mitchells until her death in 1960. She had had charge of servants in large homes in England and would often tell Mary, "This is the way we do it in England."

Mary Mitchell's sister Marguerite was survived by her four sons, Glen, Paul, John and Herbert, and her daughter, Dorothy Reese Dudley. Mary was the last of the Eby children to survive.

As Herb and Verna's four girls (Verna Elizabeth, Marianne, Ruth and Marguerite—Marty) came along, the Mitchells kept in close touch.

"We always had Thanksgiving at our place and Christmas at their place," Verna remembers. "One time there were 36 of us and we had to set up three tables in the basement. Our home was more or less of a shelter for the Mitchells. So much of their life was spent in public, and they were very private people."

At such affairs Verna Elizabeth would get teased by Uncle Jack if she dabbled with her food.

"You eat up, Verna," he would say as he rubbed the palm of his hand on the corner of the table. "My hand is getting itchy." That meant she better start eating or else she might see some long fingers creeping along the table to snatch her food. That got to be a family joke, too, and it always brought laughter.

Mary loved to tell about the times when she and Jack took Verna Elizabeth with them on trips. They loved taking her along as a "companion child." Once, at lunch in a train dining car, Verna, age three, saw a fingerbowl for the first time. Her aunt instructed her to dip her fingers in the bowl and to wipe them carefully on her napkin.

"Do I wash my face, too?" came the piping voice that reached to the end of the car—much to Auntie Mary's embarrassment at the time but her later enjoyment as it became another family story.

Ruthie and her uncle somehow managed to curl their lips into what they called a "fish kiss."

"It was something we had fun with," Ruth has said, "and other people seemed to have trouble doing it. That made it all the more his and mine. And whenever we were at their house, it was always such a happy time to be with them. There didn't ever seem to be any reprimands or anything like that. It was just sort of 'This is neat that we get to be here today.'"

Ruth would go over to the Mitchell house every Saturday, supposedly to clean house for Auntie Mary. The three of them would have lunch and Jack would interrupt his studying to take her home.

"We used to love to look at magazines," Ruth remembers. "Auntie Mary and I had a lot of fun with that. They had just built their home on the West side. For years we used to look through magazines and get ideas of decorating."

Mary would take the girls "to town" on their birthdays to have lunch out and to buy a special present.

"It was usually something to wear or a piece of jewelry," Ruth says. "Some of my special jewelry was from her. I remember I had a birthstone ring they gave me about my

16th birthday and a locket they gave me. But we had a rob-
bery one year when we were home on furlough, and all of
those things were taken. I always felt very bad because some
of those things were probably not that valuable, but they held
much memory for me."

Ruth's sister Marty Eby Katcho remembers her special
day: "She took me shopping every year for my birthday and
we'd go down and have lunch. We'd go to the tea room at
Meier and Frank—or Lipman's. It was always such a special
occasion with Auntie Mary. She was always such a lady, and it
was always an occasion to be with a lady and do lady things."

"She really made wanting to be feminine something to
look forward to and not something that was fussy," Ruth says.
"It should be a part of us, you know. She carried that on
down to the next generation even. Our kids have seen that in
her."

Marty remembers birthday parties Auntie Mary would
have for her.

*I think she lived some of her motherly desires through us
girls and we certainly benefited from it. It was wonderful. And
she was great on games.*

*I remember one party where she took a huge long ball of
string—in fact, I think she had several of them. Each girl had
one piece that she had to follow all around the whole house. She
had to roll up the ball and find whatever the prize was at the
end. Auntie Mary loved doing all of those things, and she loved
kids, too.*

Marty also remembers thumbing through one of her
aunt's cookbooks and finding some old clippings on how to
take care of babies and young children.

"I think she had probably clipped those back in her early
marriage when she was anticipating having her own children," Marty says. "Just before she died, I said something to
her about 'was that a great hurt in your life?' She said that she

had really learned to accept it. She really had. They accepted everything as being from the Lord. But that showed me one little instance of her early hope and what that must have been for her to not to be able to have children. But think of the wonderful cousins we would have had. They both had a heart for kids, and I have no doubt that their kids would have been exceptional. Some people don't relate to kids, but they did."

Verna Elizabeth, now a Portland schoolteacher, agrees: "The four of us girls always felt extra special to them because they didn't have children of their own."

The whole Eby clan is special too. She says:

I've got a pretty neat family—the Eby family. Mom and Dad and the four of us girls and their husbands and the children and now the grandchildren—every single person is walking with the Lord. My mom's parents were missionaries in Kentucky. My dad and mom were in tent ministry down in California. The first three years of their married life they went around with another couple and had tent meetings. The other fellow preached. Daddy led the singing and Mommy played the piano. They were in Christian work for a while, and then Daddy worked at Multnomah's Christian Supply Center bookstore.

Marianne and Russ were at Faith Academy in the Philippines for years and years, and then Ruthie and Bill Berg joined them. Marianne and Russ's second son is a missionary in Germany. So on and on it goes into the second and third generation.

Being on the inside of the family walls, the Eby girls were in a good position to witness what really went on in the Mitchell home.

"I'm not sure Uncle John was always easy to live with," Marty says. "He had a mind that could plan things and that was always going. He was a leader. And I think that leaders are not always aware of things that need to be done. I think Auntie Mary was able to accept him for who he was and give him room. But if he was conscious of something he needed to do, then he would do it."

Ruth remembers that "Auntie Mary always lived a very Christian example of a submissive wife, and yet she was not one to be walked on. She certainly had a mind of her own, and she wasn't afraid to let him know how she felt about something. But she very definitely let him be the head of the home. She was submissive to what he felt was right.

"But I also think because they were both such godly people, they were not trying to live their life having their own way. They thought of the other person. They put the other person first. And, having been around them so much, I really believe that was true. I think they had deep respect for one another and for what they could do because they were both gifted.

"Uncle John also gave her her rightful place. He always uplifted her before others, and she had much opportunity to use her abilities in the church work.

"I never heard her raise her voice. In fact, I never heard her raise her voice to anybody."

Marty was looking at snapshots with Mary one day.

I saw a picture of Uncle John on the prairie preaching. You could tell it was a tent-type meeting. He was standing there with his hand up. And I said to Auntie Mary, "Boy, it sure looks like he was preaching hell, fire, and brimstone."

And she looked at me and said, "Oh, he would never do that."

She didn't mean he would never preach about the reality of hell, but he would not rant and rave.

The Mitchells *were* private people. Marty has an explanation for that:

I think they were from the generation that didn't share an awful lot. They really didn't. She didn't think it was right. In fact, I don't know if anyone knows about her prayer notebook. She had a 13 x 9 looseleaf notebook she would go through each day. She would pray for people—for the family, for missionaries.

She didn't talk about that much with anybody. Even I didn't realize it was there until the very end.

An awful lot of herself she kept very, very private. She really wanted to be that way, and I think it was largely her generation. Our generation is "be who you are and show who you are to everybody," but not Auntie Mary. She figured that you could be genuine, but you didn't have to show your whole self to everybody. Not that she was hiding things, but just that she felt some things weren't to share.

Marty has other insights about life with the Mitchells:

Lots of times, when we were sitting around the table after Thanksgiving dinner, I would ask him theological questions. I would have tons to ask, but I wouldn't want to spill them all out on him at once because we're a family and he needed time to relax. So I always chose carefully what I asked him. But when I did ask him something, if it clicked—well, he would go on and on. You know how he could just take off. He'd go into detail on things, and one thing would remind him of something else. We forgot about time. He'd just take it all. . . .

They would enter into our fun. One time we went to Victoria together as a family, and we stayed overnight at the Empress Hotel. And I remember we had just gotten a new game, called "Oh, Pshaw!" and we played it that night in their room. You know how it is when you have a new game and you have a funny streak. Well, we laughed and laughed.

I remember thinking it was funny because here we were in this fancy hotel, and we were all being very noisy in their room. He and Auntie Mary were probably glad when we left, but they were always very accepting of all that went with girls. . . .

They went to Hawaii one time when I was a student at Multnomah, and they asked me what I wanted. And I said, "Oh, I want some flowers."

So they came back with a great big box full of leis and flowers and said I could give them to all my friends. We went to school with them on that day and it was really fun. They knew someone who had a lot of flowers in the backyard and they picked them. I don't know where they got the leis. But they were always doing special things like that. . . .

Have you heard of his "almost" ticket? He was driving to school in his last year, and you know how the speed on Glisan Street is 45 up near their house. And then it quickly goes down to 40 and then 35—I'm not sure at what point. He evidently was going too fast in Menlo Park and a policeman pulled him over and said, "You know, you were going over the speed limit."

Uncle John said to him, "I'm sorry. I was thinking about my class that I'm going to teach."

And he said, "Oh? You teach?"

Uncle John said, "Yes."

And the man said, "If I give you a ticket—"

I don't remember if he said they would take his license away or if his insurance would go way up. Anyway, he said he wouldn't give him a ticket, but he needed to watch it.

And Uncle John went his way, but I'm not sure if he watched it or not. But, oh, he was so proud of the driver's license he got at age 96. He would point out that it didn't have to be renewed until 1992, the 100th anniversary of his birth. I wonder what happened to it. I certainly hope somebody keeps it. . . .

He knew God. I don't know how many people really know God. To him, He was never "Jesus." He was always the "Lord Jesus." He knew Him in a way that we don't. We think that we know Him when we are on a first-name basis, but Uncle John knew Him and it was never a first-name basis. That shows that he really knew Him. . . .

He spent time in the Word. I don't think it was just to get something to give to people. It was to get to know the Saviour Whom he would be introducing to people. . . .

You know that every Saturday there was never anything planned at their house.

I can remember one time I decided to teach Sunday School. And he said he couldn't fathom anyone, including Sunday School teachers or anybody, teaching the Word and not spending quantities of time reading it. It wasn't just for the pastor who stood up in the pulpit. He couldn't imagine anyone just quickly reading over the lesson and then giving it to the kids.

I've thought of that so many times when I was preparing my lesson. If I'm under a tight schedule, I'm tempted to cut my preparation short. And then I think, "But Uncle John said no." To him the Word was so precious and it was all you needed, but you had to spend time.

So those Saturdays of his were off limits, totally. . . .

Neither of them was a Milquetoast person. I think Auntie Mary took an awful lot into her and got it resolved in prayer to the Lord and that was it. I really do. That was her whole life. That's what she did with everything and with everybody. In fact, Ruthie and I were commenting about the fact that she learned early in life to handle everything that came along including misunderstandings with people.

She mentioned once she had been hurt by somebody in the church, but she had resolved it before the Lord and she truly, genuinely loved them. She took that ability into her marriage. She resolved her problems before the Lord. I think that's one big key to Auntie Mary, and Uncle John's tremendous respect for her was another. . . .

Uncle John would never have wanted people to be like him. He would have wanted them to be like the Lord. He was like the Lord, and that's why we loved him. But he was a real flesh and blood person whom we could see that was like the Lord. But he would never have wanted anyone to be like him. Never! . . .

He wasn't comfortable with himself being in the limelight. He hated listening to his radio program. Oh, he hated it. He wouldn't ever listen to himself.

I remember one time at Multnomah. I had been listening to

him and I drove up and he happened to be standing right there. And I opened the door and I said, "Oh, Uncle John, you're on the radio. You want to listen to yourself?" or something like that.

And he said, "No!" And he was serious.

I think he listened to himself only once or maybe twice and never again. He wasn't comfortable with listening to himself. . . .

My kids would crack up at Christmas. We always sang a song before Christmas dinner, and he'd always start it way down in the basement. It was usually an old song that our kids had never heard; but we usually sang a verse and sometimes—if Uncle John wasn't really hungry—we'd sing two or three.

I remember one time we were over at Maxine Sloan's house the summer before he died, and we decided to sing songs. So we started singing "The Sands of Time." And Uncle John's voice used to be wonderful, but it wasn't wonderful any more. When he got older, he no longer had a sense of pitch.

Well, my cousin and I just lost it. We just—we just howled. And it was so funny because we were trying to control ourselves and trying not to let Uncle John know we were laughing, but it got to the point where we couldn't hide it any more.

He looked at us and he said, "You're laughing at me."

And then he just kept right on singing. It didn't matter. It was really cute. He was singing so many verses of that song that I'd never heard, but he knew them all. They were very precious to him. Music was very special to him. . . .

How did Uncle John mark my life?

He gave me a tremendous sense of the awesomeness of God. I don't know anyone who had the respect for God and love for the Word that he had.

He was very widely read. Everybody was always sending him books. You'd go over there and all these books were piled up, and it was fun to go through them. And since I like to read, I would borrow them sometimes.

I went in one time—oh, it's been several years ago now—

and I said, "Well, have you read any good books lately, Uncle John?" thinking he'd tell me one out of the big stack that was really great.

And he said, "No." And then he said, "Yeah!"

"Oh, what one?"

"The Word."

And that's all he read in his later years. He didn't read all those books that were piled up by his desk. He just didn't bother. As he got closer to the end, I saw that nothing in the world mattered but the Word and the Lord.

I even stopped asking him questions probably six months before he died because I sensed that that didn't matter. It didn't matter a bit to him. Who cares about all those questions? I mean, they're deep ones that we have to struggle with and we have to get answers to; and they deal with how we live. But when he was almost at the end, nothing mattered but the person of the Lord. And I almost felt that it wasn't a holy thing to bring up something that was truly trivial if you compared the whole thing—because he was living in glory.

I kind of wonder, you know. We always say, "That's what I'm going to ask the Lord when I get to heaven."

No way!

We're not.

Those questions are going to all seem very trivial. They may be big issues that we have to deal with here, but it isn't going to matter when we get there. I'm sure it isn't.

So, no. I can't even begin to say how he marked my life (tears). . . .

Chapter Twenty-Eight

Old Lion of God

In his book, *An Everlasting Love*, Dr. Mitchell reveled in the prospect of heaven the Lord had set before him:

We are not unknown in heaven. If you are a Christian down here with few friends, if you feel lonely, may I tell you this? There will be a reception committee waiting for you when you get there. It is home.

Isn't it a wonderful relief for you, when you leave your office or your shop or your store or whatever you're doing and you get home? You can kick your shoes off and put your slippers on and just sit down.

"Oh, boy! I'm home!"

This is the place where you are guarded. This is the place of love. This is the place where you are loved for yourself. This is the place of peace, permanency, and restfulness.

This is home!

You might be as ornery as anyone else, but you are loved just the same when you get home.

My friends, that's what it will be like when He takes us to the place He has prepared for us.

Someone asked me, "Come now, Mr. Mitchell, do you think they'll let you in?"

"*Well,*" *I said, "even if Michael the Archangel were to stand at the door of glory and say, 'Mitchell, you can't come in here,' I'll just push him to one side and say, 'Get out of my way. I'm the man Christ died for. I'm coming home!'* "

Heaven isn't a strange place to me. I'm not going there as a stranger.

I'm going Home as the son of One who is God!

Jack Mitchell was now 97; Mary was 90. Jack had an explanation for it, and so did Mary. Asked to speak briefly at the celebration of the 50th wedding anniversary of James and Anne Braga, long a faculty family at Multnomah, he told the guests, "I have to live to be 120 years of age like Moses. I got that order from the students, by the way."

Mary's version came out in a conversation with Connie Hallof, her nurse, who "asked Auntie Mary one time if she was worried when she went into that first very serious surgery. She was in ICU and unconscious for several days afterward. And I asked her if before the surgery she was concerned about not making it as far as leaving Dr. Mitchell by himself.

"And she said, 'No, I got peace from the Lord many years ago that He would keep me around long enough to take care of John.'

"'But, Auntie Mary, he told me that same thing about you.'

"And she said, 'Oh, I guess we have the Lord in a quandry, don't we?'

"I said, 'I guess that's why you're both still alive.'

"She laughed and said, 'I guess that's why.'"

Although Dr. Mitchell was teaching a reduced load, he faithfully met his classes; and it did look as if he would live forever.

The summer of 1989 he spoke several times in Sunday morning services at Central Bible Church on such topics as "Jesus Made a Little Lower than Angels for the Suffering of Death," "Jesus, Our Creator, Redeemer, and Heir of All Things," and "Through Gifts of Humility." The old lion had not changed. That old familiar growl in his voice still rang when he spoke of the glory and authority of the Lord. Here was the "faith once delivered to the saints" being delivered week by week. People noticed how much he spoke of heaven.

True, he had often woven a thread of heaven into his sermons. A page out of *Right With God*, his study on Romans, turned out to be prophetic of himself:

God always limits the tests. He will not test you beyond what you are able to endure, but will with the temptation open the way of escape that you may be able to bear it. Everyone of us has temptations and trials.

You may think, "I have so many tests and trials. Nobody goes through what I go through." Oh? Listen, my friend. You can always find somebody who is in a hotter, tighter place than you are.

I met a man years ago who had been on his back eight or ten years, and he suffered excruciating pain. The doctor told me he should have been dead six or eight times, according to medical science. I saw that fellow with sores from the top of his head to the soles of his feet, inside and outside, and he never complained.

One day, I took a missionary to see him, and when we came out of the sickroom, he said, "Mr. Mitchell, that room is a service station. I thought when I went in there that I would go to cheer him up and help him. Instead, he helped me. Why, that fellow is living so close to God that he is just full of the love of the Saviour."

Off and on, I used to go to see my friend, and I'd forget about all my trials and my little aches and pains, whatever they were. We feel so sorry for ourselves, so self-sympathetic. You know that most of us do. Here was a man just glorying in his infirmities. He was living continually in anticipation of the coming of the Lord.

He said to me, "Dr. Mitchell, I'm going to beat you to glory. Think of it! I'm going to get there ahead of you so that, when you come, I'll be there to greet you and I'll not have this old body that I have today."

Here was a man living in the presence of God, radiating the sweetness and the love and the aroma of Christ in spite of his suffering. Faith is never destroyed by tests. Faith is purified by tests. Faith is indestructible.

In what was probably his last public utterance, when he spoke February 17, 1990, at the Braga anniversary, Dr. Mitchell said:

We oftentimes ask, "Why does God leave us down here?"

I said to the students here some weeks ago, "How many of you are going to heaven?"

They all put their hands up.

Then he turned to that audience and said:

Well, I'll ask you, "How many of you are going to heaven?"

Three of you?

(Laughter)

I better start preaching the gospel here.

(Laughter)

So I said to those students, "How many of you are going to heaven?" And they all put their hands up.

And I said, "What in the world are you doing down here?"

If my citizenship is in heaven and if heaven is my home, what in the world am I doing in this world?

Because there's a job to be done. He's never sent angels to do it. He calls on you and me.

That's why we're still here.

When Mary Mitchell was diagnosed as having cancer, her treatment required two surgeries. He would visit her at the hospital daily.

Celia Wiebe said, "It was awful to see him leave the hospital. His shoulders would be drooped. Verna Elizabeth would often try to be there to pick him up and the nieces were good to meet him at the house. Maxine Sloan did what she could, and Willard was great. But he was really, really lonely without her."

It was at this point that the Hallofs became part of the family. Duane had come to Multnomah from the San Francisco Bay area as a freshman. He had met the Mitchells at the Mt. Hermon Bible conference.

"The Lord has always dropped very godly men in front of me in my Christian life," Duane said later, "men who modeled certain aspects of the character of Christ, so that I would gain a deeper understanding of Him."

He made it a point to call on Dr. Mitchell frequently in his office.

"And then he started inviting me out to lunch with Dr. Willard and himself at Holland's. He used to tease and say, 'Just being your friend I'm manifesting grace.' But it was fun. I'd just sit there and pick up the crumbs as they would talk."

Duane was driving Dr. Mitchell to the hospital after Mrs. Mitchell's first surgery when it occurred to him to say, "You know, my wife Connie is a nurse, so if we can do anything at all at any time for you just call us."

"Ten or fifteen years ago," Duane says now, "we would never have entered that type of relationship with them. But at this point in their lives, we were able to help them a little. Dr. Mitchell said, 'Mary, this is Connie. She's going to be your nurse.' And then she had her second surgery, and we were there all the time."

Mary's illness seemed to be the turning point for Jack. His stamina dropped, and he complained of great fatigue.

One time he fainted in class.

"It was during Auntie Mary's surgery," Duane says. "He hadn't been sleeping very much and probably had not eaten very well either. Connie and I were sitting right up the aisle from him in Bradley Hall, Room One, where the organ is. He was holding onto the podium like he typically did when he was teaching. It was his 'Acts Through Philemon' class. And all of a sudden he started rocking. And he went forward and his head hit the microphone. And then he bounced straight back and sat right down on the edge of the stage behind him and just held onto the podium. Nobody moved.

"We sat there because we weren't sure what to do. Were we going to be the last class in there when he died teaching?

"Connie reached over and got my hand and said, 'What do we do?'

"And I said, 'Now, just hold on for a minute.'

"And all of a sudden he stood right up as if he was 15 years younger and he just went for it. It was just like the Spirit of God came and filled his boots. Somebody went out of class and got him a cup of water so he had something to drink.

"After class, he sat down and he said, 'I'm just so tired. I haven't been getting much sleep.'

"And I said, 'Man, what got a hold of you when you stood back up? You were just going for it.'

"He said, 'Well, it happens sometimes.'

"Auntie Mary would often comment that he could be not feeling well, but once he got into the pulpit and got the Word open, he was a new man."

Dr. Tony Wiebe, for years one of Jack Mitchell's "boys," became personal physician for both Jack and Mary in their final years. He marveled how both of them went so resolutely through their final days:

"What a tremendous testimony he was to the nurses in my office and to the nurses in the hospital. I think that's where the rubber meets the road. Here's a man who walked with God, a man who was faithful in his ministry; and God let him go through the process of dying. It wasn't easy because almost everything failed. But he never wavered. He had a number of systems failing; but when he could function, he would go back to school to teach or he would preach or he would go off to see somebody or see somebody in his office. And then, as long as he could, he personally answered the radio mail."

But as Mary seemed to get better, Jack got worse. Something had snapped within him, it seemed; and he began to lose ground. Family rallied around as the deterioration became obvious, and each one tried to buoy his spirits.

His sister-in-law Verna came over one day.

"When he was first sick and Tony had been there to see him, he didn't realize at the time that this was the beginning of what came.

"Tony had said, 'What you need to do is just sit in this chair, get yourself a good book and read and just relax.'

"And so we mulled that over a lot; and, shortly after, when I was sitting on a footstool beside him, I said, 'You love Zane Gray. There are some neat books downstairs. Let me get you some that are completely off your work so you can relax and—'

"I was still talking when he said, 'You know, I started reading the Gospels and I'm through Matthew now and into Mark.'

"And he started telling me what he'd been reading. Oh, I wish I had a recording of that. It was absolutely priceless. He wasn't even listening to me when I told me I'd get a good book. He was deep in his thinking about the Gospels.

"Well, he didn't get up and go out any more. He got worse instead of better. But that is one of my best memories of him because it was just so very special to listen to him tell me what the Lord had given him after reading the Book for the umpteenth time."

His niece, Verna Elizabeth Eby, the schoolteacher, sat at the kitchen table one day and asked him, "Uncle John, what's your favorite verse?"

"He started by quoting Psalm 1," she says. "He quoted the whole psalm. Here he was 97 years old and he was quoting the whole thing. And then he started quoting verses from Psalm 27. And then he started quoting more verses from memory—the 34th Psalm and some from the 37th Psalm and the 91st Psalm and the 101st Psalm. He just loved the Bible. And my prayer was that the Lord would give me more of a hunger for His Word.

"That's what Uncle John really had. You get him talking about the Bible, and he would just go on and on and give you little nutshells and outlines of whole books of the Bible. You know, he lived it. . . .

"I'd go over there after school, and he'd be sitting in his chair by the front window reading his Bible. That's what he did. He just lived in the Bible and he just knew the Person. He spent a lot of time with the Lord. He really did.

"I wrote in my diary: 'Uncle John, how we love you. Your great capacity for love and tenderness will be missed so much. You pointed us to the Saviour. Whenever I have come to you for counsel, you would say, "Verna Elizabeth, just pray about it. Don't take matters into your own hands, but just trust the Saviour. In His time, He'll work it out. You just pray about it.' "

"I know he would tell others that same thing when they came to him for counsel. He just lived his life that way."

Dr. Wiebe noticed that, though some things about Jack Mitchell changed, his essential character remained the same: "As he was dying, our relationship changed a little in that I was sort of the father and he, the son.

"But the physicians at the hospital that impinged upon him were absolutely amazed at the man. One of my good friends who operated on him—I gave him his book on John (*An Everlasting Love*)—still talks about him. He touched his life.

"And a number of nurses came around who had been

touched by his ministry. You would go to see him to minister to him, and you always got more. You came away blessed."

Tony's wife Celia says, "The testimony they had as a couple at the hospital was pretty special. I remember sitting outside in the hall and the doctors didn't know that I was with the Mitchell party. Two of the doctors were talking and one said, 'I've never seen a couple that love each other like that.'

"In fact, one of the nurses said that most of the time there's a lot of tension. Illness doesn't always bring out the best in a marriage. Sometimes it brings out heartache. The stress brings out things that are unpleasant, and you remember bad things and you argue and you fight.

"But it was just a wonder to watch them take care of each other. I would go get her to take her to lunch sometime during the day at the hospital. I would take her downstairs, but she hated to leave him. She wouldn't go unless Verna was there or a nurse.

"She would say, 'Oh, I just don't want to be away from him because I know he needs me.'

"And I said, 'You need to eat and you need to get out of this room once in a while.'

"But she went with reluctance. And the whole time, when we'd be gone, she'd be looking at the clock, anxious to get back.

"You don't see a lot of marriages like that."

Others called on Dr. Mitchell when he was in the hospital. One visitor was Tim Malyon, who had served Central Bible Church as assistant pastor under Jack's successor, the Rev. L. Dwight Custis, for a time. Tim had been at Central Bible as a speaker when an announcement was made that Jack was in the hospital.

"I went to see him, of course, and while I was there Dwight Custis came at that moment. I saw them interact. It was really quite touching. Dr. Mitchell was very fond of Dwight."

Duane Hallof visited Jack several times and once, when

Con Robinson, for a long time Jack's radio announcer and producer, was there.

Duane said, "Uncle John, we should give you a shave. If Auntie Mary saw you come home with that beard, she would put you out on the steps with the cat."

"Well," he said, "you better shave me up then."

And so Duane went to get a razor.

"Con told me," Duane said later, "that, when I left the room, he said to Dr. Mitchell, 'You've got so many boys that have been taking care of you. It must be nice.'

"And Dr. Mitchell said, 'I only have one boy. It's that Hallof kid. He should change his name to Mitchell.'

"That meant a lot to me afterward."

Duane's wife Connie tells of Jack Mitchell, the impatient hospital patient:

I was in the hospital the last time he was in there. He was just sitting there, and he kept saying he wasn't hungry. He'd say how everything hurt. But as soon as the doctor walked in, saying, "Anything hurt?" he would say, "Oh, no. I'm fine."

"Getting okay?"

"Oh, yes. I'm fine."

As soon as Dr. Wiebe or anyone else from the hospital walked in, it was "Oh, I'm fine."

We brought him a little carton with ice cream—sugar-free ice cream—and he ate almost the whole thing.

Auntie Mary came in, "Did you eat some?"

"Oh, no. Couldn't eat a thing."

I said, "Well, you ate the whole thing."

"I didn't eat that."

"Yes, you did."

He kept his humor right to the end.

As it became obvious that a continued stay in the hospital would really not help all that much, Mary asked that he be brought home so he could be with family. A hospital bed was installed in a bedroom and he was made comfortable.

Celia Wiebe kept her eye on them:

I was there almost every single day and Tony was there too as his physician.

Auntie Mary would say, "Uncle John wants to see you. You have to go in and give him a hug and talk to him."

He was in a hospital bed in another room. He would always say something sweet—not very much. But he'd smile and not let you worry about him. He always had that twinkle.

And one time I said, "Uncle John, it's getting close, isn't it?"

And he said, "Yes, but I don't want to go until the Lord really wants me to. I'm hanging on."

He wanted to be there for Auntie Mary. But she prayed he wouldn't live beyond her. She said, "He couldn't make it without me." And he couldn't. He was totally lost without her.

Dr. Garry Friesen, who had taken over Dr. Mitchell's teaching at Multnomah School of the Bible when he could no longer manage it himself, came to visit one day. He asked Dr. Mitchell, "What shall I tell the class?"

He said, "Just tell them to make the Lord the center."

Frank Eaton, his long-time soloist on the *Know Your Bible Hour* visited one day and sang for him:

> *The love of God is greater far*
> *Than tongue or pen can ever tell,*
> *It goes beyond the highest star*
> *And reaches to the lowest hell;*
> *The guilty pair, bowed down with care,*
> *God gave His Son to win:*
> *His erring child He reconciled*
> *And pardoned from his sin.*
> *The love of God, how rich and pure!*
> *How measureless and strong!*
> *It shall for evermore endure—*
> *The saints' and angels' song.*

Jack loved that.

Saturday, May 12, Verna Elizabeth called her sister Marianne in California and told her Uncle John really wasn't doing very well. She dropped everything and flew to Portland.

Tuesday, May 15, Marianne and Marty were helping Mary care for him. He had been really failing and not talking much. Marty read to him some of his favorite Psalms—the 34th, the 46th, the 89th. That day, he roused and told Mary several times. "I love you. That's my girl."

John Van Diest called on Dr. Mitchell that day and brought him the news of his impending trip to Europe. John wrote down his remembrance of that experience, and the document was later read at the memorial service:

I'll never forget my last meeting with Dr. Mitchell. It was just last Tuesday, two days before he went Home. On other recent visits, he had seemed drowsy, slipping in and out of consciousness. And on Tuesday, he asked me what I'd been doing and I told him about my upcoming trip to Sweden, the trip I'm on at this moment.

As these words are being read, I am meeting with seven Russian Christian leaders to discuss the translation and distribution of four million Bibles in the Soviet Union.

I didn't try to explain the details to Dr. Mitchell, but I wanted him to get the idea. I had to shout the words so that he would hear.

"I'm going to Sweden to meet some men. We're talking about getting four million Bibles into Russia."

Dr. Mitchell didn't understand and he shouted back at me, "Three million women in Russia?"

I tried repeating myself several times, but I couldn't seem to get through. Finally, I wrote out the words on a 3 x 5 card: "Four million Bibles into Russia."

Immediately, his countenance brightened. He rose up in bed and gripped my hand. His grip was strong and firm. For nearly half an hour he would not let go. He began to pray for me and for this mission. Sometimes he would slip out of consciousness for a minute or two and then return immediately to his prayer without missing a beat.

I sensed how excited he was about this opportunity. I feel certain in my heart today that this is exactly where he would want me to be.

Even though I had a godly father, Dr. Mitchell was like a father to me. Our years of association go back to the early '50s through ministries of Central Bible Church, Trout Creek camp, Real Life clubs, childrens' Bible clubs, bus classes, and eventually the work at Chrstian Supply Center and Multnomah Press.

We've played innumerable golf games and countless lines of bowling. With Dr. Willard Aldrich, we've eaten scores of grilled tuna sandwiches at Holland's Restaurant.

During the past four decades his counsel, friendship, leadership, and fellowship have meant more to me than I can put into words.

So here I am in Sweden when so much of my heart and so many of my thoughts are back in Portland. What keeps me here today is the conviction that I am doing what Dr. Mitchell would have me doing—getting the Word of God to hungry hearts.

When you think about it, Moscow isn't that much different from Portland; and the lonely prairies of Canada are really no different from the wide stretches of Siberia. Where there's an open door for God's Word, that's where we need to be.

And, as Dr. Jack was fond of saying, "Any old stick will do."

Wednesday was not a good day. He slipped back again. Duane Hallof sat with him by the hour. He recalls:

He loved to have his forehead rubbed. So I'd sit back there for hours and just rub his head. I was back there the night before he died, and I thought, "You know, it's time for me to say goodbye because he's not doing well and it's just a matter of moments or hours and he'll be gone. And so I just closed my eyes. Nobody was back there. I was praying and I said out loud, "Lord, thank You for such a wonderful example of your love. Don't let him suffer. Just let him go out in his sleep. . . ."

And then Aunt Mary came back in when I was praying. She came over and put her arm around me. I said, "It's amazing when you think about it. In just a matter of minutes he'll see everything we've been waiting to see."

And she smiled and said, "I know."

She walked back into the living room, and I just kept rubbing his head.

Dr. Wiebe kept constant check on his patient with phone calls and house calls.

The last time he saw him, a few hours before he died, he said, "How are you, Uncle John?"

And he said, "I'm okay."

"I think deep in his heart he wanted to spare those about him who were so close any pain that he might cause," Tony said later.

Jack's niece, Verna Elizabeth called her sister Marianne about 7:10 Thursday morning.

She remembers that "Uncle John had slept through the night. He was kind of restless and had really shallow breathing. Marianne had been in there with him and with the night nurse they had for him. There just wasn't much response at all."

Duane was with him when the end came.

That morning, I was sitting over there again and Aunt Mary was rubbing his forehead and holding onto his hand. It was 7:30.

He just smiled.

That was it.

Aunt Mary looked back at us and said, "He's gone."

Verna Elizabeth went right over. Willard Aldrich came at once. Family members were notified. Marianne's son David came from Germany. Russ Lambert was en route from San Jose, California, to Canada. He got off the plane as soon as he could and had to be rerouted. It took him 21 hours to get from San Jose to Portland. It took David 23 hours to come from Germany.

"When everybody got together, there were lots of things to be done," Verna Elizabeth said. "But we worked in wonderful harmony and had such a wonderful time sharing memories of Uncle John, memories of what he had meant to us. He was our spiritual mentor. He really was a great influence in all of our lives. We had a precious time."

The day before the memorial service, Mary, with Marianne and Russ Lambert, her sister-in-law Verna and Verna Elizabeth went to the Gable funeral home.

Verna Elizabeth recalls: "Auntie Mary looked at Uncle John and she said, 'He graduated a day ahead.'" Multnomah's graduation was the day following his death.

"We talked a little bit.

"And then Auntie Mary said, 'Up there, he'll be able to sing in tune now.'"

Letters of condolence poured in from all over the country. Mary Mitchell answered each one. Among them were three written to her by close friends and co-workers:

Yours are the deepest and dearest memories of your loving husband. I delight in a memory, too, of his daily loving care for each of us who work at Multnomah.

Almost daily, as he headed for his office, he has paused at our window to tease, to laugh, to ask about our work and sometimes to pray. I miss him very much. Our loss is great—yours so very much greater. But loss will be gain—together forever with the Lord.

—Joyce L. Kehoe
MSB Registrar

There just aren't words to say how much your husband meant to me as an inspiration, leader, and friend. Though he accomplished great things for the Lord, the thing that stands out most in my mind as I reflect back on the years I knew him was his spirit.

There was no seeking of the limelight, no desire for retaliation when attacked, no grasping for power or privilege, no harboring of bitterness. His was a pure spirit without guile. He demonstrated love and compassion and patience. He came closer to the I Corinthians 13 definition of love than anyone I've ever known.

He had the most of the "best gift."

I am surely going to miss him. I am praying for you daily as I did for him for years. My heart goes out to you. With much love,

—F. Pamela Reeve
Multnomah professor

Arnold and I were praying for both of you during the weeks of Dr. Mitchell's frail health. How hard it is when the time actually comes to lay aside such a beloved husband and servant of the Lord. We ache right along with you for we loved him so dearly, too. It just seemed like he should be always with us.

I have delayed writing this note a number of times because words expressing what Dr. Mitchell has meant to me and to our children over the many years appeared always so inadequate. This wonderful, humble servant of the Lord, who always radiated Christ, inspired us to read and study the Word and to really know and experience Christ personally.

He was a man of integrity, a role model whose life was consistent with all he taught and preached. I am sure long down the road, the impact of his ministry will continue. He was a giant in the Lord, truly our spiritual father. How we loved and respected him. We feel God has a special place of service for him and even right now he is singing to the glory of God.

Mary, we are continuing to pray for you as you face many

adjustments in the days ahead. We are still "some of your kids" and we love you.

—Arnold and Kay Garnett

At Multnomah, reaction was universally the same.

Many found it difficult—since he had been so much a part of the school for so long—to believe he was gone.

Muriel Cook remarked:

Since he's been gone, his presence is all over. Don't you feel that? I just feel a tremendous sense of his presence. I haven't had that with very many people in my life. I almost laugh as I walk up and down the hallways thinking that he's still here.

Her husband, Norm, tells of a trip the Cooks and the Mitchells took to the Bible conference at Cannon Beach, Oregon, where both were scheduled to speak.

When he was 92 years of age, we were scheduled to go down to Cannon Beach at the same time. He came by to pick us up in his car. It was a biggie. He didn't like to ride in our little car, our little Omni. So he came by to pick us up.

Auntie Mary was standing at the door of our house, and she said softly to me, "Well, you're going to drive, aren't you?"

And I said, "Well, I'll be glad to but Uncle John has to ask me."

He was standing out by the car.

And when we got out there, he said, "I want you to drive, but let me get you through the difficult part, first."

And he jumped in the car and we backed out and went down across the freeway, through the city of Portland, over the other side, past Beaverton, past Aloha—all those places. We got on a straight stretch of highway and he pulled over to the side of the road.

Then he got out and I got out and we changed places, and I drove the rest of the way to Cannon Beach.

How do we take the measure of such a man?

We watch him drive to Cannon Beach. He takes the wheel through the hard part. We let him show us the way.

When he lets go of the wheel and jumps out of the car, we slip over and take his place.

John Greenwood Mitchell has shown us the way, having driven for 97 years through the hard part.

Now, it's our turn. We can drive the rest of the way—to our own Cannon Beach.

And we go equipped for the drive because he spent his life taking us back to those sod shacks way up in northern Canada where he had sat on an earthen floor with a homesteader who told him what he or she knew of the Saviour. He brought to us the same sweetness, the same aroma in the things of Christ that had stirred a tremendous yearning in him back then.

He spent his life giving us the one thing he himself had wanted when he said, "This is real—not something to tickle my intellect, but something to reach the need of my heart. I saw the reality of life in Christ."

We have seen the reality of life in Christ.

In his Homegoing, we have lost more than a mentor, more than a pastor, teacher, way-shower. The last of a generation has gone.

But as we let go of John G. Mitchell, may we take the final words of his young friend Duane Hallof, who spoke as a representative Multnomah student at the memorial service, as our own final words of tribute and of love:

If Uncle John were here right now, speaking to all of the students of the Book and to all the radio listeners, I think this is what he would say. And, again, I quote from Scripture because I can't get away from thinking that these would be Uncle John's thoughts.

"I solemnly urge you before God and before Christ Jesus— who will some day judge the living and the dead when he appears

to set up his kingdom—to preach the Word of God urgently at all times, whenever you get the chance, in season and out, when it is convenient and when it is not.

"Correct and rebuke your people when they need it, encourage them to do right, and all the time by feeding them patiently with God's Word. . . .

"Stand steady, and don't be afraid of suffering for the Lord. Bring others to Christ. Leave nothing undone that you ought to do."

The verse continues. . .(tears). . ."I won't be around to help you very much longer. My time has almost run out. Very soon now I will be going on the way to heaven. I have fought long and hard for my Lord, and through it all I have kept true to Him. And now the time has come for me to stop fighting and to rest. In heaven a crown is waiting for me which the Lord, the righteous Judge, will give me on that great day of his return. And not just to me, but to all those whose lives show that they are eagerly looking forward to His coming back again."

Uncle John will always be remembered by me and by many who had the chance to sit under him as embodying I Corinthians 15:10, "Whatever I am now it is all because God poured out such kindness and grace upon me—and not without results: for I have worked (hard) . . . yet actually I wasn't doing it, but God working in me, to bless me. . . .

The important thing is that we preached the gospel to you, and you believed it."

It's been said in the past that the world has yet to see a man whose heart is totally committed to Him. I can't imagine anybody more committed than Uncle John. . .(tears). . .

Let us be reminded of the witness of Uncle John and seek to be consumed with the same love and devotion to our Saviour.

He had said that of his last two sermons, if he could have given them, one would have been on the last days of our Lord's life. And the other one would have been on "Well done, my good and faithful servant."

And I can just imagine Uncle John walking into glory and having Christ, the One he had served all of his life, stand—to receive him and to say those . . . (tears) . . .

* * *

Yes, we weep. That man Mitchell is in his glory! We thank God for his present joy. But he has left us—and we weep for our present loss. Our children will never know this lion of God.

Count on it! He would have fits if he saw our tears. He would have fits if he saw this book. In a hundred years, he would not point us to himself. He would point us to the Lamb who "is *all* the glory of Emmanuel's land."

Yes, our Elijah has gone up! It's now our turn to cry Elisha's cry: "My father, my father, the chariot of Israel, and the horsemen thereof!" It's time to take his mantle and swat our Jordan. It's time to shout: "Where is the Lord God of our Elijah?"

But it's God Himself we want, not a double portion of Mitchell's spirit. We want Mitchell's God in all His glory, in all His power, in all His love to help us know the Book as Mitchell knew the Book and to tell the world as Mitchell told the world.

He wanted us to "fall in love with the Saviour" whom he loved with all his heart.

Can't you hear that man's voice ring out as he stands in our memory, closed hymnbook in hand? He has pushed his songleader aside and raised his voice:

> *Halleluyer! What a Saviour!*
> *Halleluyer! What a Friend!*
> *Saving, helping, keeping, loving,*
> *He is with me to the end.*

And then, smiling, he breaks into an impromptu chorus,

his rich voice starting low and soaring to pitch as he sings the
first line.

> *Hallelujah to the Lamb*
> *Who died on Mount Calvary!*
> *Hallelujah!*
> *Hallelujah!*
> *Hallelujah!*
> *Amen!*

And he says: "And all the people said, 'Amen.'"
And we say, "Amen."
Amen, Dr. Mitchell.
AMEN!

Chapter Twenty-Nine

The Lion's Lady

*I was talking with Mrs. Mitchell some time after he died.
She told me there was one thing that she missed.*

You get into a routine of doing things so easily.

*She said that for many years, at a certain time of the afternoon, she knew John would be about ready to come home. And so
she would have some tea ready for him and a cookie.*

*And even after he died, that time of the day would come
and she would think to herself, "Oh, I must get ready for John.
He'll be coming home from work."*

*And then she would have to stop herself and realize, "He's
not coming home."*

—Marian O'Connor

Mary Mitchell spent hours and hours in her last few
months of life researching and writing information for
this book. She would look through diaries from past years and
write out all she could.

Her niece Ruth Berg, who helped her with it, remembers:

She was very disciplined with her time. I don't think anyone would have known how ill she was just because she was able to discipline her time so well. I don't think she slept well at night, and she would get up and write then. She would write it all out longhand and she would give it to me to type. And then she was very eager to look it over and make sure it all sounded right.

I was thankful the Lord had given her something of worth to concentrate on in those days because it brought back many wonderful experiences in their life. It brought back to her memory the full life they had had. Then she would talk with different ones to get information, different ones who would know of certain times, people who had been close to them or who knew when the church was built or when Multnomah was moved. She wrote to people. She talked to people on the phone. She was very thorough in trying to remember everything.

As Mary put together 60 typewritten pages of primary research, it was inevitable that the story of her courtship would come up.

She talked about it to Connie Hallof who said later that Mary "didn't like that story about her picture being on another young man's dresser. She didn't like people to tell it because she thought it made her look bad. She said, 'It makes it look like I was two-timing men. I wasn't. I don't like that story. I wish he wouldn't tell it.'"

Duane says, "It was Dr. Mitchell's favorite story. He said, 'I set my jaw and I went after her.'"

Family members have said they learned so much from Mary Mitchell between the time her husband died and her own final illness. Though she went through some very difficult days with her cancer, her trust in the Lord never wavered.

"What a blessing it was to be around her in her hardest days," Verna Elizabeth said. "It was incredible. I've never seen anything in my life like it. I don't imagine I will again."

Maxine Sloan, her dear friend and fishing buddy for

many years, came each day to walk with Mary over to nearby Glendoveer golf course with its barkdust walkway through the trees. They worked up to walking half a mile there and half a mile back.

In early September she became ill enough to go to the hospital. Ruth and Bill Berg arrived just about that time and, when she came home, they were ready to move into the house. Mary's sister-in-law Verna Eby had been living with her from the spring before John's death.

She said, "Believe it or not, it took all three of us to keep things going because Mary had so much company. Almost every day, maybe 10 different people would come to see her. It was a high priority for her to see them and to encourage them and to let them encourage her. Actually, her ministry in this respect was a marvelous thing, and this lasted until the day she took sick before she died—right up until the last."

Ruth Berg, who was also living there, said, "I'd get up around 5:30 or 6 o'clock and, quite often in the last couple of months, she would already be up sitting. She'd be dozing probably. Other times she was praying. She would be up thinking of things. She was just more comfortable being up.

"By ten, she would be fully dressed, ready for anything whether she would go out or not. She was always prepared for company and she had a lot of it. Usually they would call, but I don't think there was a day other than the last week that she was not up and dressed. It was amazing. It was a real example to all of us around her. She was a lady—in the highest way you can say 'a lady.'"

At Christmas, Mary set her heart on three projects.

First, she sent Christmas cards to her friends and wrote personal notes on each one of them. The cancer had grown. She was very sick, and she realized that she wouldn't last long. She would have nights when she couldn't sleep so she would get up at 2 o'clock in the morning and take some of her medicine and a little food. And then she would sit at her desk and write the notes and sign the cards. She wrote so many that her hands and fingers would hurt. Ruthie would rub them with balm and wrap them, but Mary kept on until she had finished.

Second, she made a very special thing out of Christmas dinner. Verna remembers "she wanted everything absolutely tops for the family. She had Bill get a great big turkey and a big honey-baked ham with all the fixings. Duane and Connie were with us for Christmas dinner. They were part of the family.

"She sat there and ate her gelatin and broth while we gorged ourselves on the wonderful dinner. And she didn't make anything of it. That was all she could eat and that was that."

Third, one day, just before Christmas, she had a group of friends over for lunch. Ruthie and Verna fixed the food, but Mary oversaw everything. She served chicken salad, a specialty of hers, and she sat there with her broth.

She also took a notion that she wanted to make pecan rolls, another one of her specialties, for Tony Wiebe, her doctor. It gave her great pleasure to help make them, pack them up and give them to him.

Four of the girls from the Multnomah staff, including Mary Collinson, the new dean of women, often came over to visit. One day, the subject of the light rail through Portland came up. Mary Mitchell had never been on it.

"Oh, you've got to ride on it," they said.

So one afternoon they came over and took Mary, Verna and Connie for a ride downtown on the "Max." They stopped for tea in Pioneer Place and returned. Mary loved every minute.

Verna Elizabeth was with her one day, sharing a verse that had blessed her heart. She remembers:

The next time I came over, she had gone through the Bible and written down all the verses in the whole Bible on that subject. We were talking about the word "seek" and about "those that seek the Lord" and Deuteronomy 4:29—"seek him with all thy soul."

She found verses with "seek" in I Chronicles—there it was used four different times—and II Chronicles, six times. She found them in Ezra, Job and the Psalms. She had Psalm 27:4 underlined. She had a list with Psalm 27:8, Psalm 34:10, Psalm 119:2, "Blessed are they that keep my testimonies, that seek me with a whole heart." She had underlined "whole heart." She had Proverbs 8:17, Proverbs 28:5, and Isaiah 55:6, "Seek ye the Lord while he may be found." She had Hosea 5:15, "In their afflictions they will seek me early."

She was writing all those when she was really very ill. You can tell that was her goal, her desire.

After Christmas, the family noticed that she slumped a bit. She wasn't up to what she had been. Her drive was gone.

On Sunday, January 13, Verna Elizabeth spelled her mother while Verna went for a little walk. She remembers:

I'm sure Auntie Mary wasn't feeling very well, but she never did complain. She was sitting in the chair in her bedroom. This was about nine days before she died. We had no idea that it was going to be so soon.

Anyway, I went back into her bedroom to see how she was, and I started talking to her. And we just sat there and talked for four hours. We had a wonderful time. We talked about all kinds of things. We talked about the family. We talked about memories. We talked about sisters. She talked about her dear sister, Auntie Marguerite. They used to talk on the phone every day, every week, even though Auntie Marguerite lived in California and Auntie Mary lived in Portland.

We talked about when we were kids and how we used to go over to their house. I think that's when she reminded me about that story about when I went to visit her when I was a little kid. And we talked about the trip around the world when they came to Germany to visit me. And we talked about Hong Kong because

I had been to Hong Kong with Marianne. She told me about the coffee table they brought back from Hong Kong when they were over there.

Oh, we just had a special time of talking about so many things.

The following week, Mary didn't feel well at all. By Sunday, the 20th, the family knew she was really failing.

Verna Elizabeth says, "We were over there trying to help her. She was having trouble breathing. We called the nurse and tried to get some help. We called Connie and she came right over."

Her mother, Verna, says, "The girls thought it would be smart if I went home overnight. Mary called me twice that evening. She had heard from the editor about the book on John's life, and she had plans about what we were going to do from then on. I would think of things I remembered and that would get her going. She was going to write and we were going to really hit it hard. I said I'd be back in the morning.

"But Wednesday morning, when she woke up, she had had a stroke and she couldn't talk. She had lost her eyesight and couldn't see a thing. And that was the beginning of the end."

Thursday morning, Pamela Reeve and Joyce Kehoe called on her.

When Joyce and I arrived, Verna told us that if we did not get much of a response not to be surprised at that but to go in anyway. And so we did.

And when we got in, I said, "Hello;" and, as she reached up to hug me, I said, "My, oh, my, it won't be long now before you'll see the Lord Jesus face to face."

And she said, "Yes, I'll see Him face to face."

And I repeated it—"You'll be seeing the Lord Jesus face to face." I thought she might be thinking of John Mitchell.

But she just seemed to grab hold of those words and she said,

"I'll be seeing—Him—face to face. I'll be—seeing Him—face to face. I'll be seeing Him—"

A smile broke out over her face that was beatific—something you haven't seen before. I felt like there was a Presence in the room—it was so different. She repeated that a number of times for several minutes. She seemed to be so enraptured with the fact that she was going to see the Lord face to face. She was transported with unbelievable joy. And then she slowly leaned back on her pillows and drifted into sleep.

As we left the room, I commented to Joyce about it; and she said she sensed another Presence in the room. She—who is much more matter-of-fact than I—she sensed it, too.

On Friday, Verna felt Mary was trying to tell them goodbye. She found that she could talk, not easily, but clearly enough to be understood. The pastor of the Southwest Bible Church in Beaverton, Scott Gilchrist, dropped in with his wife, Christie, to visit. They had been favorites of John's and had come over quite often.

Verna says, "She just talked and talked to him, telling him appreciative things. She talked to me. Then that night she went into a coma. . . ."

Bill Berg, her son-in-law, told the congregation at Mary's memorial service what happened that night:

Friday—before she slipped into the sleep that she never came out of—it was a good day. It was really a special day. She had had a little rally. Maxine had come over in the morning and Celia was there in the afternoon and Connie and Duane and several people had come and she was responsive. But on Friday night about 10:15 or so, she was really beginning to struggle. She had some pain and was thrashing about.

And so we came in. She had been medicated and we read Psalm 19 to her. And then I asked for another Psalm or some other area that we might read in the Scriptures that might give her a sense of comfort.

The nurse that had been helping had indicated that "even if you don't get a response, the hearing is the last thing to go. Continue to share and to speak."

So Mom suggested Psalm 103, "Bless the Lord, O my soul."

So I read Psalm 103 nice and loud down by her ear and she began to relax.

And, when I was done reading it, I said, "Well, we ought to sing this." There were seven of us—Ruthie and myself and our daughter Linda, Mom, Duane and Connie and Auntie Mary. So we started to sing "Bless the Lord, O my soul" and Auntie Mary joined right in, line for line. She sang every word nice and strong. And when we came to the 'Amen" she was down in there and Duane said, 'That's just like Uncle John would do it.'

And then when we finished, she decided to keep singing. And so she paraphrased the song, "Bless the Lord, O my soul," and she sang several phrases after we had stopped. Our daughter Linda joined in, singing with her, and then she began to drift off into sleep.

Verna Eby sat with her that night.

I was in the room where she was sleeping and she started talking.

And she called, "Honey!"

No one can say "Honey" like she did. It was a low inflection that simply was just—her.

She said, "Honey, it's time! We have to go! Come on, Honey! We HAVE to go. Come on!"

She kept saying "Honey" and, oh, I just about burst inside.

Verna Elizabeth didn't know what to do that last morning:

On Tuesday, I really didn't know whether to go to work or not. I thought, Well, I don't know. Auntie Mary could be this way for several days. I just can't skip work because when she dies I know that I'm going to need to take time off work. I really didn't know whether to go to work or not, but I did.

At 10:15, our kids have a recess break. So I sent the kids out to recess and I went into the teachers' room. It was about 17 minutes after 10. I called up at the house to see how she was doing.

Bill answered the phone and he said to me, "She's taking her last breath right now."

My immediate feeling was, "Oh, she's with the Lord and Uncle John." I couldn't even cry. At least not then. She'd been so brave and she had suffered so through that illness.

I can't put into words how I felt. I just had a great desire to love the Lord all the more because of the way I saw her loving the Lord. She really depended on Him in her time of adversity.

Uncle John was very protective of Auntie Mary. He gave her strength to carry on and to minister to all of us. We'd go over to minister to her, and we would all come away cheered up because she was so positive. She was so strong. I know it had to be the Lord's strength because physically she was so weak. But she was so strong. She was always mentally alert and emotionally just a stronghold. She always helped everybody else with their problems. She really didn't ask for much help with hers.

Her favorite song was "In the Secret of His Presence."

After she died, I wrote it in the front of my diary.

I wrote down: Auntie Mary, April 7, 1900 to January 27, 1991.

> "In the secret of His presence
> how my soul delights to hide!
> Oh, how precious are the lessons
> which I learn at Jesus' side!
> Earthly cares can never vex me,
> neither trials lay me low;
> For when Satan comes to tempt me,
> to the secret place I go,
> To the secret place I go."

That's the verse that everybody knows. But the last verse I think is the key to Auntie Mary's beautiful spirit.

"Would you like to know the sweetness
of the secret of the Lord?
Go and hide beneath His shadow;
This shall then be your reward;
And when-e'er you leave the silence
of that happy meeting place,
You must mind and bear the image
of the Master in your face,
Of the Master in your face."

Isn't that neat? It makes me cry to think about it. Because the reason she was so sweet was because she spent time with the Lord.

And she showed forth His sweet spirit. It was her sweet spirit.

She was quite a lady.

Mary Mitchell's printed Christmas card her last Christmas was an engraving of one of her own poems:

I am looking for that bright and glorious morning
When the Sun of Righteousness shall rise,
With healing in His wings;
When we shall know the fulness of His promise
In all the blessed joys His coming brings.

The precious joy of being in His presence,
Of seeing our dear Saviour face to face,
Of knowing all the radiance of His glory
And the full riches of His love and grace.

The joy of meeting loved ones who are waiting,
When separation, pain and sorrow all are past;
When leaving all earth's transient joys and shadows
We are together, safely home at last.

M.M.